John Wesley Hales

Essays and Notes on Shakespeare

John Wesley Hales

Essays and Notes on Shakespeare

ISBN/EAN: 9783337055684

Printed in Europe, USA, Canada, Australia, Japan

Cover: Foto ©Thomas Meinert / pixelio.de

More available books at **www.hansebooks.com**

ON

SHAKESPEARE

BY

JOHN W. HALES, M.A.

PROFESSOR OF ENGLISH LITERATURE IN KING'S COLLEGE, LONDON;
EXAMINER IN ENGLISH AT LONDON UNIVERSITY;
CLARK LECTURER AT TRINITY COLLEGE,
AND LATE FELLOW OF CHRIST'S COLLEGE, CAMBRIDGE.

NEW EDITION

LONDON
GEORGE BELL & SONS, YORK ST., COVENT GARDEN
AND NEW YORK
1892

CHISWICK PRESS:—C. WHITTINGHAM AND CO., TOOKS COURT,
CHANCERY LANE.

1, OPPIDANS ROAD,
PRIMROSE HILL, LONDON.
May 19*th*, 1884.

MY DEAR SEELEY,

When I asked you to let me connect this booklet with your name, you replied at once: "You surely cannot doubt for a moment that I shall think your dedication a great honour." No words could be kinder; few, if any, could make me prouder. Only, would they were better deserved!

I have always thought, and shall always think, your friendship, enjoyed ever since I a Freshman looked up with reverence to you a 'Senior Soph', as one of the chief pleasures and distinctions and blessings of my life.

And so it is with no ordinary satisfaction that I avail myself of your permission to inscribe this volume to you.

Believe me, my dear Seeley,
To be always
Very sincerely yours,
JOHN W. HALES.

To J. R. SEELEY, Esq., LL.D.,
Regius Professor of Modern History in the University of Cambridge.

ESSAYS AND NOTES ON
SHAKESPEARE

CONTENTS.

	PAGE
I. From Stratford-on-Avon to London. (From the *Cornhill Magazine*)	1
II. Round about Stratford in 1605. (From *Fraser's Magazine*)	25
III. Chaucer and Shakespeare. (From the *Quarterly Review*)	56
IV. Shakespeare's *Greek Names*. (From the *Cornhill Magazine*)	105
V. Hazlitt's *Shakespeare's Library*. (From the *Athenæum*)	120
VI. Mr. and Mrs. Cowden Clarke's *Shakespeare Key*. (From the *Athenæum*)	129
VII. Dr. Elze's *Essays on Shakespeare*. (From the *Academy*)	134
VIII. Some Conditions of the Elizabethan Drama. (From the *Saturday Review*)	145
IX. Mr. Halliwell-Phillipps' *Papers referring to Shakespeare*. (From the *Athenæum*)	152
X. Mrs. Furness' *Concordance to Shakespeare's Poems*. (From the *Academy* and the *Athenæum*)	165
XI. Dr. Schmidt's *Shakespeare-Lexicon*. (From the *Academy* and the *Athenæum*)	174
XII. *Shakespeare Scenes and Characters*. (From the *Academy*)	185
XIII. Bell's, and Singer's Editions of *Shakespeare's Dramatic Works*; and Mr. Watkiss Lloyd's *Critical Essays on Shakespeare*. (From the *Academy*)	189
XIV. Shakespeare and Satire. (From the *Antiquary*)	198
XV. Milton's familiarity with Shakespeare's Plays. (From the *Athenæum*)	201
XVI. *King Richard the Second*. (From the *Academy*)	205
XVII. *Wily Beguiled* and *The Merchant of Venice*. (From the *Athenæum*)	209

CONTENTS.

		PAGE
XVIII.	A certain Edition of *The Merchant of Venice*. (From the *Athenæum*)	215
XIX.	"With good capon lined." (From the *Antiquary*) .	219
XX.	"Cæsar doth bear me hard." (From the *Academy*) .	224
XXI.	Mr. Furness' *New Variorum Edition of Shakespeare: Hamlet*. (From the *Athenæum* and the *Academy*)	228
XXII.	Hamlet's Age. (From the *Academy*) . . .	237
	"An aery of children, little eyases." (From the *Athenæum*)	237
	"That cry out on top of question." (From the *Athenæum*)	239
	"Assume a virtue, if you have it not." (From the *Academy*)	240
XXIII.	*King Lear*. (From the *Fortnightly Review*) . .	242
XXIV.	Cordell Anslye. (From the *Athenæum*) . . .	271
XXV.	The Porter in Macbeth. (From the New Shakspere Society's *Transactions*)	273
XXVI.	Macbeth a good Churchman. (From the *Academy*) .	291
XXVII.	"The Coal of Fire upon the Ice." (From the *Academy*)	292
XXVIII.	"The Washing of Ten Tides." (From the *Academy*)	294

I.

FROM STRATFORD TO LONDON.

(From the *Cornhill Magazine*, Jan., 1877.)

SEEING our dearth of information about Shakespeare is so great, nothing that may be of the slightest value ought to be neglected; and so it may be worth while to consider what scenes and sights may have been familiar to him in his journeyings to and fro from Stratford to London. The transit can be accomplished now in four or five hours; but it was no such light matter in the Elizabethan age. The distance is some 100 miles (by Oxford 94), and probably under ordinary circumstances would occupy four or five days to traverse, though no doubt, under pressure, a less time might suffice. These periods would certainly form notable epochs in the poet's life. What a change from "the smoke and uproar and riches of Rome"! No doubt he would seldom travel alone. Perils from robbers were too common and too serious to encourage that practice. But yet he would often be lonely enough; and many a thought afterwards embodied in immortal shape must have occurred to him during these long hours. It would make a fine picture —the author of *Hamlet*, his "season" over, amidst the woody solitudes of the Chilterns, or slowly wending his way through some lowland marsh. We may be sure he was not idle at these times. The rough rude simple life he saw around him would not be unsuggestive. There is a tradition, as we shall see, that he "studied" his Dogberry in some village he passed through. His tablets must often have been called into requisition. And when the days were fair, and all the landscape wore the beauty of the sunshine, many a "session of sweet silent thought" must have been holden. We cannot doubt that in those long quiet journeys his spirit found for itself nurture and strength. The true poet is like that "bright flower, whose home is everywhere." Often travel-tired, he would find rest for himself in contemplating the face of nature and the humours of men. Indeed, with all their discomforts and annoyances, these may have been precious times for him; and he may have arrived at his destination a wiser, if a weary, man.

There are two or three sonnets in which he speaks of journeys, possibly of these journeys. The following may have been written at Stratford, at the close of one of them :—

> "Weary with toil, I haste me to my bed,
> The dear repose for limbs with travel tired;
> But then begins a journey in my head,
> To work my mind when body's work's expired;
> For then my thoughts (from far where I abide)
> Intend a zealous pilgrimage to thee,
> And keep my drooping eyelids open wide,
> Looking on darkness which the blind do see;
> Save that my soul's imaginary sight
> Presents thy shadow to my sightless view,
> Which, like a jewel hung in ghastly night,
> Makes black night beauteous and her old face new.
>   So thus by day my limbs, by night my mind,
>   For thee and for myself no quiet find."

In others we see him in the midst of a journey, weighed

down with that strange sorrow whose history seems likely to remain inscrutable :—

> "How heavy do I journey on the way,
> When what I seek—my weary travel's end—
> Doth teach that ease and that repose to say,
> 'Thus far the miles are measured from thy friend!'
> The beast that bears me, tired with my woe,
> Plods dully on, to bear that weight in me,
> As if by some instinct the wretch did know
> His rider loved not speed, being made from thee.
> The bloody spur cannot provoke him on
> That sometimes anger thrusts into his hide,
> Which heavily he answers with a groan
> More sharp to me than spurring to his side;
>   For that same groan doth put this in my mind,
>   My grief lies onward, and my joy behind."

There are others in which he speaks of absences from his friend. Of course Shakespeare made other journeys, besides between Stratford and London; occasionally he "strolled" with his company; but in any case these sonnets may be of assistance in picturing him to us as he passed along the roads that we propose to specify. We can see that it was not without knowledge he made Autolycus sing :—

> "A merry heart goes all the day;
> Your sad tires in a mile-a."

II.

We need scarcely remind our readers that facilities of locomotion in the Elizabethan age were scanty enough. They are probably well aware how scanty such facilities were a century later, and even a century later still. It was much worse in the Elizabethan age. Public coaches did not begin to run, or to stick fast, till nearly half a century after

Shakespeare's time. The art of road-making was not yet known; Metcalfe and Telford, and their worthy biographer Mr. Smiles, belonged to a far distant posterity. What they were pleased to call roads then were mere deeply-rutted tracks, almost or altogether impassable in bad weather; wide-spreading sloughs with no Mr. Hope at the further edge to lend the splashed and mired traveller a hand. The country was still generally unenclosed; and all that could be done when the ruts became too deep for endurance was to essay a fresh track by the side of the old one. Some statutes indeed had been passed in the reign of Henry the Eighth, designed to improve certain thoroughfares of notorious badness, and an Act of a more general application had been passed in the reign of Queen Mary; but little or nothing had come of them. The description given in the preamble of the statute of 1555 remained still true: "Highways are now both very noisome and tedious to travel in, and dangerous to all passengers and carriages." We have not yet learnt to control our rivers, and it is still possible sometimes to see wide lakes extending over the land: but this was a common Elizabethan spectacle. Often then, and many a time after, locomotion was completely intercepted by floods. Not so very seldom might it be said that the "contagious fogs"

> "Falling in the land,
> Have every pelting river made so proud
> That they have overborne their continents:
> The ox hath therefore stretch'd his yoke in vain,
> The ploughman lost his sweat, and the green corn
> Hath rotted ere his youth attain'd a beard;
> The fold stands empty in the drowned field,
> And crows are fatted with the murrion flock;
> The nine men's morris is filled up with mud,
> And the quaint mazes in the wanton green
> For lack of tread are undistinguishable."

At such times one's journey could only be pursued by the help of skilful guides, and even so at some risk. To take a late illustration, Thoresby, who died in 1715, tells us in his diary how the rains had "raised the washes upon the road near Ware to that height that passengers from London that were upon that road swam, and a poor higgler was drowned, which prevented me travelling for many hours; yet towards evening we adventured with some country people who conducted us over the meadows, whereby we missed the deepest of the wash at Cheshunt, though we rode to the saddle-skirts for a considerable way, but got safe to Waltham Cross, where we lodged."[1]

Such being the roads—so "founderous," as someone calls them—what would the vehicles be?

Carriers' carts[2] of a sort did struggle along; but for the most part movement was accomplished on foot or on horseback, and conveyance of goods by pack-horses. Horse-litters were occasionally used. Coaches are said to have been introduced by Boomen, Queen Elizabeth's own coachman; but they were little better, as Mr. Smiles remarks, than carts without springs, the body resting solid upon the axles. And those who used them paid a bitter penalty for the luxury.[3] At one of the first audiences which the Queen

---

[1] See Smiles' *Lives of the Engineers:* Metcalfe and Telford, p. 19, ed. 1874.

[2] Fynes Morison speaks (*temp.* James I.) of "carriers who have long covered wagons, in which they carry passengers from place to place; but this kind of journeying," he adds, "is so tedious, by reason they must take wagon very early and come very late to their inns, that none but women and people of inferior condition travel in this sort."

[3] See a picture of this invention in Mr. Roberts's *Social History of the Southern Counties.* Perhaps those who have known what it is to be hauled in a bathing-machine across a fine shingly beach can best appreciate the delights of such a means of locomotion.

gave to the French Ambassador, in 1568, she feelingly described to him "the aching pains she was suffering in consequence of having been knocked about in a coach which had been driven a little too fast, only a few days before." About a century later, the public vehicles were popularly known as "hell-carts," and no doubt well deserved the name. One grave objection to wheels was, it seems, that they broke up the roads! "King James," says Mr. Roberts, "proclaimed that carts and wagons with four wheels, carrying excessive burthens, so galled the highways and the very foundations of bridges, that the king denounced them to the judges as common nuisances, against the weal public, and the use of them an offence. By this proclamation of James I., in the year 1622, no carrier was to travel with a four-wheeled wagon, but only with a cart having two wheels, and only to carry 20 cwt. Anyone transgressing this was to be punished." At Weymouth, in 1635, "the authorities passed a bye-law, that no brewers were to bind the wheels of their carts with iron, as it wore away the pitching of the streets. Precisely similar was the complaint against hackney-coaches, 1638— viz. that they broke up the streets. . . . It having been thought proper to ordain in the year 1662, that the wheels of each cart or wagon should be four inches in the tyre, this was found to be impracticable, for in some parts the ruts could not receive such wheels, nor could the carriages pass. A proclamation stayed the prosecution of offenders till the further order of Parliament." In the Elizabethan age the fact was that the roads could not bear the coaches, and the coaches could not bear the roads; so there was but little traffic in that way, that fearful institution the stage-coach being a later birth of time.

On foot then, or on horseback, Shakespeare would perform his journeys. That he would ride when he could afford it is the more probable from the fact we gather from certain sonnets that he was lame, for we see no reason to take the words in any non-natural or heterobiographical sense. There is ground for believing that this defect was of no very serious nature; it has been compared with that of Scott, and that of Byron; but it would probably make him prefer riding to walking. And we might just ask in passing whether pedestrianizing is not a quite modern English taste? A German, who made a walking tour in this country not a hundred years ago, found such a method of progress not at all practised, and indeed one which exposed him to much suspicion and discomfort. He unbosomed his wonder that it should be so to a coach-fellow-traveller, for he did sometimes indulge himself in a lift. "On my asking him why Englishmen, who were so remarkable for acting up to their own notions and ideas, did not, now and then, merely to see life in every point of view, travel on foot; 'Oh!' said he, 'we are too rich, too lazy, and too proud.'" But, if a quite modern taste, it was, no doubt, an old necessity for many a traveller. See Walton's account of Hooker's walking from Oxford to Exeter.

Horses could be hired at 12d. the first day, and 8d. a day after till re-delivery. "Mr. John Garland, merchant, mayor of Lyme in 1569, rode to London on town business. His whole charge for himself and horse in London was 3l. 5s.; the hire of the horse was 5s." Also, it was possible to post, at least in some parts. It was so in Norfolk as early as 1568, as we learn from Blomefield *apud* Roberts. The charge was 2d. a mile for the horse, and 6d. for the guide "to go and carry back the horse; and the said horses were not to carry any cloak-bag of above ten pounds' weight." A common arrangement for those who did not keep a horse of their own was to buy one at the beginning of a journey and sell it at the end. So late as 1753 a Dr. Skene, of Aberdeen, travelled from London to Edinburgh in this way. He bought a mare for eight guineas in London, rode her nineteen days, and sold her in Edinburgh for what he had given for her.

We have an incidental picture of the travelling equestrian of the seventeenth century, in a book quoted by Mr. Smiles, called *The Grand Concern of England explained in several Proposals to Parliament*, published in 1673, denouncing stage-coaches and caravans. The writer, said to be one John Gressot, of the Charterhouse, insists that stage-coaches were ruinous to trade, " for that most gentlemen, before they travelled in coaches, used to ride with swords, belts, pistols, holsters, portmanteaus, and hat-cases [a heavy cargo this !], which in these coaches they have little or no occasion for; for, when they rode on horseback, they rode in one suit and carried another to wear when they came to their journey's end, or lay by the way; but in coaches a silk suit and an Indian gown, with a sash, silk stockings, and beaver hats, men ride in and carry no other with them, because they escape the wet and dirt, which on horseback they cannot avoid; whereas in two or three journeys on horseback their clothes and hats were wont to be spoiled; which done, they were forced to have new very often, and that increased the consumption of the manufactures and the employment of the manufacturer, which travelling in coaches doth in no way do."

Certainly it was not all plain sailing for the equestrian. It was often as much as he could do, nay more, to get along. Here is a fourteenth century instance: Archbishop Islip, riding from Oxford Palace to Mayfield, Sussex, in 1362, fell from his horse in a wet and miry lane between Sevenoaks and Tunbridge, so that he was wet through all over. In that pitiable state he rode on without any change of clothes, and was seized with paralysis. Think of his poor Grace, the Primate of All England, utterly dank and bemudded! And things were scarcely a whit better three centuries after. "Eight hundred horse were taken prisoners in the civil wars in Lincolnshire while sticking in the mire."

Add to all the perils from ruts and sloughs and floods those from highwaymen. The waters were only sometimes out; the robbers always were, professionals or amateurs. The woods that then abounded afforded these gentlemen an excellent cover, which they turned to good account. So early as 1285 some attempt was made to circumscribe this accommodation. It was enacted, says Mr. Smiles, "that all bushes and trees along the roads leading from one market to another should be cut down for two hundred feet on either side, to prevent robbers lurking therein." On the Buckinghamshire proverb, "Here if you beat a bush it's odds you'ld start a thief," Fuller, in his *Worthies*, observes, "No doubt there was just occasion for this proverb at the original thereof, which then contained satirical truth, proportioned to the place before it was reformed; whereof thus our great antiquary: 'It was altogether unpassable in times past by reason of trees, until that Leofstane, Abbot of St. Alban's, did cut them down, because they yielded a place of refuge for thieves.' But this proverb is now antiquated as to the truth thereof, Buckinghamshire affording as many maiden assizes as any locality of equal populousness. Yea, hear how she pleadeth for herself that such highwaymen were never her natives, but fled thither for their shelter out of neighbouring counties." We may quite admit the truth of Fuller's latter remark, without believing that highway robbery was at all rare in the county of which he speaks. Certainly in the olden times the Chiltern Hills were notorious for the bandits that haunted them. "We passed through many woods," writes Brunetto Latini, Dante's tutor, of his journey from London to Oxford, "considered here as dangerous places, as they are infested with robbers, which indeed is the case with most of the roads in England. This is a circumstance connived at by the neighbouring barons on consideration of sharing in their booty and of these robbers serving as their protectors on all occasions, personally and with the whole strength of their band. However, as our company was numerous, we had less fear." It was to establish order, or do what he could in that line in this thieves' lair, that the Steward of the Chiltern Hundreds was originally appointed. But in all parts of the country a meeting with those who

> "With a base and boisterous sword enforced
> A thievish living on the common road"

was a very common travelling experience. And so it was common to go armed; as appears from the extract given above, from *The Grand Concern*, &c., and could be shown still more fully, if our space permitted, from Harrison's *Description of England.* See the New Shakspere Society's edition, edited by Mr. Furnivall, Part I., p. 283.

III.

Having said just as much on the ways and means of Elizabethan travelling as may help us to form a picture of our poet *en route*, let us now name specially the roads which he in all probability followed in passing between his home at Stratford and "his place of business" in London.

There are two main routes between Stratford and London: one by Oxford and High Wycombe, the other by Banbury and Aylesbury. And there are traditions which indicate that Shakespeare used them both. At least that he used the former one may be regarded as fairly certain. For the latter one it is to be said that certainly at a later time it became the recognized route from London, and that one tradition seems to connect him with it.

There would seem good reason for believing that in the Elizabethan age, and later still, that the common route was by Oxford. Mr. Halliwell-Phillipps, to whose researches we all owe so much, prints in his *Life of Shakespeare* the following account of some Stratford people who went to London on the business of the Corporation in 1592.

Charges laid out when we went to Court:

Paid for our horsemeat the first night at Oxford .	ii*s.*	viii*d.*
And for our own charges the same night . . .	ii*s.*	ii*d.*
The second night at Islip for our supper . . .	ii*s.*	iiii*d.*
And for our horsemeat the same night at Islip . .	ii*s.*	viii*d.*
The third day for our bait and our horses at Hook Norton		xii*d.*
And for walking our horses at Tetsworth and elsewhere		iii*d.*
Sum for this journey . . . xi*s.* i*d.*		

We are told by Anthony Wood that Shakespeare in his journeys between Warwickshire and London frequented "the house of John Davenant, a sufficient vintner." It was, and is, a tavern known as the "Crown," in the Corn Market, not far from Carfax Church. And so Aubrey: "Mr. William Shakespeare was wont to go into Warwickshire once a year, and did commonly in this journey lie at this [Davenant's] house in Oxon, where he was exceedingly respected." And so Oldys, on the authority of Pope, who quoted Betterton: "If tradition may be trusted, Shakespeare often baited at the Crown Inn, a tavern in Oxford, in his journey to and from London." Davenant, the poet, son of the publican, is said to have been Shakespeare's godson, and to have boasted, or at least suggested, that he stood in a yet closer relation to him.

The tradition that connects Shakespeare with the other route mentioned, or rather with a variety of it, is given only by Aubrey :—

"The humour of the constable in *Midsummer Night's Dream* [he means *Much Ado about Nothing*] he happened to take at Grendon, in Bucks, which is the road from London to Stratford; and there was living that constable about 1642, when I first came to Oxon. I think it was Midsummer night that he happened to lie there. Mr. Jos. Howe is of that parish, and knew him. Ben Jonson and he did gather humours of men daily wherever they came. . . . He was wont to go to his native country once a year."

The *Variorum* version gives Crendon (see iii. 213, ed. 1813), and there is a place called Long Crendon in Bucks, not far from Thame; but we follow the reading of Mr. Halliwell-Phillipps as more probably sound.[1] Grendon, or to give it its full style, Grendon Underwood, lies just to the north of the road—the old Akeman Street—from Aylesbury to Bicester, about six miles from the latter town; and so travelling by the Banbury and Aylesbury route, mentioned above, Shakspeare might easily make the worthy constable's acquaintance. At a later time the coaches, it would seem, did not go by Bicester, but by Buckingham, as may be learned from Owen's *Britannia Depicta, or Ogilby Improv'd*, 1749. No doubt the equestrian traveller would perpetually vary his route, for the sake of companionship, or some special flood or other danger, or for mere variety's sake.

That Shakespeare then did not always go *viâ* Oxford is

---

[1] That Grendon is right is proved—if any proving is wanted—by the fact, known from other sources, that Mr. Jos. Howe was of Grendon, not Crendon. He was born at Grendon Underwood, Bucks, March 29, 1612, and died August 28, 1701, ætat. ninety. See Bishop Pearson's *Vind. Ignat.*; Hearne's *Robert of Gloucester*, ed. 1810.

probable enough, and has a tradition in its favour; but we seem justified in believing that *viâ* Oxford was certainly his ordinary route; and so to it we will now give attention.

IV.

For the sake of convenience, we will divide the journey into four stages, two between Stratford and Oxford, two between Oxford and London.

(i) *From Stratford to Chipping Norton*, 20 miles. A most pleasant expedition, now-a-days, over a finely undulating country, up the valley of the Stour, by the side, for some miles at least, of noble parks, which in Shakespeare's time, perhaps, were not enclosed. Probably no English county surpasses Warwickshire in quiet loveliness. Nature does not reveal herself there in her more terrible forms, but in a sweet, tranquil beauty, balm-like to the spirit, and deliciously restful. Scott calls "Caledonia stern and wild"—Caledonia, with its brown heaths and shaggy woods, with its mountains and floods—"meet nurse of the poetic child." But the greatest of all poetic children was nursed amid far other scenes—not amidst excitement and grandeur, but amidst calm and peace. The Avon, no doubt, could and did rise at times, and sweep the labours of men and oxen before its swollen current; but for the most part it flowed on, not chafing and mutinying against its restraints, but content and gentle; and Gray, with his fine tact, touches the right chord when he speaks of "lucid Avon" straying. It was amidst sweet silences, which Avon's murmur and Arden's whisperings scarcely broke, that Shakespeare was cradled and nurtured,—that the mighty mother did unveil her awful face to her "darling." So too it was with the Jewish prophet. "A great and strong wind rent the mountains and brake in pieces the rocks before the Lord; but the Lord was not in the wind; and after the wind an earthquake; but the Lord was not in the earthquake; and after the earthquake a fire; but the Lord was not in the fire. And after the fire"—after all those tumults and terrors —"a still small voice."

"One said no less truly than merrily," writes Fuller of Warwickshire: "'It is the heart, but not the core of England,' having nothing coarse or choaky therein. The wooded part thereof may want what the fieldon affords; so that Warwickshire is defective in neither. As for the pleasure thereof, an author [Speed] is bold to say, that from Edgehill one may behold it another Eden, as Lot did the Plain of Jordan; but he might have put in: 'It is not altogether so well watered.'"

Shakespeare would leave Stratford by the Clopton Bridge, and then presently turn his face due southward. Soon the road rises. When it falls slightly again, amidst noble trees, he would lose sight of Trinity spire, and feel that his native town was really left behind. At Alderminster, if the day was bright, he might linger a few minutes by the church, so picturesque and picturesquely situated. And then on, beneath trees that, some of them at least, still lend a grateful shadow, by Newbold to Tredington, little dreaming as he passed by the point where a road strikes off to Lower Eatington, that there some day on a cross would be inscribed doggrel mentioning him:—

> "6 miles to Shakspere's Town whose name
>   Is known throughout the earth
> To Shipton 4, whose lesser fame
>   Boasts no such poet's birth."

What comfort even this feeble quatrain might have ministered to him, could he have seen it that first journey, when he was setting forth to try his fortune in strange fields; when, whatever the confidence with which his genius inspired him, his course was yet dim and uncertain; and who knew whether "when the surly sullen bell," which gave warning to the world that he was fled from it, had ceased tolling, any one would care his "poor name" to rehearse? Just where that cross now stands, he may one day have stood, faint and weary, hesitating, despondent. It is, however, quite as probable that when he reached the bifurcation he was in the highest possible spirits, and punned villanously on the name of the neighbouring hamlets.

He might turn a quarter of a mile or so from the high road to look at the fine church at Tredington, with its Norman doorway and its monuments; and, perhaps, gossiping with some native—"he was a handsome, well-shaped man," quoth Aubrey, "very good company, and of a very ready and pleasant smooth wit"—would hear, and would himself crack some joke about the ever hard-up rector. "I have heard Mr. Trap say," so writes the Rev. John Ward, sometime (1662-1679) vicar of Stratford, "that the parsons of Tredington were always needy. One Dr. Brett, who was parson before Dr. Smith, was to marry one Mr. Hicks; and Mr. Hicks, in a vapour, laid a handful of gold and silver upon the book; and he took it all. [Why should not he? What was it put on the book for?] Whereupon Mr. Hicks went to him, and told him of it that he did not intend to have given him all: it was about ten pound. Says he, 'I want, and I will pay thee again;' but never did."

The first place worthy of the name of town he would arrive at would be Shipston-on-Stour, situated on a somewhat bleak upland. A quiet place in these days, but once, as is shown by the inns which still abound, lively enough with coaches and traffic. They gape in vain now, the yard gates, except haply on market-days and at the mop-fair; and the horns that once made the old streets ring are blown, if blown at all, on the banks of the Styx, no longer of the Stour. "In this bleak ill-cultivated track,"[1] writes one who traversed it not quite a century since, "the lower class of labouring poor, who have very little other employment in winter than thrashing out corn, are much distressed for the want of fuel, and think it economy to lie much in bed, to save both firing and provisions."

Now on to Long Compton. "The intervening country is open, exposed, and not very rich," says the writer just quoted, and his description may serve for the earlier time. "It is deficient in planting, which in course of time would generate warmth to the atmosphere, and convert the various influences of the heavens into a nutritive vegetable mould that would eventually enrich it." The water-shed of the Stour is now reached. Long Compton[2] lies straggling in a way that justifies its adjective across a valley, from either edge of which are obtainable fine views, those to the north from above Weston House especially so. Crossing the Combe, which gives the village its name, even the most uninterested and uninteresting tourist would, we should suppose, turn a few steps aside to see the antiquarian glory of Oxfordshire, for we are now in Oxfordshire—the Rollrich-stones.[3] They probably show less well now than in Shakespeare's day, for Time and the farmers have been busy. We may certainly

---

[1] See *Tour in England and Scotland in* 1785. By Thomas Newton, Esq.

[2] At Barton-on-the-Heath, some two miles from Long Compton, lived Robert Dover, of Cotswold games celebrity. (*Merry Wives*, I. i. 92.) See Britton's *Beauties of England and Wales: Warwickshire.*

[3] See Drayton's *Polyolbion*, the 13th Song, and Selden's note.

imagine him lingering in that mysterious circle, wondering what faith or what sorrow or what triumph it was that had once arranged it, hearing perchance from some old shepherd the stories of the Whispering Knights and of the disappointed King. Here indeed were "sermons in stones." The original language was dark and hidden; yet, for all that, they were rich in significance, in suggestion, in pathos. An old MS., quoted by Hearne in his edition of Robert of Gloucester's *Chronicle*, describing the *Mirabilia Britanniæ*, ends thus: "Sunt magni lapides in Oxenfordensi pago, manu hominum quasi sub quadam connexione dispositi, set a quo tempore vel a qua gente vel ad quid memorandum vel signandum factum fuerit, ignoratur. Ab incolis autem voca tur locus ille Rolendrych."

Dropping across another valley, we presently reach Chipping Norton, for no longer can one put up at Chapel House at Cold Norton, a well-known hostelry once—" a most excellent inn, and fitted up in the first style of accommodation," says a last century traveller. "The Chapel" originally belonged, as we learn from Murray, to an Augustinian priory, founded *temp.* Henry II. When Shakespeare passed by, this priory had been suppressed only some fifty years; and, probably enough, ruins were yet standing, and the Chapel looked not altogether unlike itself. At Chipping Norton he would find accommodation in abundance; for it must have been then, as it had been long before (so its name shows) an important market town, and as it was long afterwards, an important station for travellers. When, in 1749, a coach was started to run from Birmingham to London, *viâ* Oxford, "It breakfasts," writes Lady Luxborough to Shenstone, whom she wishes to avail himself of it, "at Henley [in Arden], and lies at Chipping Norton." The town consists mainly of one long street, which it would seem

C

consisted mainly of inns. The church, not much changed probably since the sixteenth century, with its picturesque site, its double north aisle, its hexagonal south porch, and its old monuments, is well worth a visit.

(ii) *From Chipping Norton to Oxford*, 20 miles.—Regaining the high road, Shakespeare would, as far as Woodstock, follow the course of the Glyme, which flows into the Evenlode, which flows into the Isis. The first village encountered is Neat Enstone, half a mile south of Enstone. He might turn aside to see Enstone church, and smile over the legend of the murdered Kenelm, son of Kenulphus, to whom it is dedicated, having, perhaps, Latin enough to interpret the old leonines—always provided he came across them :—

"In Clene sub spina jacet in convalle bovina
Vertice privatus, Kenelmus fraude necatus."

At least let us think of him visiting the Hoarstone, as it is called, the Giant's (A.S. *Ent* = a giant) stone, that is said to give the village its name, for it would lie but a few yards out of his way. We say "it," but in fact there are four other stones, the Hoarstone alone surviving upright. They formed once, it may be believed, a rude tomb with four cumbrous sides and a cumbrous roof, with earth heaped all round them or over them. How long might a giant lie i' the earth ere he rot? He must, surely, have an extra allowance of years.

Passing now on through the hamlet of Over Kiddington, with its ruined cross—at Nether Kiddington, a mile on the left, is a church said to be worth seeing, but we cannot see everything—by Ditchley Park,[1] home of the Lees, who were

---

[1] "Hence [from Cornbury] we went to see the famous wells, natural and artificial grotts and fountains, called Bushell's Wells, at Enstone. This Bushell had been secretary to my Lord Verulam. It is an extraordinary solitude. There he had two mummies; a grott where he lay

destined to be celebrated hereafter by a brother-genius; then, after perhaps a slight detour, to Glympton, and passing on the right the road to Cornbury Hall (only five miles off), where Leicester, Elizabeth's Leicester, perished by the poison prepared, it is said, for his wife; keeping by the old wall of Woodstock Park—it is said to have been the first park enclosed with a wall—our poet would arrive at Woodstock town. For him, obvious associations here would be the Fair Rosamond and the poet Chaucer. The story of the former has been shown to be much mixed with fable; the connection of the latter with Woodstock need not be doubted, for, after all, we may disbelieve that Thomas Chaucer was the son of the poet without disbelieving that the poet, who was connected with the court and with princes of the blood, visited a palace so famous in his time and so much frequented. Shakespeare would enjoy the Chaucer memory, at least, with no allaying scepticism; and as he strolled through that glorious park, might have a vision of Theseus, to be portrayed perhaps by himself some day, "to the laund riding him full right," or of Palamon and Arcite madly fighting—fighting

"breem, as it were boares two."

in a hammock like an Indian. Hence we went to Dichley, an ancient seat of the Lees, now Sir Hen. Lee's; it is a low, ancient timber-house, with a pretty bowling-green. My lady gave us an extraordinary dinner. This gentleman's mother was Countess of Rochester, who was also there, and Sir Walter Saint John. There were some pictures of their ancestors not ill-painted; the great-grandfather had been Knight of the Garter; there was the picture of a Pope, and our Saviour's head. So we returned to Cornbury."—Evelyn's *Diary*, Oct. 20, 1664. This Sir Henry Lee would be, so far as date goes—Bevis belonged to the grandfather—Scott's hero. It would have pleased the author of *Woodstock* to know, that the Will whom his hero is for ever quoting, must often have passed close by Ditchley Park, and might have patted the head, or pinched the ear, of his admirer when a boy.

Or, perhaps, in a realistic vein, he drew a grotesque picture to himself of the royal lover losing the thread and finding himself involved in his own labyrinth, with his Rosamond close by, yet inaccessible, so near and yet so far, while the queen sat fuming and frowning outside, unable to discover the aperture through which her truant spouse had disappeared.

Woodstock would have also associations with his own time. The palace had been one of the places of the queen's confinement during her sister's reign. It was here she heard the milkmaid singing, and envied her happy lot. The verses she is said to have written upon that occasion may have been still decipherable in Shakespeare's time, and he may have perused them on their extraordinary tablet:—

> "O Fortune, how thy restless, wavering state
> Hath fraught with cares my troubled wit!
> Witness this present prison whither fate
> Could bear me, and the joys I quit.
> Thou caused'st the guilty to be losed
> From bands wherein are innocents enclosed;
> Causing me guiltless to be straight reserved,
> And freeing those that death hath well deserved.
> But by her envy can be nothing wrought;
> So God send to my foes all they have thought."

A.D. 1555.   ELIZABETH, Prisoner.

And so, by Begbrooke and Wolvercote, with a drink, perhaps, at Aristotle's well, into Oxford by St. Giles's Street, to the Crown, or, perhaps, on his first visit, to some humbler shelter.

What a revelation of delight and beauty to the youth from Stratford! It would form an epoch in his life, this first passing under the spell of Oxford. It was like entering the Presence. The colleges, already venerable, seemed the very homes of learning and thought. His shrewd observation would, indeed, presently suggest to him that folly and ignorance had here and there intruded themselves, and that often the Muses must be blushing for those called their sons; but so broad and wise a critic would never make the blunder of forgetting in certain abuses the magnificent uses and the magnificent fruits of the great school within whose precincts his heart beat with a new rapture. It was a temple dedicated to Wisdom, and we may believe he bowed his head in it with a sincere worship. To say nothing else, the mere outward beauty of the place, its halls and quadrangles and groves, its antiquity, which showed as "a lusty winter, frosty but kindly," its stately towers, the majestic river on whose waters its fair face was mirrored—the mere outward beauty of the place would gladden his inmost soul.

(iii) *From Oxford to High Wycombe*, 25 miles.—The common route from Oxford to London was by Tetsworth, High Wycombe, and Beaconsfield. It was by this route that Brunetto Latini, from whom we have already quoted, proceeded in the thirteenth century. Harrison, in the Elizabethan age, in his chapter on Thoroughfares, mentions it. This is his list of the intermediate places: "Whatleie, Thetisford, Stocking-church, East Wickham, Becconsfield, Uxbridge." The Stratford citizens went this way on the occasion referred to above. So Evelyn, in 1664, going "with my lord visct. Cornbury to Cornbury in Oxfordshire, to assist him in the planting of the park and bear him company, with Mr. Belin and Mr. May, in a coach with six horses; dined at Uxbridge, lay at Wickam." Returning from Oxford, "we came back by Beaconsfield; next day to London, where we dined at the lord Chancellor's with my lord Bellasis." And endless other instances might be given. But the route by Henley is scarcely four miles longer, and no doubt was often taken.
. Shakespeare would pass down "the High," and beneath Magdalen Tower, across Magdalen Bridge, and then turn to

the left. He might keep to the main road, go on up Heddington Hill, and so pass near Forest Hill, where the Powells lived, with whom Milton was to be one day connected, perhaps exchanging a "good morrow" with the future father of Mary; or, more probably, he would take the nearer road which runs just north of Horspath, and so to Wheatley. Then crossing the Thame, on to Tetsworth, where he might pause to look at the rude sculptures over the south doorway of the church. Then mounting the hill in front of him, he would find the Chilterns now close at hand, stretching from north to south before him like a wall, here richly beech-wooded, there bare down. Near Aston Rowant, which lies a little to the north of the road, there were objects of interest on either hand that might well have attracted him, did his leisure serve. Some two miles to the south there was Shirburne Castle, looking much as we see it now, much as the men of the fourteenth century had seen it, with its towers and moat and drawbridges, as perfect a representation of the Middle Ages as exists, we suppose, at least exteriorly; the interior is modernized. It was here, but not in the present building, which dates from 1377 according to Murray, that Brunetto Latini passed a night. Some eight miles to the north from Aston Rowant, he would find localized traditions of a king on whom he was himself to confer immortal distinction; for the Kimbles—Great Kimble, Little Kimble, and Kimblewick—near Princes Risborough, are said to have derived their name from Cymbeline, or Kimbelinus *apud* Geoffrey of Monmouth, Kimbel *apud* Robert of Gloucester. A yet older form of his name—the form found on certain coins—is found close by in Cunobelin's Camp. The mound by Great Kimble church, the Whiteleaf Cross on Green Holly Hill, and the earthwork just mentioned, all give to the neighbourhood a strange traditional interest. And it has other charms. The view to the west, from near Cunobelin's

Camp, is of unusual extent and beauty; and it is good to be there for a summer's evening.

> "He looked and saw wide territory spread
> Before him, towns and rural works between."

Let us now go on our way from Aston Rowant to the Chilterns, by Stokenchurch Hill to Stokenchurch. Thick wood still covers the sides of the Chilterns here; the thieves that once swarmed in them are no more, or rather have transferred themselves to some other beat, for we cannot flatter ourselves or them that they have grown honest. They only do not rob here because there is no one to rob, and because that way of doing the business is something out of date. Stokenchurch has now a deserted look; it seems created for coaches to drive through, and at the present time they are like angels' visits. On now across the Common into Buckinghamshire, to West Wycombe, not in Shakespeare's time deformed by a church so unsightly and in such vile taste, with its "hypæthral mausoleum," which looks rather like an overgrown pound. And so to High or Chipping Wycombe, called also by Harrison, as we have seen, East Wycombe, whose most interesting feature is its large and handsome church, with its fine Perpendicular tower.

(iv) *From High Wycombe to London*, 29 miles.—The road runs alongside of the Wick till, when a mile beyond Loudwater, that streamlet turns south towards the Thames; and then makes for Beaconsfield, to be made famous in after days by the residence of Waller (at Hall Barns) and Burke (at Gregory's, or Butler's Court, as he named it). The church lies close by the wayside, and might well attract the traveller's notice. And now on by a gentle descent, passing on the right of Bulstrode Park, with its old earthwork and legend of Saxon daring, and then across the common by Gerard's or Jarrett's Cross. And so crossing the Colne into

Middlesex, to Uxbridge, in whose main street still stand many houses that, to judge from their appearance and style, were there when Shakespeare passed through. The place has long outshone its mother village. "Though," says a writer[1] in 1761, "it is entirely independent, and is governed by two bailiffs, two constables, and four head-boroughs, it is only a hamlet to Great Hillington" [*sic*].

The road would now, no doubt, begin to give evidence of the proximity of the metropolis in an increasing number of passengers. The attractive force of the great centre would be more manifestly shown, and Shakespeare would see a striking illustration of one of his own similes:—

> "As many arrows, loosed several ways,
> Come to one mark; as many ways meet in one town;
> As many fresh streams meet in one salt sea;
> As many lines close in the dial's centre;
> So may a thousand actions, once afoot,
> End in one purpose, and be all well borne
> Without defeat."

From Hillingdon Hill, with Harrow on his left and Windsor in the distance on his right, he would look down on the champaign in which London lies. And then, now on the very threshold of his Promised Land, across Hillingdon Heath, and through Northcote, near Southall; over Hanwell Common, through Ealing dean to Acton, by Kensington Gravel Pits, through Tyburn, all along what is now Oxford Street as far as High Street, when, following the old line, he would turn south by St. Giles'-in-the-Fields (then really so), and along Broad Street, and so along Holborn, houses now beginning to multiply around him, and so, at last, into LONDON.

---

[1] *London and its Environs*, &c., 6 vols. Printed for R. and J. Dodsley. 1761.

II.

ROUND ABOUT STRATFORD-ON-AVON IN 1605.

(From *Frazer's Magazine*, April, 1878.)

NOT many other distinctions belong to Stratford-on-Avon besides its sovereign honour of being Shakespeare's birthplace and home; which, indeed, is distinction enough and to spare. "I am sure, sir," said a worthy inhabitant, who was showing us something or other supposed to be of Shakespearian interest; "I am sure, sir, we ought to be very much obliged to Mr. Shakespeare for being born here, for I don't know what we should have done without him." The trade of the place may be described as Shakespeare; and we believe it is not a bad business. The entire town might not inaptly put up above it a gigantic signboard inscribed with the single name of that supreme article of commerce. No town in the Middle Ages ever turned its saint to better account. Nowhere and never have relics been more zealously sought after and treasured up. To think what a single shoe of the hero would now fetch, if only devouring time had spared one; or a doublet—who shall calculate the present market price of a Shakespearian doublet?

The other notabilities of the place are few; not many could be expected, its size and importance considered. It is said to have produced three eminent ecclesiastics in the fourteenth century, two brothers and a kinsman—John Stratford, Archbishop of Canterbury; Robert, Bishop of

Chichester; and Ralph, Bishop of London. Southern, too, the dramatist, has been stated to be a native, by Nuttall, editor of Fuller's *Worthies;* but Southern was born in Ireland, co. Dublin. Perhaps the most remarkable historical association that is commonly known, is Queen Henrietta's temporary residence in the town, and at New Place, in the house that had been Shakespeare's, in June and July, 1643.

We propose now to speak of another historical association that may be claimed for Stratford. Strangely enough, it has been little noticed, though an acquaintance with it cannot fail to add interest to a visit there, especially when we remark that it belongs to Shakespeare's own time. There is nothing said of it in Wheler's *History of Stratford;* nor, it need perhaps scarcely be said, in such minor compilations as Black's *Warwickshire,* or Wise's *Shakespeare, his Birthplace and its Neighbourhood;* nor yet in such really well-informed and valuable volumes as Knight's *Biography* and Halliwell-Phillipps' *Life* of the poet, though we have no doubt Mr. Halliwell-Phillipps knows what there is to be known about it. Nor is there a word respecting it in the poem that has for its subject the locality specially concerned —Jordan's *Welcombe Hills,* published just a century ago. Perhaps the knowledge of such an interest might have imparted some vigour into at least one paragraph of that nerveless production. What we mean, and propose now to show, is that Stratford and its neighbourhood are very intimately connected with Gunpowder Plot.

II.

Where Shakespeare was in 1605 it is impossible to say. Possibly, he was the greater part of the year in London and the rest at Stratford. " He was wont to go to his native country once a year," says Aubrey. More probably, perhaps, he was the greater part of the year in Stratford and not in London; but he may have been "strolling" with his company, if the common opinion is not accepted that he gave over acting early in King James's reign. He "frequented the plays all his younger time," says Ward, in his Diary, 1662; "but in his elder days lived at Stratford, and supplied the stage with two plays every year." Wherever he was, there can be little question that he shared the general horror the discovery of the Powder Treason, as Bacon calls it, excited throughout the land; and that his interest in that hideous affair would be deepened by the fact that one of its chief nurseries lay close by his own home, and another but a few miles off.

The one close by his own home was Clopton House, about a mile north of Stratford, lying at the foot of the western slope of the Welcombe Hills. It belonged at this time to the Baron Carew of Clopton (for so Sir George had been created in the preceding May) in right of his wife Lady Joyce, daughter of William Clopton; but it was let, or rather sublet, to Ambrose Rookwood, one of the chief conspirators, some weeks before the fatal November; and there, during those weeks, Rookwood resided, and from time to time received in his house his partners in the intended crime. Clopton House then was one of the headquarters of the treason.

Only a few miles off was Norbrook, of which we will speak presently, and at no great distance were two other spots concerned in the same infamy—Lapworth and Coughton. All these four places are in the hundred of Barlichway, in which Stratford is situated.

At Bushwood, near Lapworth, was born the chief concoctor of the plot, the heart and soul of it, Robert Catesby. Other estates were possessed by his family, notably at Ashby St.

Legers in Northamptonshire; but it was at Bushwood (which, oddly enough—who wishes, may see an explanation in Dugdale—was a part of the parish of old Stratford) that his father, Sir William, had mostly resided, and here, in 1573, was born he who was to achieve the notoriety of a Catiline. He was the direct descendant of the Catesby whom Shakespeare had represented in his play of *Richard III.*—the first item of the old doggrel :

> "The Cat, the Rat, and Lovell that Dog,
> Rule all England under the Hog."

His mother was a daughter of Sir Robert Throckmorton of Coughton, and so the sister of the Throckmorton on whom the pains of persecution for religion's sake had pressed so heavily. Thus, by race on both sides, as well as by place, he was linked to Warwickshire. These links were further strengthened by his marrying a daughter of Sir Thomas Leigh of Stoneleigh. According to Lingard he was originally a Protestant; and, as has been pointed out, his marriage seems to countenance the statement, as the Leighs were so. Whatever check on his tendencies towards the old faith his matrimonial alliance may have imposed, was presently removed by his wife's death; and he threw himself with all the ardour of a vehement, headstrong nature into the Recusant cause. As we shall mention again presently, he took part in the Earl of Essex's insurrection. He was afterwards involved in all the treasonable projects of the discontented Roman Catholics during the last two years of Queen Elizabeth's reign; and it appears from a letter of Camden's dated only nine days before the Queen's death, that Catesby and several other gentlemen, "hunger-starved for innovations," among whom were Sir Edward Baynham and the two Wrights (all of them conspirators in the Gunpowder Treason), were at that time committed by the Lords of the Council for some seditious movements. Such was the restless, intriguing spirit to whom must be assigned the chief authorship of the Powder Plot. "At his death," says Stow, " he said that the plot and practice of this treason was only his, and that all others were but his assistants, chosen by himself to that purpose, and that the honour thereof only belonged to himself." We must not forget that the wrongs he saw daily inflicted around him on his co-religionists were sorely oppressive, and such as might well goad him to a fierce indignation. Shortsighted and diabolical as his scheme was, it is yet credible that the motives that instigated it were not altogether base. Certainly he seems to have kindled an admiration and enthusiasm that no merely ignoble nature could have kindled. There is a certain lustre about him, even in the midst of his obstinate folly and horrible guilt. Something of what is Divine, however devilish the work his hands are set about, is yet present in the man for whom and near whom others are ready to die. His comrades seem to have been drawn and attached to him by a singular fascination. He might truly say with Edmund, when "the wheel had come full circle," "yet Catesby was beloved." King he was amongst them.

Also Lapworth-born was another of the conspirators, of humbler rank—Thomas Bates, an old servant of Catesby's. He was not one of the original sharers of the scheme; but as he had been employed about Vinegar House—the house hired in the Palace Yard, Westminster—and so had inevitably seen something of what was going on, it was thought well to take him into full partnership.

Lapworth is some eleven miles from Stratford; but we have given it precedence of Norbrook because of its connection with the leading conspirator. Norbrook is only some five miles from Shakespeare's town. It lies a little off the Warwick road, to the left, very near Coplow Hill. It was an old manor-house, wherein at the time that concerns us resided John Grant with his brothers, who also were implicated in the plot, though not to the same extent as John; for John was one of the thirteen chief traitors. "This mansion-house was conveniently placed for the purpose of the conspirators, being in the centre of their proposed rendezvous and of the most populous part of Warwickshire, between the towns of Warwick and Stratford-on-Avon. It was walled and moated, and well calculated from its great extent for the reception of horses and ammunition. At the present day, little remains of it but the name. Some fragments of massive stone walls are, however, still to be found, and the line of the moat may be distinctly traced; an ancient hall of large dimensions is also apparent among the partitions and disfigurations of a modern farmer's kitchen. The identity of the house is fixed, not only by its name and local situation, but by a continuing tradition that this was the residence of one of the gunpowder conspirators; and still more conclusively by the circumstance that an old part of the building, which was taken down a few years ago, was known by the name of the Powder Room."

To understand the statement that Norbrook was "in the centre of their proposed rendezvous," it must be remembered that the blowing up of the House of Lords was to be followed by a general Papist insurrection. The existing Government having been summarily disposed of, a new one was to be formed, at the head of which was to be placed the Princess Elizabeth, she who was in after years the "Winter Queen" of Bohemia. At this time she also was living in Warwickshire—at Combe Abbey, some four or five miles east of Coventry, in the care of Lord Harington; and the design of Catesby and his party was, immediately after the explosion, to seize her at Combe and proclaim her accession to the throne. Of all such subsequent operations Warwickshire was to be the base; and Norbrook was to be the Warwickshire magazine.

Lapworth and Norbrook, then, as the homes of three of the chief ringleaders in the Plot, are places of no slight importance in its history. They and the district in which they lie are further distinguished by the temporary sojourn of others of the notorious thirteen. At Catesby's instance the Wrights—John and Christopher—took up their abode at Lapworth; Ambrose Rookwood, as we have seen, at Clopton House; and Sir Everard Digby at Coughton Court, about eleven miles to the west of Stratford, near Alcester. Coughton Court was the seat of the Throckmortons. The present owner was a minor, and it may readily be supposed that Catesby, whose mother, as we have mentioned, was a Throckmorton, would have no difficulty in arranging for its temporary occupation by one of his friends. So thither, in October, proceeded Sir Everard and his family, along with Father Garnet and others, quitting for the nonce, as he thought, his own seat at Gayhurst, or Gothurst, near Newport Pagnell in Buckinghamshire, in effect quitting it for ever.

Thus, shortly before the day fixed for the explosion, no less than seven of the arch-traitors, to say nothing of minor persons, might have been found in the hundred of Barlichway. As the time drew near, Catesby sold his property at Bushwood (to Sir Edward Grevile of Milcote, near Stratford) in order to provide funds for his enterprise. But none the less did Warwickshire remain the general rendezvous.

One other part of the county was to be made memorable by its connection with this wild, execrable folly. This was

Dunsmore Heath, on the other side, a few miles south of Rugby, stretching to the east of Dunchurch. "The bloody hunting match at Dunchurch" was the name given to "the meet" to which Sir Everard Digby invited the Roman Catholic gentry for Tuesday, November 5th. To do these gentlemen justice, it must be noticed that they knew little or nothing of the iniquity that had been concocted, or of what was to follow it. There was a general impression that some Recusant movement was afoot, but no particulars had been vouchsafed. One cannot but believe that, had the scheme of the conspirators been disclosed to them in all its enormity, they would at once have repudiated and denounced it. It is true that they were smarting beneath grievous injustice, heavy and perpetual fines exacted from them, personal penalties occasionally inflicted, but all this persecution had not divested them of humanity and rendered them capable of an atrocity that would justify the old adage, "homo homini lupus," or a fresh reading of it, "homo homini diabolus." The conspirators themselves had not attained such hardness of heart with "no compunctious visitings of nature." Even of Catesby so much may be believed, and of the others with scarcely an exception so much is known. They recoiled when Catesby first revealed his horrid purpose. Not at once were they "settled," and could—

> "Bind up
> Each corporal agent to this terrible feat."

Nature, says the old poet, in giving men tears, confesses she gives them most tender hearts.

> "Mollissima corda
> Humano generi dare se natura fatetur
> Quæ lacrumas dedit."

And tears cannot harden into frost in an instant; petrifaction, thank Heaven, is a slow process, and ofttimes may be retarded, may be prevented. Certainly, those Recusant gentlemen who mustered at the Lion Inn at Dunchurch and the Bull at Coventry that Monday and Tuesday in November, 1605, were not so lost to all sense of sound patriotism and true manhood, as that they would have aided and abetted such devilry as Catesby and his gang had brought themselves to believe was of God, godly. But there they were, uninformed, wondering, probably expecting that their game was to be something more than hares, and assuredly ready to strike a good blow, if opportunity was given, for what was in their eyes the cause of Heaven.

In this same part of the county, at Shelford, lived John Littleton, who it was hoped would join Stephen and the others on the Heath.

Thus intimately was Warwickshire associated with the Gunpowder Conspiracy. We may just add that Huddington, or Uddington, the home of the Winters—Thomas and Robert, two more of the chief Thirteen—lies but just beyond the western frontier of this same county, no great distance from Alcester and Coughton; that Ashby St. Legers is situated just over the eastern border, but a few miles from Dunchurch; and that Holbeach, where at last the ringleaders were brought to bay, is in Staffordshire, the county which bounds Warwickshire on the north-west.

III.

It is clear that the conspiracy would excite a very special interest in every Warwickshire man and in Shakespeare. Counties were more sharply distinguished, and county feeling ran far higher in the old days than now, though it is by no means extinct yet, nor likely to be. Wherever Shakespeare was in the autumn of 1605, there can be no question, as we have already said, that the horrid tale at which men stood aghast would affect him the more deeply for its association with his own neighbourhood. Had a Romanist rising taken place, Stratford itself might have been the scene of bloodshed and outrage. And, as a fact, conspiracy had found close by

> "A cavern dark enough
> To mask" its "monstrous visage."

In the midst of the peaceful hills that rose almost within sight of New Place (the poet's property since 1597) treason had made its lair. Besides the interest of locality, it is fairly certain that he must have felt another interest in the plot, arising from personal knowledge of some of its members. We are not about to advance a theory that Shakespeare was himself a powder plotter—that Guy Fawkes was his "sworn brother;" though, indeed, there is quite as much —not to say more—to be said for such a theory as for many with which the world is favoured. We commend it to the attention of the brilliant ready-made critics with whom our age is abundantly adorned; and, for ourselves, all we wish to point out is, that Shakespeare must in all probability have been brought into personal contact with several of the traitors. If at Stratford in September and October, he would grow familiar, by sight at least, with Rookwood and his brother and their visitors—amongst others Grant, "Mr. Winter," "Mr. Wright" (the document we quote does not specify which of the Winters, or which of the Wrights), Catesby. Grant, too, he may have seen at other times in the streets of Stratford, or on the Warwick road. But it is of a possible acquaintance in London that we are thinking; it is of the fact that Catesby, Grant, Tresham, the Wrights, and Thomas Winter, had all been actively concerned in the rebellion, or miserable failure of a rebellion, attempted by the Earl of Essex in February, 1601.

Here again is a fine opening for a theory. What a temptation to prove that Shakespeare was an uncompromising partisan of that unfortunate nobleman. However, as we do not believe he was so, we shall deny ourselves the pleasure of proving it, and be content to remark that, without being a rabid partisan, he yet was attracted by a nature which with all its faults—they were neither few nor slight—seems to have been singularly winning and lovable. The mention of Essex in *Henry V.* deserves especial notice and consideration. It is quite unique in its kind. The poet is wishing to suggest parallels to the enthusiastic welcome the victor of Agincourt received from his people on his return from that famous field. He says, even so did the people of Rome greet their Cæsar when he came home triumphant; and even so would the people of England greet their Essex, were he now returning in glory from his Irish campaign.

> "But now behold,
> In the quick forge and working-house of thought,
> How London doth pour out her citizens!
> The mayor and all his brethren in best sort,
> Like to the senators of the antique Rome,
> With the plebeians swarming at their heels,
> Go forth and fetch their conquering Cæsar in;
> *As by a lower but loving likelihood,*
> *Were now the general of our gracious Empress,*
> *As in good time he may, from Ireland coming*
> *Bringing rebellion broached on his sword,*
> *How many would the peaceful city quit,*
> *To welcome him!* Much more, and much more cause,
> Did they this Harry."

This "loving likelihood"—observe that "loving"—was never to be fulfilled. It was rather himself than rebellion that poor Essex brought back "broached on his sword."

But such an introduction of him, and in such language, by a writer so chary of such allusions, is surely significant of a more than common feeling of interest and affection. There is another fact pointing decisively in the same direction. It is Shakespeare's intimate friendship with the Earl of Southampton, who was Essex's most intimate friend. "The love I dedicate to your lordship," runs the brief letter to Southampton that prefaces *The Rape of Lucrece*, "is without end. . . . . What I have done is yours; what I have to do is yours; being part in all I have, devoted yours. Were my worth greater, my duty would show greater. Meantime, as it is, it is bound to your lordship, to whom I wish long life still lengthened with all happiness." These words, which surely sound a note of sincerity often unheard in such epistles, were written in 1594; but there is good ground for believing that the feeling they express was no transient emotion, but deep-rooted and flourishing to the end. This dear friend was, we repeat, also Essex's dear friend. He was one of his truest and faithfullest supporters that fatal Sunday when Essex, halting between ever so many opinions, half paralyzed it would seem by the fearful difficulties amidst which he found himself, confused and confounded by the clamour and fury of the followers who filled the court of his house, and were eager for action, however foolish and desperate, "extremely appalled as divers that happened to see him then might visibly perceive in his face and countenance, and almost moulten with sweat, though without any cause of bodily labour, but only by the perplexity and horror of his mind," passed forth into Fleet Street on the way to inevitable disaster and ruin. At his trial, which soon followed, Southampton stood side by side with him, and was condemned at the same time. And, though he did not share his fate—in death they were divided—for two long years he lay in the Tower under sentence of death. Such being Southampton's devotion to Essex, and such Shakespeare's to Southampton, Shakespeare's confessed relation to Essex being also such as we have seen, we cannot doubt that Shakespeare would have some personal knowledge of Essex's chief partisans, amongst whom, as has been mentioned, were several of the Powder Plotters.

That extreme and violent Papists should rally around Essex may seem not a little surprising, when we call to mind his Puritan sympathies and connections. During the weeks that ushered in the end, "the most eminent Puritan divines preached daily at Essex House, to hear whose sermons the citizens flocked in great numbers." We wonder if Catesby and his intimates "sat under" these orators? We presume that, with a dispensation, they might lawfully do so. The whole history of the Essex riot, or whatever it is to be called, is far from clear. Probably the misguided leader scarcely knew himself what he would be at. He was a governor who did not govern, a leader that was led; and so all kinds of unquiet folk gathered around him. His house was a very cave of Adullam, and with but slight variation one might quote the well-known description: "Everyone that was in distress, and everyone that was in debt, and everyone that was discontented, gathered themselves unto him; and he became a captain [a merely nominal one] over them; and there were with him about" three "hundred men." An odd, ill-assorted conflux. "Misery acquaints a man with strange bedfellows." But indeed there would be much in these Puritan discourses that the Recusant party would hear with thorough complacency and satisfaction. "The Puritans were in the habit of justifying resistance to authority, and one of the preachers at Essex House went so far as to say that the great magistrates of the kingdom had power, in case of necessity, to control and restrain the Sovereign."

Again, the Earl and his friends had a great liking for theatrical entertainments. "My Lord Southampton and Lord Rutland come not to the Court," writes Rowland White towards the close of 1599; "the one doth, but very seldom; they pass away the time in London merely in going to plays every day." We might be pretty sure, if there was no evidence on the point, that the company whose services would be called into requisition, or whose theatre would be frequented, would be that of which Shakespeare was a member. But one piece of evidence there is. "The afternoon before the Rebellion, Merrick, with a great company of others that afterwards were all in the action, had procured to be played before them the play of deposing 'King Richard II.' When it was told him by one of the players that the play was old, and they should have loss in playing it, because few would come to it, there was forty shillings extraordinary given to play, and so thereupon played it was." Whether the play thus performed by special request and arrangement was Shakespeare's *Richard II.* or some other, it was certainly Shakespeare's company that was thus negotiated with; for in another account of the transaction is given the name of the player with whom the bargain was struck. It was Philips, and Philips was one of Shakespeare's company.

Thus Shakespeare was probably brought into contact with several of the Plotters, not only socially but professionally. He had acted before them, and his plays no doubt had been acted before them again and again.

We may confidently believe, then, that besides the general interest in the conspiracy he would feel as an Englishman, there would be for Shakespeare other special interests, springing both from local and personal associations. The thing would have for him a singular nearness and reality.

IV.

Having now pointed out fully enough for our purpose the close connection of the Plotters with Shakespeare's county and with himself, we will for a short space turn our eyes again towards Clopton, the suburb of Shakespeare's own town, and see what little is to be seen of what went on there.

It was there, as has been already twice mentioned, that Rookwood and his family located themselves in September, 1605.

The house stands in a neighbourhood where Shakespeare possessed property, and with which he had in the very year that especially concerns us formed a fresh monetary connection. In May, 1602, he had bought land in that part from William and John Combe—107 acres of arable land. "In July, 1605," writes Mr. Halliwell-Phillipps, in that treasure-house of sound and accurate information, bar the acceptance of certain forgeries, his *Life of Shakespeare*, "Shakespeare made the largest purchase he ever completed, giving the sum of £440 [equal to some £1,750 of our money] for the unexpired term of a moiety of a lease, granted in 1544 for ninety-two years, of the tithes of Stratford, Old Stratford, Bishopton, and Welcombe. In the indenture of conveyance he is described as of Stratford-upon-Avon, gentleman; and, as he is similarly designated three years earlier, when we know that he was in London, we may conclude that after the purchase of New Place he had taken up his permanent abode in his native town." This would of course be consistent with long visits to London from time to time. Probably enough his home had been at Stratford all along, only he had been mostly away from it. "It appears from a letter," written by Abraham Sturley, January 24, 1597-8, "that as early as 1598 the subject of Shakespeare becoming the purchaser of these tithes had been mooted at Stratford, and the management of them would probably require great prudential care. It is not impossible that confidence was entertained in Shakespeare's tact and judgment, and that this, as well as his command of capital, produced the desire of the Council of Stratford, who received a rent from these tithes, that he should become the purchaser." And then follows a copy of the indenture (pp. 210-6). Mr. Phillipps also quotes from a copy of a rent-roll of the borough of Stratford the following note: "Mr. Thomas Combes and Mr. William Shakespear do hold all manner of tithes of corn, grain, and hay in the towns, hamlets, villages, and fields of Old Stratford, Welcomb, and Bishopton, and all manner of tithes of wool, lamb, hemp, flax, and other small and privy tithes, for the yearly rent of xxxiiij li., payable at our Lady Day and Michaelmas."

According to the *Beauties of England and Wales*, 1814, " Clopton House is a venerable mansion, probably erected in the latter part of the fifteenth century; but some modern exterior alterations detract much from the general effect of the building. In different apartments are preserved a few pictures, and some curious articles of ancient furniture, among which is a bed, *said* to have been given to Sir Hugh Clopton by King Henry VII." Not far from it—a furlong or two—at Welcombe, lived Shakespeare's friend John Combe. His house (the present one standing there is "quite a recent erection") nestled in a southern recess of the hills that derived their name from it, or rather from the " cwm " where it stood. "To the west of Alveston," says Britton, " are Welcombe Hills, the celebrated scene of warlike operations between the Britons and Saxons. Here are extensive entrenchments, termed the Dingles, which appear to have been formed by the latter people [they are probably British, to begin with at least], and numerous other earthworks, some of which were probably thrown up to cover the remains of those who fell in battle. The rugged features of this neighbourhood are softened by Welcombe Lodge, the handsome residence of George Lloyd, Esq.," "John a'Combe's" successor. It was in this vicinity that an inclosure was attempted in 1614, and successfully resisted by the Corporation, with whom Shakespeare seems to have cordially acted. There is a brief glimpse of him in that year, in a memorandum made by one Thomas Green, clerk of the Corporation, who had been despatched to London about this business: "1614 Jovis 17 No. My cousin Shakspear coming yesterday to town, I went to see how he did. He told me that they assured him they meant to inclose no farther than to Gospel Bush, and so up straight (leaving out part of the dingles to the field) to the gate in Clopton Lodge, and take in Salisbury piece; and that they mean in April to survey the land, and then to give satisfaction and not before; and he and Mr. Hall say they think there will be nothing done at all." Nor was the great poet's sagacity at fault in the matter. Nothing was done at all; though he did not himself live to see the common ground secured to his fellow citizens. "A petition on the subject was presented to the Privy Council; and in 1618 an order was made, not only forbidding the inclosure, but peremptorily commanding that some steps which Combe actually seems to have commenced in it should be at once retraced." The other memorandum of Green's is as follows: "23 Dec. A hall. Letters written to Mr. Manyring [Mainwaring], another to Mr. Shakspear, with almost all the company's hands to either. I also writ myself to my cousin Shakspear [he was still in London?] the copies of all our acts, and then also a note of the inconveniences would happen by the inclosure." Clearly, for private reasons if not for public, Shakespeare was much interested in this Welcombe district.

In the heart, then, of a neighbourhood so well known to and intimately connected with Shakespeare, came Rookwood to reside, as we have said. The official duties of Lord Carew must have seldom permitted any protracted occupancy of his house by himself, even since his return from Ireland. In his absence at this time, Robert Wilson, Lord Carew's tenant, was persuaded to admit the stranger from Suffolk, Grant and one of the Winters assuring him of the stranger's intimacy with his master.

He came from Coldham Hall, in the parish of Stanningfield, where his house, built in 1574, still stands. He "was born of Roman Catholic parents," says Jardine, "and carefully brought up from his childhood in the Roman Catholic faith. He had received his education at one of the Roman Catholic universities in Flanders; and when he succeeded to his inheritance upon his father's death, in 1600, his house in Suffolk became, as it had been in his father's time, a common asylum for persecuted priests, and mass was constantly performed there; in consequence of which he was subjected to repeated prosecutions and penalties. It is remarkable that he had been indicted for recusancy at the London and Middlesex Sessions in February, 1604-5, after the Gunpowder Plot had been contrived and arranged. He married a daughter of Sir William Tyrwhit, of Kettleby, in Lincolnshire, by whom he had two or three children. He possessed an ample estate, and was specially remarkable for his fine stud of horses, a circumstance which made him a particularly desirable acquisition to the conspirators. At the period of which we are speaking he was twenty-seven years of age. He had been long the intimate friend of

Catesby, whom he says 'he loved and respected as his own life;' and attachment to him, and the contagion of religious enthusiasm, drew Rookwood from the bosom of his family, and bound him to this rash and desperate conspiracy."

It was not till about Michaelmas, 1605, that Rookwood was admitted into the horrid league, which had then existed for some year and a half, it being in Lent, 1604, that Catesby and John Wright and Thomas Winter first formed it. This admission must have taken place about the time of the first of the two eclipses, which to the superstition of the age threatened evil things. In September was a lunar, early in October a solar, eclipse; and the popular mind held with Gloucester in *King Lear* that "these late eclipses in the sun and moon portend no good to us"—a passage we shall consider again by-and-by. It was in London that same September that "Catesby told him that 'for the ancient love he had borne unto him, he would impart a matter of importance unto him;' and then, after administering the oath of secrecy, he revealed to him the design of blowing up the King and the Parliament House with powder. Rookwood states that he was 'somewhat amazed' at the proposal, and asked 'how such as were Catholics and divers other friends should be preserved;' Catesby answered that 'a trick should be put upon them.' Then Rookwood objected that 'it was a matter of conscience to take away so much blood.' But Catesby assured him that 'he might be satisfied on that head, for though he had not yet put that case in particular to any, he had put the like case, and had been resolved by good authority that in conscience it might be done.' Rookwood still expressing scruples of conscience respecting the lawfulness of the action, Catesby told him 'that he had also asked advice, whether if the act could not be done without the destruction of some innocents, it might still be done, and was resolved that rather than the action should fail they must also suffer as the rest did.' By these assurances Rookwood's scruples were quieted ; " and he at once fell in with Catesby's machinations. Thus were his better instincts overborne ; thus the voice of conscience smothered ; and a gallant gentleman degraded into a base assassin. Alas for him that he should have surrendered those Divine remonstrances of his soul to any so-called authority of priest or Jesuit or " bejesuited " friend. Alas that he was not " to his own self true," and obedient to those natural promptings which would have saved him from falsehood and shame. Alas that he ignobly placed himself at the bidding and in the hands of others, and submitted to believe that what was inhuman could be religious, that villainy could be holy, that impiety could be pious.

Such was Shakespeare's new neighbour in the autumn of 1605. It would seem to have been just after his joining the plot that the well-known pilgrimage to St. Winifred's Well in Flintshire was made—made, we suppose, to procure a blessing for the nefarious work then in hand. An odd, strange God, the God of these people ; or did they confound God and devil? " The ladies of the company went barefoot from Holt to the Well, where all remained a whole night." To think of the prayers these pilgrims were praying !

"Tantum religio potuit suadere malorum."

It was probably after their return that Rookwood settled at Clopton.

In a list of letters "come about this treason," made by Levinus Munck, one unluckily lost is thus described—it is the document we referred to above: "A paper reporting that at Clopton there hath been with Ambrose Rockwood [sic], John Grant, Mr. Winter [Thomas?], Mr. Ross, Mr.

Townshend [of Broughton, Suffolk], Mr. Cee, Mr. Wright [John?], Sir Edward Bushall, Robert Catesbye." We know also that Rookwood's brother Thomas was there. So the house was often pretty full of traitors. A strange fierce company this in the bosom of the Welcombe Hills.

Rookwood seems scarcely to have outgrown a young man's vanity in dress and such matters. There is mention of a sword of his with its hilt, or hilts, as they used to say, engraved with the passion of Christ; and Sir William Wade, Lieutenant of the Tower, writes about "a fair scarf that Rucwood [*sic*] made," a sort of badge, perhaps, as Sir William speaks of "figures or ciphers on it from which something might be gathered." "Rucwood made also a very fair hungarian horseman's coat lined all with velvet and other apparel exceeding costly, not fit for his degree." Thus he would be a notable object in the streets of Stratford, if ever he rode that way, and one that would exercise the minds of Dogberry and Verges if haply they espied him.

But though the burghers might have their suspicions about their new neighbours, no one would credit them with any design so fiendish as they were presently discovered to have entertained and matured. Some ten or eleven days before Tuesday the 5th, Rookwood disappeared from those parts. He had gone up to London to be in at the death. Then the news reached Stratford of some Papist outbreak near Warwick. There had been some sort of muster, horses had been stolen; and the county was up. Suspicion at once fell on the tenant of Clopton House, especially as his brother Thomas had been seized attempting escape, as it seemed, and his associates Grant and Winter were known to have been actively concerned in the horse robbery at Warwick. The bailiff of Stratford at once proceeded to search the house at Clopton. Mrs. Rookwood was still there. He found a "cloak bag" of crosses and "massing reliques," but nothing that threw light on the disturbance, the rumours of which spread general alarm. Presently came the news of what had been intended at Westminster. A few days later Mrs. Grant, Mrs. Percy, and the wives of other conspirators were apprehended and sent up to London, Mrs. Rookwood amongst them, we suppose; and so there was an end of the traitors' occupancy of Clopton House.

Here, before we quit the scene, is a copy of two documents that mention it preserved at the State Paper Office, in the Gunpowder Plot Book.

"The examination of Thomas Rookwood, gent., of Clopton, in the county of Warwick, taken before Sir Fulk Grevil, day and year aforesaid [Nov. 8, 1605]: This examinate being demanded upon what occasion he passeth into these parts, saith he was going to Worcester to meet with one Ingram that had sold him a hawk. Being demanded why he fled from his way at Alcester, said because Townsend and Johnson that were of his company said the town was disquieted, which made them return out of the way to Bidford, when he was with the rest apprehended.

"The examination of William Johnson, servant to Mr. Rookwood of Clopton in the county of Warwick, yeoman: This examinate being demanded for what cause he past this way saith he was going to Worcester to see a kinsman he had there. Being demanded how young Mr. Rookwood and Townsend came into this county, saith that they both had a purpose to deal with a hawk with a gentleman in Hereford. ['Young Mr. Rookwood,' said Worcester.] Being demanded why he fled when he came to Alcester after the troops were past, saith when he came and saw the town disturbe [*sic*], he went with Mr. Rook [*sic*] and Townsend the contrary way out of the way to Bidford, when he was apprehended."

There are "examinations" of other servants of Rookwood, appointed to go from Suffolk to meet him at Norbrook.

Meanwhile the master was fleeing for his life. Early on Tuesday morning those of the Plotters who were in town were aware that their plot was discovered. "Richard Johnson" had been seized the preceding midnight, and, though he had disclosed nothing, it was clearly time to be gone. One Henry Tatnall met two gentlemen, afterwards thought to be conspirators, in Lincoln's Inn Fields that morning, and heard one say: "God's wounds! we are wonderfully beset, and all is marred." They were soon tearing along the road for Dunchurch. Rookwood started last, but, better mounted, soon overtook the others—overtook Keyes about three miles beyond Highgate, then Catesby and John Wright beyond Brickhill; then a little farther on Percy and Christopher Wright; and "they five rode together; and Percy and John Wright cast off their cloaks and threw them into a hedge to ride the more speedily." And so to Ashby St. Legers, Rookwood having covered the eighty miles in seven hours. Then on to Dunchurch, where it soon got out that the grand blow that was to be struck, whatever it was, had been thwarted, and all was lost. The assembly rapidly dissolved; and the ringleaders, left almost alone, and it would seem wellnigh planless and desperate, dashed on through the night by or through Warwick—Grant and the others went through, and stole fresh horses, Rookwood went round—to Norbrook, reached about daybreak, where they rested awhile, as they well had need; then, on the Wednesday, through Alcester to Huddington, the Winters' house; on the Thursday, at sunrise, to Whewell Grange, where they helped themselves to Lord Windsor's arms and armour; then, with yet thinner numbers, on to Holbeach, the house of Stephen Littleton, where, during the night, they made what preparations they could for the assault certain to be made on the morrow. It was here, on Friday the 8th, that some powder that was drying exploded, and Rookwood and others were severely burnt. Sir Richard Walsh, Sheriff of Worcestershire, with the *posse comitatus*, was soon at the gate. "When I came," says Th. Winter, who had been outside at the time of the explosion—"I found Mr. Catesby reasonable well, Mr. Percy, both the Wrights, Mr. Rookwood, and Mr. Grant. I asked them what they resolved to do; they answered, 'We mean here to die.' I said again I would take such part as they did. About eleven of the clock came the company to beset the house, and as I walked into the court I was shot into the shoulder, which lost me the use of my arm; the next shot was the elder Wright shot dead; after him the younger Mr. Wright; and fourthly, Ambrose Rookwood [shot, not shot dead]. Then said Mr. Catesby to me, standing before the door they were to enter: 'Stand by me, Tom, and we will die together.' 'Sir,' quoth I, 'I have lost the use of my right arm, and I fear that will cause me to be taken.' So, as we stood close together, Mr. Catesby, Mr. Percy, and myself, they two were shot, as far as I could guess, with one bullet; and then the company entered upon me, hurt me in the belly with a pike, and gave me the other wounds, until one came behind and caught hold of both my arms."

One more scene we will look at, in which Mr. Rookwood, of Clopton, plays a signal part. Let us pass over his trial with his surviving fellows—the heads of Catesby and Percy had for some time been grinning "upon the side of the Parliament House," that of Tresham on London Bridge; how he spoke of his attachment to Catesby; how he begged for mercy, that he might be punished "*corporaliter non mortaliter;*" and see the last act in his miserable tragedy.

The old sentence in such cases was carried out in all its barbarity, at which, in the then state of public feeling, one can scarcely wonder. Indeed, according to a letter of the time, "there were some motions made in Parliament about a more sharp death for the gunpowder conspirators." Four—Sir Edward Digby, Robert Winter, Grant, and Bates—were executed at the west end of St. Paul's Churchyard; the others—Th. Winter, Keyes, Fawkes, and he in whom we are here specially interested—in the Old Palace Yard at Westminster, opposite the Parliament House, now grimly decorated, as we have just mentioned, with the heads of Catesby and Percy. The procession to the Old Palace Yard "passed by a house in the Strand in which Rookwood's wife lodged. She had placed herself at an open window, and Rookwood, raising himself as well as he could from the hurdle on which he was drawn, called upon his wife to 'pray for him.' She replied in a clear, strong voice, 'I will! I will! And do you offer yourself with a good heart to God and your Creator! I yield you to Him with as full an assurance that you will be accepted of Him as when He gave you to me.'" So a contemporary MS. Evidently of a high and inflexible spirit was this lady—something of the antique Roman in her—who could look on such a sight and speak so firmly as she looked. The rough journey was soon completed. Then kneeling and often bowing their heads to the ground, the doomed men prayed, "but no voice heard, saving now and then 'O Jesu, Jesu, save me and keep me,' &c., which words they repeated many times upon the ladder," and soon all was over.

Such were the ends of Mr. Grant of Norbrook, and Mr. Rookwood, late of Clopton.

V.

As Gunpowder Plot was thus brought near, so to speak, to Shakespeare, those scenes at the west end of St. Paul's and in Old Palace Yard, so linked, as we have seen, with Stratford-on-Avon, it might be expected that we should find in his plays special allusions to an event that was in such a manner intruded upon his special notice. For our own part, we think that expectations of this kind are based upon ignorance of Shakespeare's way of working. But there are one or two passages—we ourselves shall lay no great stress upon them—which have been supposed to be suggested, and may have been suggested, by this same conspiracy.

There is a passage in *King Lear*—we have already quoted a few words from it—which is possibly not impertinent. Certainly it should be remembered that it was in all probability about the close of 1605, or in the course of 1606, that *King Lear* was written. Likely enough it was begun in the one year and finished in the other. "These late eclipses in the sun and moon," says Gloucester, who is ready to explain what goes wrong by any theory but that of personal culpability, "portend no good to us. Though the wisdom of nature [*i.e.* natural philosophy] can reason it thus and thus, yet nature finds itself scourged by the sequent effects: love cools, friendship falls off, brothers divide: in cities, mutinies: in countries, discord: in palaces, treason: and the bond cracked 'twixt son and father. . . . . We have seen the best of our time; machinations, hollowness, treachery, and all ruinous disorders follow us disquietly to our graves." Surely this speech would have a very curious significance in 1606; and it can scarcely be accidental that it was written in or about that year.

The Porter in *Macbeth* amuses himself by fancying that he is, for the nonce, the janitor of hell. Knocks come pretty frequent at that door; and amongst other arrivals "here's an equivocator that could swear in both scales against either scale; who committed treason enough for God's sake, yet could not equivocate to heaven. O come in, equivocator." The exact date of the composition of *Macbeth* cannot be absolutely ascertained. Malone assigns it to 1610, which is certainly too late; Dyce to 1606, which is probably not far out. That it is not later than 1606 could be shown pretty definitely, if our space permitted. One could not wish for a truer description of the Powder Plot than that it was a committing of treason for God's sake. That flattering unction the unhappy plotters laid constantly to their soul; it was their misguided boast, that they were championing the true faith.

And then the mention of equivocation. It is true that great scandals had been previously caused by the Jesuits and their practice of this art; but Father Garnet had surpassed his predecessors. To the average Englishman of the day who watched that worthy's proceedings, the distinction between equivocating and what is vulgarly termed lying seemed impossible to recognize. To subtly discriminate between propositions, mental, verbal, written, mixed, was quite beyond his feeble capacity. And in considering the question of Garnet's complicity in the Plot, we must plainly assert we do not see how, all things considered, any weight whatever can be attached to his own denial of it. We know that on one occasion—we refer to his denying that he had had an interview with Hall—he saw his way to absolutely deny a fact, and what he knew to be a fact; and to his contemporaries his conscience seemed to be remarkably elastic in such respects. Equivocation sank into the worst repute; and that equivocators could by no means "equivocate to heaven," but verily would succeed in equivocating to a very different region, was certainly the general impression and feeling. On the whole, the passage looks very like an allusion to the Plot, and especially to Garnet, as Malone long ago pointed out. It is just what would be commonly said of him wherever his participation in the Plot was believed; and it was generally believed, nor has it yet been successfully contradicted. He "committed treason enough for God's sake, yet could not equivocate to heaven."

Probably written about the same time, about 1606, *Timon of Athens* contains a passage that the Plot illustrates, if it did not suggest. It is held, and not without reason, that this play is not all by Shakespeare; and it may be that the passage we are about to quote may not be from his hand, though in our opinion it is fully in his manner. Anyhow it appears in a play of which he was joint author, and so we may believe received his assent and approval, if it was not actually penned by him. Sempronius, applied to by Timon for help, has just cloaked the baseness of his refusal with the pretence that he is affronted at not having been applied to earlier. "Who bates mine honour," says the mean creature, making a show of dignity, "shall not know my coin;" and so *exit*. "Excellent!" cries Timon's servant, when his back is turned; "your lordship's a goodly villain. The devil knew not what he did when he made man politic; he crossed himself by 't; and I cannot think but in the end the villanies of man will set him clear. How fairly this lord strikes to appear foul! takes virtuous copies to be wicked, *like those that under hot ardent zeal would set whole realms on fire.*"

Possibly enough other relevant quotations might be made.

Knight quotes in this connexion certain well-known lines in the *Winter's Tale*, a play of later date, viz. I. ii. 357-61, but the reference there seems rather to the recent assassination of Henry IV. of France.

But what is more important than any such references, real or fancied, is to consider how Shakespeare illustrates the conspiracy in a more general way; to notice how it not unnaturally belongs to such an age as he depicts for us; how the men who were conspicuous in it are of the same breed with those whom his supreme art has made so strangely familiar to all posterity.

Or, instead of using Shakespeare to illustrate it, we may, with not less convenience and profit, use this conspiracy to illustrate Shakespeare. There is, indeed, an aspect of it which is merely distressing and horrid. When we view it as a masterpiece of bigotry—bigotry at its fiercest and worst—it simply inspires disgust and loathing; we must bow our heads with shame that human beings can fall so low, that the name of religion can be so foully misused, so grossly profaned. But there are other features that inspire rather pity and admiration, and remind us that these Plotters, too, were the children of the great Elizabethan age.

It was an age of passion; of passionate hates and passionate loves; of eager devotions, of fervid abhorrences; of infinite tenderness, implacable fierceness; of the keenest readiness to do or die—to do and die.

These violent, excitable, ardent, faithful, wild, impetuous spirits, are they not, then, the children of their age? Writhing with a fierce impatience beneath the intolerant tyranny which would fain have torn from them the old religious creed of their race—a creed deeply rooted in their nature and with tendrils intertwined with their heart-strings—stung to a burning resentment by the wrongs daily inflicted on them and theirs; mad for revenge; reckless mutineers against the order that oppressed them; defiant of law and defiant of fate; true unto death to each other and their cause; still intrepid and fixed in the midst of desperate fortunes; in the very jaws of ruin unconquered and unconquerable—it is impossible to observe these men without seeing that they are of the same flesh and blood with those heroes that won for the reign of Queen Elizabeth its honour and glory; that, however deluded and damnable were the uses to which they unworthily lent themselves, they were not unendowed with the splendid energy and valour and devotion which on other fields achieved triumphs that to this day we Englishmen cannot remember without a thrill of joy and pride.

What especially characterised the Shakespearian age, both for good and evil, was the comparatively free play of life—the unfettered movement of nature. It was this characteristic that made it so favourable to art. As in the public exercises of their gymnasia and palæstræ the Greek sculptor studied the physical form, and attained that intimate familiarity with it that enabled him to reproduce it with a faithfulness and power never equalled; in the same manner in our Elizabethan age our dramatists studied mind and character, and were enabled to represent the humours and the passions of their time with an insight and force that place their works amongst the most precious records of humanity. Shakespeare saw "the very pulse of the machine." The springs of action were disclosed to him. He looked into the inmost heart of things. "Off, off, you lendings;" and nature stood revealed before him, disguiseless, not "sophisticated."

We say that the study of Gunpowder Plot, stamped as its

chief agents are with certain characteristics of their age, may be of no mean service in helping us to appreciate Shakespeare. Into what close neighbourhood with it he was brought it has been the special purpose of this paper to show.

III.

CHAUCER AND SHAKESPEARE.

(From the *Quarterly Review*, January, 1873.)

IT is now about a century since the study of Chaucer began to revive. Between the time of Verstegan and Tyrwhitt—the *Restitution of Decayed Intelligence* was published in 1605, Tyrwhitt's memorable work in 1775—he had, by slow degrees, fallen nearly altogether out of the general knowledge of men. He, whom Spenser called "the well of English undefiled," was vulgarly accused of having poisoned and corrupted the springs of his native tongue. He whom that same Spenser—the sweetest melodist of our literature—looked up to as his verse-master and exemplar, was stigmatized as a very metrical cripple and idiot. And what little acquaintance there was maintained with him was due to versions of certain of his poems made by the facile pens of Dryden and of Pope; so completely had he fallen on what were for him "evil days" and "evil tongues." To Tyrwhitt belongs the honour of first reinstating the old poet on the pedestal from which he had been so rudely deposed so long a time. Proper consideration being made for the age in which that admirable scholar lived, his edition of Chaucer's *Canterbury Tales* must be pronounced a wonder of erudition and of faithful labour. Certainly the figure of Chaucer which he presented to the eyes of his time is not a quite genuine thing; there are traces on it of the whitewash or the paint with which the eighteenth century thought it well to "touch up" ancestral images; but yet it is not easy to overstate the importance or the merit of the service he performed. From the publication of his volumes may be dated the renewal of the critical and the appreciative study of the greatest literary productions of the English Middle Ages. The impulse they gave has been perpetually strengthened and multiplied by various tendencies and movements, both of a general and a particular character. At the present time a Chaucer Society has been formed, and under the zealous leadership of Mr. Furnivall, its founder and organizer and almost sole worker, is doing excellent service [1] in bringing within common reach the original texts of the great poet. Of various other ways in which in the course of this century, and especially in our own generation, some popular, as well as scholarly, familiarity with one of our greatest minds has been encouraged and promoted, it is not our purpose now to speak. Let it suffice to say that Chaucer has never been known since his own day more intelligently and more admiringly than he seems likely to be during the last quarter of this nineteenth century.

It is certain that this Chaucerian revival is not the result of any mere antiquarianism, but of a genuine poetic vitality. There can be no better testimony to the true greatness of the old poet than that half a thousand years after the age in which he wrote he is held in higher estimation than ever; that, whatever intermissions of his popularity there may have been in times that cared nothing for, as they knew little of, the great Romantic School to which he belonged, and that were wholly incapable of understanding the very language in which he expressed and transcribed his genius, he this day speaks with increasing force and power. Through all the obsoletenesses of his language, and all the lets and impedi-

[1] So far as its funds, which, we are sorry to say, are by no means flourishing, allow it.

ments to a full enjoyment of his melody caused by our ignorance of fourteenth-century English, through all the conventional and social differences which separate his time from ours, we yet recognize a profoundly human soul, with a marvellous power of speech. We are discovering that he is not only a great poet, but one of our greatest. It is not too much to say that the better acquaintance with Chaucer's transcendent merits is gradually establishing the conviction that not one among all poets deserves so well as he the second place.

Chaucer and Shakespeare have much in common. However diverse the form of their greatest works, yet in spirit there is a remarkable likeness and sympathy. Their geniuses differ rather in degree than in kind. Chaucer is in many respects a lesser Shakespeare.

Chaucer lived generations before the dramatic form was ripe for the use of genius. In his day it had scarcely yet advanced beyond the rude dialogue and grotesque portraiture of the Miracle-play.[1] In fact at that time that rare growth, which two centuries later was to put forth such exquisite imperishable flowers, had hardly yet emerged from its

---

[1] Absalon of the *Milleres Tale*:—

"Sometime to shew his lightnesse and maistrie
He plaieth Herode on a skaffold hie."

In the Elizabethan age this part of Herod had become a proverb of rant; so that Hamlet uses the name as the very superlative of noise (act iii., scene 2). The Miller himself cries out "in Pilate's voice." The wife of Bath, with Clerk Jankin and her gossip dame Ales, goes to *Playes of Miracles*. Shakespeare laughs at the rough amateurs of the old stage in the by-play of the *Midsummer Night's Dream*. In Chaucer's age perhaps Bottom would have been regarded as a very Roscius, and that interlude of Pyramus and Thisbe might have drawn genuine tears down medieval cheeks.

native earth; it was yet only embryonic. Chaucer stands in relation to the supreme Dramatic Age in a correspondent position to that held by Scott. Chaucer lived in the morning twilight of it, Scott in the evening. There can be little doubt that both would have added to its lustre—that England would have boasted one more, and Scotland at least one great dramatist—had they been born later and earlier respectively; but Chaucer could not even descry it in the future, so far off was it, and it was Scott's fortune to look back upon it in the swiftly receding distance.

But although the form which was to receive such splendid usage from Shakespeare, and to prove the very amplest and fittest and noblest body for the highest dramatic spirit, was not yet ready for wear in the culminating epoch of the Middle Ages, yet that dramatic energy which blazed out so brilliantly at a later period was already at work, and insisting on some representation. It worked with vehemence in Chaucer. He is pre-eminently the dramatic genius, not only of mediæval England, but of mediæval Europe. The great Italians of the bright dawn of modern literature were not of the dramatic order. Much as Chaucer undoubtedly owed to them, they furnished him with no sort of dramatic precedent or example. He is the first in time of modern dramatical spirits; and one must travel far back into the ancient times before one meets with anybody worthy of comparison with him. Certainly if, as has been remarked, it was in Dante that Nature showed that the higher imagination had not perished altogether with Virgil, it was in Chaucer that she showed that dramatic power had not breathed its last with Plautus and Terence.

In respect of means of expression Chaucer was placed in a much more unprovided and destitute position than was Shakespeare. We have already seen that neither Tragedy nor Comedy,[1] in the strict sense of those terms, was known in his day; whereas nothing can be falser than to make Shakespeare say, as Dryden makes him say,—

"I found not, but created first the stage."

The stage was already not only in existence, but occupied by wits of no contemptible rank, when Shakespeare appeared in Town. Shakespeare had in Marlowe a dramatic master. The pupil presently outshone the master; but of the influence of that master there can be no doubt, though perhaps it has not been, and is not, as adequately recognized and acknowledged as it should be by Shakespearian critics and commentators. And Marlowe did not stand alone; he was one, certainly the most eminent one, of a group, whose starry lights it is not easy to see in the intense brightness flowing from the great sun that uprose amongst them; but there they were and are, of no faint brilliancy, so long as they had the firmament to themselves, unsuffused by an overpowering glory. But for Chaucer there were no such predecessors at home or abroad. Naturally enough, it would seem that it was not till comparatively late in life that he discovered the best vehicle of self-expression. For many years his genius struggled for a fitting language. Like all

[1] See the prologue to *Monkes Tale*:—

"Tragedis is to seyn a certyn storie,
As olde bookes maken us memorie
Of hem that stood in greet prosperite
And is y-fallen out of heigh degre
Into miserie, and endith wrecchedly;
And thay ben versifyed comunly
Of six feet, which men clepe exametron.
In prose been eek endited many oon;
In metre eek, in mony a sondry wise."

As to the term Comedy, observe, for instance, Dante's use of it.

poets, he began by imitating the models he found current. He dreamed dreams, and saw visions in the conventional mode. He echoed whatever sweet sounds reached his quick sensitive ears from any quarter. He translated, with a quite touching humble-mindedness, received masterpieces of French and of Italian literature. Through all these labours his originality was gradually developing. For all his efforts his genius would not keep to the beaten path, but would perpetually strike out some new way for itself and forget the appointed route. At last he started altogether alone, looking no longer for old footprints to retrace or any established guide-posts. He discovered a fair wide country that had lain untrodden for ages, over whose tracks the grass or the moss had grown, and here he advanced as in some fresh new world :—

> "Parnassi deserta per ardua dulcis
> Raptat amor ; juvat ire jugis, qua nulla priorum
> Castaliam molli devertitur orbita clivo."

Chaucer's great work is but a noble fragment. It seems certain that many troubles beset the declining years of his life. We think it may be doubted whether he was endowed with that excellent commercial prudence which so eminently distinguished Shakespeare. It was certainly a happy circumstance for Shakespeare—a circumstance due in a great measure, it may be believed, to his own sound judgment—that he never became in any way a satellite or retainer of the Court, but could escape from the unwholesome atmosphere of Whitehall to his home at Stratford. Chaucer was not so fortunate. He was attached to one of the most extravagant and frivolous circles that ever gathered round a monarch of a like description. However noble-natured, he could scarcely live in such company without some contamination. Assuredly his works have stains upon them contracted in that evil air, much as Beaumont and Fletcher are flushed and spotted by the contagions of James I.'s time. And with that Court connection it is impossible not to associate the extreme pecuniary difficulties, of which there are only too manifest signs at a certain period of Chaucer's life. Probably it was these piteous, but seemingly not inevitable or reproachless, distresses that impeded the completion of the *Canterbury Tales*. The original design, indeed, is in itself too vast for realization. Chaucer commits the same error in this respect as Spenser does. But it may well be believed that had Chaucer matured his work, he would either have retrenched his plan, or by some device have brought its execution within tolerable dimensions. The part that happily was written has evidently not received the finishing touch. The Prologue itself, perhaps, was never finally revised; as it stands it contains incompatible statements as to the number of the pilgrims; in the case of the "Persoun" it deviates from the programme in not telling us—

"in what array that" he "was inne."

Had the work been fully completed, especially had more of those Inter-prologues been written, in which Chaucer's dramatic power more particularly displays itself, and the figures portrayed in the initial Prologue are with admirable skill shown in self-consistent action, being permitted to speak for themselves and develop their own natures, there can be little doubt that the claims upon our admiration would have been greatly multiplied.

Chaucer then stands at a considerable disadvantage as compared with Shakespeare, both in respect of the dramatic appliances of his time and in respect of the works representative of his genius. Chaucer, as we have seen, found ready to hand no literary form such as should worthily interpret his mind, and was many years searching before he found one, and, when at last he found it, was somewhat obstructed in the free use of it by troubles and cares that divorced him from his proper task. Moreover the English of his day, though already a copious and versatile tongue, was something rude and inflexible in comparison with the Elizabethan language. In several passages it is clear that he is conscious of certain difficulties attendant on the use of such an instrument. A true instinct led him to choose English for his service rather than French, which his less far-seeing contemporary Gower chose at least for his early piece, the *Speculum Meditantis*, and for his *Balades;* but his choice exposed him to various perplexities inseparable from the transitional condition of the object of it.

Fragmentary as his great work is, it is enough to show how consummate was his genius. Not more surely did that famous footprint on the sands tell the lonely islander of Defoe's story of a human presence than Chaucer's remains assure us that a great poet was amongst us when such pieces were produced.

We have said that his genius exhibits a remarkable affinity to that of Shakespeare—a closer affinity, we think, than that of any other English poet. To Chaucer belongs in a high measure what marks Shakespeare supremely—a certain indefinable grace and brightness of style, an incomparable archness and vivacity, an incessant elasticity and freshness, an indescribable ease, a never-faltering variety, an incapability of dulness. These men "toil not, neither do they spin," at least so far as one can see. The mountain comes to them; they do not go to it. They wear their art "lightly, like a flower." They never pant or stoop with efforts and strainings. They are kings that never quit their thrones, with a world at their feet. The sceptre is natural in their hands; the purple seems their proper wearing. They never cease to scatter their jewels for fear of poverty; the treasury is always overflowing, because all things bring them tribute.

For skill in characterization who can be placed between Chaucer and Shakespeare? Is there any work, except the "theatre" of Shakespeare, that attempts, with a success in any way comparable, the astonishing task which Chaucer sets himself? He attempts to portray the entire society of his age from the crown of its head to the sole of its foot—from the knight, the topmost figure of mediæval life, down to the peasant and the cook; and the result is a gallery of life-like portraits, which has no parallel anywhere, with one exception, for variety, truthfulness, humanity. These are no roughly drawn, rudely featured outlines, without expression and definiteness, only recognizable by some impertinent symbol, or when we see the name attached, like some collection of ancient kings, or of "ancestors" where there prevails one uniform vacuity of countenance, and, but for the costume or the legend, one cannot distinguish the First of his house from the Last. They are all drawn with an amazing discrimination and delicacy.[1] There is nothing of caricature, but yet the individuality is perfect. That the same pencil should have given us the Prioress and the Wife

---

[1] Chaucer's sound taste shrunk altogether from every form of caricature. His humour, boisterous enough sometimes, at others wonderfully fine and delicate, is always truthful. His *Tale of Sir Thopas* is one of the best parodies in our language. He tells it with the utmost possible gravity, looking as serious as Defoe or Swift in their "driest" moments; and, only if you watch well, can you detect a certain mischievous twinkle in his eyes. Some worthy people, indeed, have not detected this twinkle, and have soberly registered Sir Topas amongst the legitimate heroes of chivalrous romance.

of Bath, the Knight and the Sompnour, the Parson and the Pardoner! These various beings, for beings they are, are as distinct to us now as when he who has made them immortal saw them move out through the gates of the "Tabard," a motley procession, nearly five hundred years since. So far as merely external matters go, the Society of the Middle Ages is perpetuated with a minuteness not approached elsewhere. We know exactly how it looked to the bodily eye. Chaucer addresses himself deliberately to this exhaustive portrayal:—

> "But natheles whiles I have tyme and space,
> Or that I ferthere in this tale pace,
> *Me thinketh it accordant to resoun*
> *To telle yow alle the condicioun*
> *Of eche of hem, so as it semed me,*
> And which they weren and of what degre,
> And eek in what array that they were inne."

Surely a quite unique programme; and it is carried out with profound conscientiousness and power.

We ask, who among our poets, except Shakespeare, shall be placed above Chaucer in this domain of art? In our opinion there is not one of the Elizabethans that deserves that honour. There is an endless variety of creative power, and the offspring is according. Spenser is, in a way, a great creator; he fills the air around him with a population born of his own teeming fancy; but these children of Spenser are not human children, but rather exquisite phantoms, with bodies, if they may be called embodied, of no earthly tissue, mere delicate configurations of cloud and mist. They are very ghosts, each one of whom pales and vanishes if a cock crows, or any mortal sound strikes their fine ears :—

> "Ter frustra comprensa manus effugit imago,
> Par levibus ventis volucrique simillima somno."

And yet, as man is made in the image of God, so certainly the creatures of the poet should be made in the image of man. There is no higher model to be aimed at. Man is the culminating form of the world as we know it, or can know it. Spenser's creatures may thrive in their native land of "Faerie;" but their "lungs cannot receive our air." Something more existent and real are the lovely presences that owe their being to Beaumont and Fletcher—Aspatia, Bellario, Ordella. Assuredly Ordella is rich in sons and daughters such as she spoke of in that high dialogue with Thierry:—

> "He that reads me
> When I am ashes, is my son in wishes;
> And those chaste dames that keep my memory,
> Singing my yearly requiems, are my daughters."

But scarcely are she and that passing fair sisterhood of which she is one formed of human clay. They stand out from the crowd with whom they mix as shapes of a celestial texture. One can only think of them as white-robed sanctities. In fact, they are the natural counterparts of those grosser beings that are only too common in the plays of the authors who drew them. A painter of devils must now and then paint angels by way of relief. Perhaps it is not too much to say that all the characters of these writers are either above or below human nature. They cannot show us humanity without some sort of exaggeration. Ben Jonson has hardly succeeded better in this respect. One grave defect in all his creations is what may be called their monotony. There is no flexibility of disposition, no free play of nature. Moreover, his works exhibit too plainly the travail and effort with which they were composed. One seems to be taken into his workshop, and see him toiling and groaning, and, in the very act of elaboration, shaping now this limb and now that.

The greatest master of characterization of that age next to Shakespeare is certainly Massinger. Sir Giles Overreach and Luke are both real men. Luke is a true piece of nature, not all black-souled, nor all white, but of a mixed complexion. But the area which Massinger could make his own was of limited dimensions. When he stepped across its limits, his strength failed him, and he was even as other men.

To pass on in this necessarily rapid survey to a later period. Goldsmith alone amongst our later poets has left us a portrait that deserves to compare with one by Chaucer. It is that ever-charming portrait of the Village Preacher, a not unworthy *pendant* of the "Parson," by which, indeed, it was indirectly inspired. He has given us duplicates of it in prose in the persons of the Vicar of Wakefield and of the Man in Black. There is a tradition that he who sat to Chaucer for the Parson was no other than Wicliffe. It seems fairly certain that Goldsmith's original was his own father. That was the one figure he could draw with the utmost skill, the deepest feeling. Since Goldsmith there has arisen in our literature no consummate portrait-painter in verse, unless an exception be made in favour of Browning. Scott's creative power did not come to him when he wrote in metre. Shelley's creations are of the Spenserian type—fair visions, refined immaterialities,

> "Shapes that haunt Thought's wildernesses."

Has Tennyson's Arthur human veins and pulses? He lived and lives somewhat, perhaps, in that earliest of the Arthurian books—the *Morte d'Arthur*—the supposed relic of an Epic; but in the later treatments he has become more and more impalpable and airy, and only visible to us as to Guinevere when

> "more and more
> The moony vapour rolling round the king,

> Who seem'd the phantom of a giant in it,
> Enwound him fold by fold, and made him gray
> And grayer, till himself became as mist
> Before her, moving ghostlike to his doom."

The Arthur of the *Idylls*, looking at his younger self in the earliest Tennysonian poem that celebrates him, might say of himself what Marlborough in his old age is reported to have said when he looked at a picture of his youth: "I was once a Man!" He has become a thinly clothed Idea.

Perhaps Mr. Browning possesses the highest dramatic power amongst the poets of this century, but his power is rather analytical than constructive. Mr. William Morris, the professed disciple of Chaucer, affords a striking contrast to his master in this regard. *The Life and Death of Jason* and *The Earthly Paradise* have many charms and excellencies; but amongst these the lifelike delineation of character is not to be numbered.

We must turn to our prose writers if we would find out of Shakespeare any parallel to the excellence and, at the same time, to the variety of Chaucer's personæ; for it is in prose, since the Elizabethan age, that the highest creative power of our literature has expressed itself. The Massingers and Fletchers and Fords have turned novelists in the latter days. Addison and Steele, those genial literary partners, the Beaumont and Fletcher of the prose period in this respect of collaboration, have sketched a group which it is not uninteresting to compare with that of the Prologue. As in the time of Richard II. men went on pilgrimage in companies, so in Queen Anne's reign they formed clubs. The *Spectator*, it will be remembered, in his opening papers describes the members of the Club by a committee of which his delightful serial was to be conducted. The account of himself comes first; he is as reserved as the poet of the *Canterbury Tales* is social, only like him in the keenness of his powers of observation. Then comes the knight Sir Roger, who is to be the real hero of the work. Sir Roger is far beyond praise. On him Addison lavishes all the wealth of his exquisite humour. In Chaucer's day the knight was too awful a personage to be trifled with. There are only three characters in the Prologue in whose painting the overflowing fun of the artist is checked and repressed, and the gentle mockery dies out of his eyes for a while, and he is all gravity and reverence; and of these the Knight is one. But, in fact, knight does not answer to knight. Sir Roger rather corresponds to the Franklin of Chaucer; and perhaps the nearest equivalent to Chaucer's Knight in the *Spectator's* list is Captain Sentry, but there is no quite correspondent figure, so utterly had society shifted and changed since the Middle Ages. Then comes the Templar who, if he pairs off with any one of the Chaucerian society, must go with the Clerk of Oxenford; but the one is a real student, the other something of a mere dilettanti. Next in order is Sir Andrew Freeport, the merchant, a figure that can never be absent from any English circle that is meant to be at all representative, of much greater note in the early eighteenth century than in the late fourteenth, and accordingly treated with deeper respect by Steele than by Chaucer, though there is a curious similarity of traits, showing that both writers drew from nature. Then there is Captain Sentry, who, in some sort, as we have said, is to be matched with the Knight of the Pilgrimage. Sixth is Will Honeycomb, a man about town, a young, frivolous, and unprofitable being, for whom, to the honour of the older age be it said, there is no responsive type whatever. Lastly is recorded "a clergyman, a very philosophic man, of general learning, great sanctity of life, and the most exact good breeding;" with whom, of course, "a pore Persoun of a toun" is to be compared or contrasted. Observe the order of the characteristics of the "Augustan" divine: he is learned, pure-lived, and well-bred! Is there not something piteously significant in this bathos? He had a high sense of holiness, and of etiquette! Chaucer never commits such a frightful anticlimax. On the whole, it is clear, if we compare these groups, that the moral superiority belongs to the older one. It is true that there are "highly objectionable" persons in the Chaucerian catalogue, whose souls, to adopt the Pythagorean faith, do not re-appear in fresh bodies in the later epoch as represented by Addison and Steele; but this is because that epoch is not represented exhaustively. The Pardoner and the Sompnour and the Friar were certainly "going to and fro in the earth, and walking up and down in it" as busily under the last of the Stuarts as under the last of the Plantagenets, though they had altered their titles and employments; but it did not fall within the plan of the great essayists to depict them. Looking away from this matter of moral superiority, which it may be truly said is due rather to the difference between the ages than to that between the writers, to the artistic merits of the two performances, it is surely impossible to deny the palm to Chaucer as to the deeper and wider genius. Addison conceived and incorporated one immortal figure. His sympathies scarcely extended at all beneath a certain social level. What are called "the lower classes" hardly found a literary patron and introducer till Goldsmith arose. It was not unnecessarily that Gray forbade "Grandeur" to

> "hear with a disdainful smile
> The short and simple annals of the poor."

The noble declaration that Terence puts in the mouth of Chremes—

> "Homo sum; humani nihil a me alienum puto,"

though often quoted by the wits of the last century, was seldom, if ever, sincerely adopted and made the principle of action. One infinite glory of Chaucer is the capacity of his moral, no less than of his intellectual nature; he is not the painter of a class—his courtesy and interest know no such mean circumscription; he makes friends with all his fellow pilgrims, not only with those of his own rank and distinction as the Knight and the Squire and the Prioress and the Man of Law, but

> "Schortly when the sonne was to reste
> *So hadde I spoken with her everychon,*
> *That I was of here felawschipe anon,*
> And made forward erly to aryse
> To take oure waye ther as I yow devyse."

Defoe has created a man, the brave, resolute, self-contained, invincible, but withal somewhat untender and dry-natured Robinson Crusoe. About the middle of the last century creative genius abounded. Richardson, Fielding, Smollett, Sterne, and Goldsmith, all in various degrees added to that spirit-born population that will be known and familiar through all times. Generations will come and go, but Squire Western, and Parson Adams, and Uncle Toby, and Dr. Primrose will live on insensible of the weight of years, still hale and vigorous, still moving all who approach to laughter or to tears. Chaucer represents Nature regarding with pride her handiwork, in the shape of the daughter of "the knight" Virginius, and speaking in this wise:—

> "Lo, I, Nature
> Thus can I forme and peynte a creature
> Whan that me lust; who can me counterfete?
> Pigmalion? Nought, though he alwey forge and bete
> Or grave or peynte; for I dar wel sayn
> Apellis, Zeuxis, schulde wirche in vayn
> Other to grave, or paynte, or forge or bete,
> If they presumed me to counterfete.

> For He that is the Former principal
> Hath maad me his vicar general
> To forme and peynte erthely creature
> Right as me lust. Al thing is in my cure
> Under the moone that may wane and waxe.
> And for my werke no thing wol I axe;
> My lord and I ben fully at accord;
> I made hir to the worschip of my Lord;
> So do I alle myn other creatures
> What colour that they been, or what figures."

It is to the reverence for Nature so finely expressed in this passage that the success of the great Masters is due.

When that galaxy faded away just a century since, Nature found no faithful and cunning copyists for the space of a generation, for it was not Nature that Miss Burney and Mrs. Ratcliffe copied, but some false goddess whom they mistook for her. And hence their men and women, however much admired on their first appearance, soon sank into obscurity when Jane Austen and Sir Walter Scott began to write. Then once more the mirror was held up to Nature, and the reflected images caught and eternized with supremest skill. Miss Austen is without a rival in the field she occupied. In any of the highest creative ages Scott would assuredly have taken an eminent place. But in comprehensiveness of power can either of these immortal artists be ranked above Chaucer? What we wish to emphasize is not only the depth but the breadth of Chaucer's genius. It was a mere fragment of human life that Miss Austen saw with a clearness and an intelligence and a reproductive power that defy panegyric.

Scott's canvas is more thickly and variously crowded; it is inexpressibly admirable both in quantity and in quality; but in our opinion it does not betoken a genius either so wide-embracing or so deep-piercing as that of the old poet whom the author of *Waverley* himself studied with such enthusiastic delight.

Passing on, now, to the second generation of novelists who have graced and glorified this current century. Thackeray's creative power was scarcely co-extensive with his humour, or his sympathy. He mused and moralized more frequently than he created. Like Hamlet, he was afflicted with a tendency to think and reflect rather than to act. Dickens certainly possessed more abundant creative power. Beings sprang up at his call, as it was said the legions would arise at the stamp of Pompey. And amongst these there are undoubtedly genuine specimens of the human race, who will live for ever; but he has left behind him scarcely anything that is not marred by caricature. The mirror held up by him to Nature was certainly not provided with a properly even surface, and consequently all the images he saw in it, and drew from it, were apt to be distorted and out of proportion. He gives us at times a very masque of hobgoblins; one seems to have dropt into the country of

"The Anthropophagi and men whose heads
Do grow beneath their shoulders;"

there is nothing normal or calm, but incessant eccentricity and theatricalism. In this respect Dickens strikingly contrasts, to his disadvantage, with Chaucer, whose fidelity to nature is far too sincere to permit him to take such liberties with her fair works, or to select her monstrosities as her types. Both writers are pre-eminently realistic; no Englishmen, perhaps, exhibit more clearly that intense realism which it may be lies at the basis of the Low German mind, and which produced that school of painting amongst our own nearest kinsmen on the Continent which may compete with photography in the minute accuracy and exactness of its representations. Chaucer and Dickens are as precise in their delineations of external life and manners as are Hooge or Teniers. We know the outside look of the Miller and the Reeve just as we know that of Mr. Pickwick and Sam Weller. But even in wardrobe matters the modern is not seldom fantastic and grotesque, which Chaucer never is. To some extent the difference between these two great writers is one of culture. Chaucer was of the highest culture to be reached in his age, and all his works are fragrant with evidence of it. Dickens could have drawn certain of the Pilgrims with excellent success; but he could not have drawn the Knight or the Prioress. But the difference is not only of culture; it is also of soil.

Of what may be termed the third, the now reigning generation of novelists appertaining to this century, certainly the only one that in point of characterization merits naming with Chaucer is that most accomplished and profound writer known as George Eliot; of whom, as it is almost impossible to speak with undazzled judgment whilst we are actually in the midst of his—or may we say her?—fascinations, we will not attempt any comparative review.

In our opinion, then, to Chaucer may worthily be assigned the place next, we do not say close, to Shakespeare as a maker of men. By no other writer, with that illustrious exception, have so many real fellow-creatures been given to us; by no other has been exhibited such wellnigh universal knowledge and comprehension of mankind.

With regard to Chaucer, as to Shakespeare, it has been disputed whether he is greater as a humorous or a pathetic writer. It is a common observation that the gifts of humour and pathos are generally found together, a statement that, perhaps, requires some little qualification. Ben Jonson, Addison, and Fielding, for instance, are humorous without being pathetic; on the other hand, Richardson is pathetic and not humorous. Sterne's pathos is a mere trick. Let those who please weep by the death-bedside of Le Fevre; for our part we will not be so cheated of our tears. Sterne, in that famous scene, is nothing better than an exquisite "mute"—a masterpiece of mercenary mourning. One may see him, if one looks intently, arranging his pocket-handkerchief in effective folds, with one eye tear-streaming, while the other watches that all the proper manœuvres of woe are duly executed. *Flet nec dolet.* And something of this is true of Dickens. In the great masters of pathos our tears are not drawn from us; they flow of themselves. There is no design on the softness of our hearts, no insidious undermining, no painful and elaborate besiegement. For writers to kill, merely to melt their readers with a scene of tender emotion, is unjustifiable manslaughter. There is, in short, nothing to be said for those whose delight it is with malice aforethought to spread a feast of woe and serve up little children, or any sweet human thing they can lay hands on, that their guests may enjoy the luxury of tears. These are the Herods of literature. Shakespeare never slays or butchers after this fashion. He would have saved Cordelia if it had been in his power; but it was a moral necessity that she should die. He could no more have kept alive and blooming the fair flowers of the field when evil winds blew than preserved that lovely form from perishing amidst the wild passions that Lear's sad error had let loose. "Sin entered into the world, and death by sin;" and this death falls not only on the guilty. Goneril and Regan perish; and so the true daughter, though with all our hearts we cry with the old "child-changed" father, "Cordelia, stay a little." It cannot be otherwise. And so always there is nothing arbitrary in the pathetic scenes of the supreme artists. Of purely pathetic writing there are, perhaps, no better specimens in all our literature than the tales of the Clerk of Oxford and of the Man of Law. Both poems aim at showing how the "meek shall inherit the earth"—how true and genuine natures do in the end triumph, however desperately defeated and crushed they may for a time, or for many times, seem to be. Chaucer weeps himself, or grows, indeed, something impatient, as he conducts his heroines along their most sad course. The thorns of the way pierce his feet also; and he would fain uproot them, and scatter soft flowers for the treading of his woeful wayfarers. But he knew well that all pilgrimages were not as easy as that one he sings of to Canterbury, that was lightened with stories and jests; but that certain spirits must go on in darkness and weariness, with aching limbs and breaking hearts, through much tribulation. In both works, perhaps, surveyed from the purely æsthetic point of view, there is an excess of woeful incident; the bitter cup which Constance and Griselda have to drain seems too large for mortal lips. In this regard we must remember that both these tales, though inserted into the grand work of Chaucer's maturity, yet were certainly written in his youth. The Man of Law, in his Prologue, gives us to understand that the tale he proposes to narrate was written by Chaucer, of whose writings he speaks, both expressly and fully, in that highly interesting and important passage "of olde time." A careful study of the *Clerk's Tale* undoubtedly demonstrates that it, too, was an earlier production. In both cases, so far as the mere facts go, Chaucer closely follows his authorities, much after the manner of Shakespeare. In the latter case the closeness—Petrarch's well-known letter to Boccaccio is the authority—is so strict that Chaucer is compelled to speak for himself in an *envoy* at the conclusion. Perhaps the most pathetic passage in Chaucer's later writings is in the *Knight's Tale*, which also, however, was first written before the noon of his genius. This passage is, of course, the death of Arcite. The event is necessary.[1] Arcite had been untrue to that solemnest of the pacts of chivalry—to the pact of sworn brotherhood (see especially Palamon's words to him in vv. 271-293, and the quibble with which the other palliates his conduct, vv. 295-303); and Arcite must die. His triumph in the lists had been but as the flourishing of a green bay-tree. The final scene is described with the utmost simplicity. The evil spirits that ought never to have found a harbour in his heart have at last been expelled from it, and the old fealty has returned; and the last words of his speech to Emily, whom he has bade take him softly in her "armes twaye" "for love of God," and hearken what he says, are a generous commendation of his rival:—

> "I have heer with my cosyn Palomon
> Had stryf and rancour many a day i-gon
> For love of yow, and eek for jelousie.
> And Jupiter so wis my sowle gye,
> To speken of a servaunt proprely
> With alle circumstaunces trewely,
> That is to seyn, truthe, honour, and knighthede,
> Wysdom, humblesse, astaat, and hye kinrede,
> Fredam, and al that longeth to that art,
> So Jupiter have of my soule part,
> As in this world right now ne knowe I non
> So worthy to be loved as Palomon,
> That serveth you, and wol do al his lyf.
> And if that ye schul ever be a wyf,
> Forget not Palomon, that gentil man."

Assuredly Chaucer was endowed in a very high degree with what we may call the pathetic sense. It would seem to have been a favourite truth with him that

---

[1] Prof. Ebert is of opinion that Chaucer's grasp of the moral intention of the *Knight's Tale* is less vigorous and firm than that of Boccaccio, and it may be so.

"Pite renneth sone in gentil herte."[1]

It ran "sone" and abundantly in his own most tender bosom. But he is never merely sentimental or maudlin. We can believe that the Levite of the Parable shed a tear or two as he crossed over to the "other side" from where that robbed and wounded traveller lay, and perhaps subsequently drew a moving picture of the sad spectacle he had so carefully avoided. Chaucer's pity is of no such quality. It springs from the depths of his nature; nay, from the depths of Nature herself moving in and through her interpreter.

Another respect in which Chaucer is not unworthy of some comparison with his greater successor is his irony. We use the word in the sense in which Dr. Thirlwall uses it of Sophocles in his excellent paper printed in the *Philological Museum* some forty years ago, and in which Schlegel, in his *Lectures on Dramatic Literature*, uses it of Shakespeare, to denote that dissembling, so to speak, that self-retention and reticence, or, at least, indirect presentment, that is a frequent characteristic of the consummate dramatist, or the consummate writer of any kind who aims at portraying life in all its breadth. We are told often enough of the universal sympathy that inspires the greatest souls, and it is well; but let us consider that universal sympathy does not mean blind, undiscriminating, wholesale sympathy, but precisely the opposite. Only that sympathy can be all-inclusive that is profoundly intelligent as well as intense; and this profound intelligence is incompatible with any complete and unmitigated adoration. The eyes that scrutinize the world most keenly, though they may see infinite noblenesses that escape a coarser vision, yet certainly see also much meanness

---

[1] This line occurs in several of his poems—in the *Knight's Tale* and in the *Legend of Good Women*, &c.

and pravity. Hence, to speak generally, for exceptions do not concern us, there is no such thing amongst the deep-seeing and really man-learned as unqualified and absolute admiration. And thus the supremest writers have no heroes in the ordinary acceptation of that term. There is not a hero in all Shakespeare; not even Harry the Fifth is absolutely so. For a like reason, there is no quite perfect villain. Neither monsters of perfection nor of imperfection find favour with those that really know mankind. Thus a real master never completely identifies himself with any one of his characters. To say that he does so is merely a *façon de parler*. They are all his children, and it cannot but be that some are dearer to him than others, but not one, if he is wise, is an idol unto him. His irony consists in the earnest, heartfelt, profound representation of them, while yet he is fully alive to their failings and failures. It is observable only in the supremest geniuses. Men of inferior knowledge and dimmer light are more easily satisfied. They make golden images for themselves and fall down and worship them. Shakespeare stands outside each one of his plays, a little apart and above the fervent figures that move in them, like some Homeric god that from the skies watches the furious struggle, whose issue is irreversibly ordered by Μοῖρα κραταιή—that cannot save Sarpedon or prolong the days of Achilles. Chaucer, too, in a similar way abounds in secondary meanings. What he teaches does not lie on the surface. He never resigns his judgment or ceases to be a free agent in honour of any of the characters he draws. He never turns fanatic. He hates without bigotry; he loves without folly; he worships without idolatry. This excellent temper of his mind displays itself strikingly in the Prologue, which, with all its ardour, is wholly free from extravagance or self-abandonment.

It is because his spirit enjoyed and retained this lofty freedom that it was so tolerant and capacious. He, like Shakespeare, was eminently a Human Catholic, no mere sectary. He refused to no man an acknowledgment of kindred; for him there were no poor relations whom he forbade his house, or neighbours so fallen and debased that in their faces the image of God in which man was made was wholly obliterated. And it is because his understanding is thus wide and deep, and his sympathies commensurate with that understanding, that his ethical teaching is, for all time, sound and true. He is no formal or formulating moralist; he never adds his voice to the mere party cries of his day, or concentrates his energies on any dogma. To speak of him as a zealous religious reformer is ridiculous;[1] far other was his business. But yet he was a great moral teacher, one of our greatest—$\mu\epsilon\tau'$ $\dot{a}\mu\acute{v}\mu o\nu a$ $\Pi\eta\lambda\epsilon\acute{\iota}\omega\nu a$. All the world's a school, if we may adapt Jaques' words, and all the men and women merely school-children. Chaucer is a teacher in this great world-school, and in no lesser or special seminary; and the lessons he gives are "exceeding broad." They are such as life itself gives. They breathe out of his works in a natural stream, no mere accidents, but the essential spirit of them, to be discovered not by the labels but in the works themselves:—

> "Oh! to what uses shall we put
> The wildweed-flower that simply blows?
> And is there any moral shut
> Within the bosom of the rose?
>
> "But any man that walks the mead,
> In bud, or blade, or bloom may find,

---

[1] Chaucer was just as much of a Lollard as Shakespeare was of a Puritan. A recent writer has, we believe, demonstrated—to his own satisfaction—that Shakespeare was the latter. Certainly he was no Anti-Puritan; nor was Chaucer an Anti-Wicliffite.

> According as his humours lead,
>   A meaning suited to his mind.
> And liberal applications lie
>   In Art like Nature, dearest friend;
> So 'twere to cramp its use, if I
>   Should hook it to some useful end."

There is just one point of personal likeness between Chaucer and Shakespeare that we wish to notice. Of each man, as his contemporaries knew him, the chief characteristic was a wonderful lovableness of nature. The special epithet bestowed on Shakespeare by the men of his day was not the Wise, or the Witty, but the Gentle.[1] Thus Ben Jonson, in his lines " To the Memory of my Beloved the Author, Mr. William Shakespeare, and what he has left us "—lines which surely must have been forgotten by those critics, long since routed by Gifford, who gave the great-hearted " Ben " so little credit for generosity and affection :—

> "Yet must I not give Nature all; thy Art,
> *My gentle Shakespeare*, must enjoy a part."

And, after saying that—

> "the father's face
> Lives in his issue,' .

he apostrophized the " Sweet Swan of Avon." Again, in his lines prefixed to the portrait of the 1623 folio, he speaks of "The gentle Shakespeare." In his *Timber*, he writes— " I loved the man, on this side idolatry, as much as any. He was indeed honest, and of an open and free nature," &c. That Chaucer inspired a similar affection and love appears

---

[1] One cannot but remember here the εὔκολος, by which Aristophanes makes Dionysus describe Sophocles :

> ὁ δ' εὔκολος μὲν ἐνθάδ', εὔκολος δ' ἐκεῖ.
> Aristoph. *Frogs*, p. 82.

And might not Goethe be described by some such epithet?

from the warm-hearted language in which both Occleve and Lydgate make mention of him. It is the language of real attachment, kindled by no mere brilliancy of wit, but by a kindly genial love-winning nature. Occleve, when the great poet had passed away, wails thus with an unwonted fervour :—

> " O maister dere and fader reverent
> My maister Chaucer, floure of eloquence,
> Mirrour of fructuous entendement,
> O universal fader in science,
> Allas ! that thou thyne excellent prudence
> In thy bedde mortalle myghtest not bequethe ;
> What eyleth dethe, alas ! why wold he sle thee."
>
> * * * * *
>
> "Allas ! my worthy maister honorable,
> This londes verray tresour and richesse,
> Dethe by thy dethe hath harme irreperable
> Unto us done."
>
> * * * * *
>
> " That combre-world that thee my maister slow—
> Wolde I slayne were !—dethe was to hastyfe
> To renne on the and reve the thy life."
>
> * * * * *
>
> " O maister, maister, God thy soule reste ! "

And so the verses of Lydgate, in his *Troye-book*, which for the most part flow but dull and languidly, thrill with a sincere emotion when he speaks of him, whom he, too, calls his "dear master." The old "pantographer's" voice breaks, so to say, as he names the loved name, and recalls that vanished presence as he knew it, so sensitive, unexacting, self-disparaging, so "charitable, and so pitous."

Did Shakespeare read the works of Chaucer ? This is of course a question which has little or nothing to do with the unanimity of their geniuses. Wordsworth was by no means a poet of the Chaucerian type ; yet he tells us how

> "Beside the pleasant Mill at Trompington
> I laughed with Chaucer in the hawthorn shade:
> Heard him, while birds were warbling, tell his tales
> Of amorous passion."

And he has reproduced three[1] Chaucerian pieces with a reverent manner that contrasts forcibly with the freedom with which Dryden and Pope handled the old master. Neither is Tennyson a cognate spirit; and yet *A Dream of Fair Women* is an inspiration of the elder poet:—

> "I read, before my eyelids dropt their shade
> The *Legend of Good Women*, long ago
> Sung by the morning star of song, who made
> His music heard below.
>
> "Dan Chaucer, the first warbler, whose sweet breath
> Preluded those melodious bursts that fill
> The spacious times of great Elizabeth
> With sounds that echo still.
>
> "And, for a while, the knowledge of his art
> Held me above the subject, as strong gales
> Hold swollen clouds from raining, tho' my heart,
> Brimful of those wild tales,
>
> "Charged both mine eyes with tears."

And at last he dreams, as we know, of Iphigenia and Helen, and the other disastrous or ill-starred beauties of bygone ages.

This question of Shakespeare's knowledge of Chaucer has as yet received no proper attention whatever. Godwin, at the beginning of this century, noticing "the high honour the poem of *Troylus and Cryseyde* has received in having been made the foundation of one of the plays of Shakespear," remarked that "there seems to have been in this respect a

---

[1] The best authorities now incline to agree that the *Cuckoo and Nightingale* is not the work of Chaucer.

sort of conspiracy in the commentators upon Shakespear against the glory of our old English bard." This "conspiracy" was perhaps scarcely deliberate; it was rather a mere concord of ignorance. Now that Chaucer is becoming better known, signs of Shakespeare's familiarity with him are occasionally discerned.[1] But not yet, as we have said, has this matter been properly investigated. Yet it is quite certain that there is much valuable illustration of the great Elizabethan dramatist to be derived from the great Plantagenet tale-teller.

Apart from any overt facts to be found in the works of Shakespeare, would it not be incredible that he should not have known the writings of the highest preceding English genius, especially when we consider what we have already discussed—the profound congeniality that exists between the two minds? Would not "deep call unto deep"?

When Shakespeare "came of age," the one great name of English literature was Chaucer. Spenser had not yet put forth all his strength. Wyatt, and Surrey, and Sackville were but lesser lights. To Spenser and to Shakespeare, looking back into the past, the one great prominent figure was that of Chaucer. He bestrode the world of English literature like a Colossus, and the Gowers, and Occleves, and Lydgates, and Barclays, "petty men, walked under his huge legs." It would be less difficult to believe that Virgil did not know Ennius, than that Shakespeare did not know Chaucer. English literature then without Chaucer would be simply *Hamlet* without Hamlet. Shakespeare read the *Confessio Amantis*, if *Pericles*[2] is in part at least his work,

---

[1] We are glad to see some illustrations from Chaucer are given in Messrs. Clark and Wright's edition of *Hamlet*, just published by the University of Oxford.

[2] Oddly enough, the story of King Antiochus's incest which occupies

and it is not easy to deny it to be so in the face of the evidence for connecting it with him. That he should read Gower and ignore Chaucer would be as extraordinary as if the coming great genius of the close of the twenty-first century—whoever and whatever he is—should study his Tupper, and let Browning grow mouldy on his shelf; or—not to go too far into the future, although we have not a shadow of doubt as to the verdict of posterity, unless, indeed, there presently sets in a millenium of platitudes—as if the Brownings and Tennysons of our own day should prize Kyd above Shakespeare himself, or, to be quite definite, delight in the perusal of *Jeronimo* rather than of *Macbeth*. Surely Chaucer's language could be no insuperable barrier to Shakespeare's acquaintance with him. It is, perhaps, slightly more obsolete than that of Gower; but it is only slightly so.

Chaucer was accessible. Editions of him were published in 1542, 1546, 1555, and 1598.

It may be well, perhaps, before proceeding any further, to notice a little more fully how predominant was the fame of Chaucer in the latter half of the sixteenth century. The best collection of commemorations of him yet made is that prefixed to Urry's edition of his works; but even that is extremely meagre. It would not be difficult to collect Chaucerian tribute from Latimer, Ascham, and others of the age immediately preceding the age of Shakespeare. But it is more important to show that such tribute was voluntarily paid by the very circle in which Shakespeare himself moved, or with whose works he could not but have been familiar. There is every probability that Shakespeare knew

the first part of *Pericles*, is especially reprobated by the "Man of Law" in his Prologue, as one that Chaucer would in no wise tell. Chaucer evidently thinks that he whom he himself calls "the moral Gower" should have known better than to meddle with it.

Spenser personally; one can scarcely doubt that they met, during Spenser's London visits, at the house of the Earl of Essex, the close friend of the Earl of Southampton; for Lord Essex was an intimate friend of Spenser's, and the love Shakespeare "dedicated" to Lord Southampton was "without end." Ben Jonson, Daniel, Drayton, Fletcher, were amongst Shakespeare's closest friends, according to traditions of value, as well as amongst his most eminent contemporaries. Now, all these five great poets confess, in one way or another, their knowledge and admiration of Chaucer. Spenser, in his *Shepherdes Calendar*, in his *Faerie Queene*, in his *View of the Present State of Ireland*, either refers to or expressly mentions him; in *Mother Hubberds Tale* he essays his manner, with such success as might be expected. Most noticeable is the passage in the last book of the *Shepherdes Calendar*, which tells us Colin, that is, himself—

"Wel could pype and singe,
For he of Tityrus his songs did lere"—

that Tityrus was Chaucer we know on the authority, if any authority is wanted, of his friend and annotator, Edward Kirke—and the passages in the *Faerie Queene*, in which he gives full voice to his delight and love. One is the well-known canto (the second of book iv.), in which, not without fear and trembling and a cry for pardon, he sets himself to conclude the "half-told" "story of Cambuscan bold;" in the other, not so generally noticed, which occurs in one of the fragments of book vii., he speaks of—

"Old Dan Geffrey, in whose gentle spright
The pure well-head of Poesie did dwell."

There can be no doubt that the antique cast of Spenser's language is mainly attributable to Chaucer's influence. To him the language of Chaucer seemed to be the proper language of poetry. As the grammarian, L. Ælius Stilo, is said to have declared that had the Muses written Latin, they would have adopted the dialect of Plautus, so Spenser held that, had they spoken the English tongue, they would have modelled themselves on Chaucer. To Ben Jonson, Chaucer was the chief English classic of the older time; see his *Grammar, passim.* Daniel, in his *Musophilus*—a poem full of fine thought and fluent expression " containing a general defence of learning "—grieving to think that a time may be coming when Chaucer may fall out of remembrance— speaks with high enthusiasm of the triumphs he has already won :—

> "Yet what a time hath he wrested from time,
> And won upon the mighty waste of days
> Unto th' immortal honour of our clime
> That by his means came first adorn'd with bays?
> Unto the sacred relics of whose time,[1]
> We yet are bound in zeal to offer praise."

Then follows a curious general prophecy,[2] that, in fact, precisely applies to Chaucer. It anticipates that revival of which we have spoken in the beginning of this paper :—

> "the stronger constitutions shall
> Wear out th' infection of distemper'd days,
> And come with glory to outlive this fall
> *Recov'ring of another spring of praise,*

---

[1] For *time* in this line we should, perhaps, read *rime*, or *rhyme*, as we corruptly spell the word.

[2] There is another striking prophecy, an imagined possibility, in this poem. It relates to the spread of the language :—

> "And who in time knows whither we may vent
> The treasure of our tongue? To what strange shores
> This gain of our best glory shall be sent
> T' enrich unknowing nations with our stores?
> What worlds in th' yet unformed occident
> May come refin'd with th' accents that are ours."

> Clear'd from th' oppressing humours wherewithal
> The idle multitude surcharge their lays."

Drayton, in his epistle *To my dearly-loved friend, Henry Reynolds, Esq., of Poets and Poesy*—a survey, of singular interest for us now, of the poetry of his day, preceded by a rapid retrospect—begins his splendid catalogue with the name of Chaucer:—

> "That noble Chaucer in those former times
> The first enrich'd our English with his rhymes,
> And was the first of ours that ever brake
> Into the Muses' treasure, and first spake
> In weighty numbers, delving in the mine
> Of perfect knowledge, which he could refine,
> And coin for current, and as much as then
> The English language could express to men,
> He made it do; and by his wondrous skill
> Gave us much light from his abundant quill."

Still more interesting in connection with our special topic is the Prologue of the *Two Noble Kinsmen*, a play, as is well known, founded on the *Knight's Tale*, mainly written by Fletcher, but in whose composition it seems highly probable Shakespeare himself took some part. Says the Prologue of the play it introduces:—

> "It has a noble breeder, and a pure,
> A learned, and a poet never went
> More famous yet 'twixt Po and silver Trent.
> Chaucer, admired of all, the story gives;
> There constant to eternity it lives!
> If we let fall the nobleness of this,
> And the first sound this child hear be a hiss,
> How will it shake the bones of that good man,
> And make him cry from underground : 'Oh! fan
> From me the witless chaff of such a writer
> That blasts my bays, and my famed works makes lighter
> Than Robin Hood.' This is the fear we bring;
> For, to say truth, it were an endless thing

> And too ambitious, to aspire to him,
> Weak as we are, and almost breathless swim
> In this deep water. Do but you hold out
> Your helping hands, and we will tack about
> And something do to save us; you shall hear
> Scenes, though below his art, may yet appear
> Worth two hours' travel. To his bones sweet sleep !
> Content to you ! "

It would be easy to multiply these praises of Chaucer, did the limits of our space allow us; but surely we have quoted enough to show what an object of real veneration and love the old poet was in Shakespeare's time, and how sincere and earnest celebrations of him must have perpetually sounded in Shakespeare's ears. *A priori*, therefore, it might have been concluded that Shakespeare was familiar with the greatest English pieces of characterization, and humour, and pathos, that had appeared before him. But we need not rest content with an inference. If we turn to the plays themselves, we have abundant evidence of that familiarity.

Chaucer, it is true, is not represented in the picture Shakespeare gives of Chaucer's age, in his plays of *Richard the Second* and *Henry the Fourth*. Falstaff, it seems, was on speaking and jesting terms with John of Gaunt, who was Chaucer's great friend and patron. "John a Gaunt," as we learn, had once "burst" Shallow's head, and Falstaff had told him he had beaten his own name. But we see no Chaucer in the retinue of "time-honoured Lancaster." He is not by any means, however, conspicuous by his absence, any more than Lydgate in *Henry the Fifth*, or Skelton and Surrey in *Henry the Eighth*. Indeed, known in the Elizabethan age only as a poet, and not as a diplomatist or a politician, he would have seemed something out of place in a "History," when all the interest centres on the throne and its occupants; for Shakespeare's "Histories" do not aim at giving complete descriptions of the times with which they deal. They are regal rather than national pieces. In that very play of *Richard the Second* we hear nothing of Wat Tyler; just as in *King John* we hear nothing of Magna Charta.

It must also be noted that there was much material common to the times both of Chaucer and Shakespeare, which both have used. There were common authors, as Ovid, and common legends. With regard to the Romances of Chivalry, it is striking to notice how both poets declined to use them. Chaucer's taste anticipated the taste of Shakespeare. And so with regard to allegory. Chaucer soon outgrew that form of writing, so fashionable in his age; Shakespeare scarcely ever adopted it, for he does not seem to have cared to write masques.[1] It would seem contrariwise that many things attracted them both. They both tell the story of Lucretia —Chaucer in his *Legend of Good Women*, following Ovid, Shakespeare in his *Tarquin and Lucrece*, partly under the influence, as we shall see, of a quite different work of Chaucer's. Chaucer briefly recounts the fall of Julius Cæsar in his *Monkes Tale*, as Shakespeare so splendidly in his great play, both committing an error as to the scene, which they make the Capitol (so Polonius in *Hamlet*); both portray the tragic ends of Pyramus and Thisbe, in the *Legend of Good Women* and the *Midsummer Night's Dream* respectively, Chaucer translating Ovid with all submission, Shakespeare giving his humour free play at a story, which is absurd enough, notably in the matter of that cracked wall, if one

---

[1] Neither poet had any liking for profuse alliteration; see the "Parson's"

"Trusteth wel, I am a Suthern man,
I cannot geste rum raf ruf by the letter:"

and Shakespeare's ridicule in the *Midsummer Night's Dream*, v. 1, and *Love's Labour's Lost*, iv. 2.

lets one's self realize it. Cleopatra is another of the *Saints of Cupid* in the Legend already twice mentioned, as she is also a famous Shakespearian " person ; " both Chaucer and Shakespeare holding a far too favourable opinion of her lover, whom the former describes

> "a ful worthy gentil werreyour."

Dido, Ariadne, Medea, Philomela, are well-known figures to both, though only the older poet, who, as living in the first glimmering of the Renaissance, lay humbly at the feet of the author of the *Heroides*, honours them with special celebrations.

The true power of Chaucer is not displayed in any one of the pieces just mentioned; for of the *Saints Legend of Cupid*, as the Man of Law intitules it, undoubtedly the most valuable part is the Prologue; and as for the *Monk's Tale*, we weary of it, even as the Knight, with all his courtesy, wearied, and half agree with the free-spoken host—the very " able " chairman of the Pilgrim party—

> "Such talkyng is nought worth a boterflye,
> For therinne is noon disport ne game."

Certainly not in Shakespeare's treatment of the just-mentioned stories is his knowledge of Chaucer, or Chaucer's influence upon him, obviously manifested. The two works of Chaucer which evidently attracted Shakespeare most were *The Knight's Tale* and *Troylus and Cryseyde;* and the tokens of this attraction are to be seen in the *Midsummer Night's Dream* and in *The Two Noble Kinsmen*, in *Venus and Adonis*, *Tarquin and Lucrece*, *Troilus and Cressida*, and *Romeo and Juliet*. The *Cokes Tale of Gamelyn*, as everybody has long agreed, is not by Chaucer; but in the Elizabethan age it was believed to be so. Shakespeare was certainly acquainted with it, as well as with the prose version of it incorporated in Lodge's *Rosalynd*, the source of *As You Like It*. Besides these connections, there are scattered throughout Shakespeare's plays and poems various other indications that the writings of Chaucer were anything but a sealed or an unopened book to him.

To mention a few of these latter echoes : the Man of Law, as we have mentioned, names *The Legend of Good Women*, *The Seintes Legende of Cupid*, and Chaucer, in the Latin heading of the various parts of the Legend, styles each heroine "a martyr." Compare *Pericles* i. 1, where Antiochus describes the fallen suitors of his daughter as

"martyrs, slain in Cupid's wars;"

and the Princess's *Saint Denis to Saint Cupid*, in *Love's Labour's Lost*, v. 2.

Compare *The Assembly of Foules*—

"And brekers of the law, soth for to saine,
And likerous folk, after that they been dede,
Shal whirle about the world alway in paine,
Til many a world be passed, out of drede," &c.

with Claudius's—

"To be imprisoned in the viewless winds,
And blown with restless violence round about
The pendent world."—*Measure for Measure*, iii. 1.

Again, compare from the same poem—

"The wery hunter slepynge in hys bed,
To woode ayeine hys mynde gooth anoon;
The juge dremeth how hys plees ben sped;
The cartar dremeth how his cartes goone;
The ryche of golde, the knyght fyght with his fone;
The seke meteth he drynketh of the tonne;
The lover meteth he hath hys lady wonne,"

with that marvellously brilliant speech of Mercutio, of Queen Mab's doings :—

"She gallops night by night
Through lovers' brains, and then they dream of love : "

* * * * *

"O'er lawyers' fingers, who straight dream on fees : "

* * * * *

"Sometime she driveth o'er a soldier's neck," &c.[1]

Compare *Legende of Good Women*, Prologue—

"My worde, my werkes, ys knyt so in youre bonde
That as an harpe obeieth to the honde
That makith it soune after his fyngerynge,
Ryght.so mowe ye oute of myne herte bringe
Swich vois, ryght as yow list, to laughe and pleyne,"

with Hamlet's rebuke of those unfortunate catspaws, Rosencrantz and Guildenstern :—

"*Hamlet.* Will you play upon this pipe ?
Guil. My lord, I cannot.
Hamlet. I pray you.
Guil. Believe me, I cannot.
Hamlet. I do beseech you.
Guil. I know no touch of it, my lord.
Hamlet. 'Tis as easy as lying. Govern these ventages with your finger and thumb, give it breath with your mouth, and it will discourse most eloquent music. Look you, these are the stops.
Guil. But these cannot I command to any utterance of harmony ; I have not the skill.

[1] Comp. Lucretius, iv. 965 *et seq.* :—

"In somnis eadem plerumque videmus obire ;
Causidici causas agere et componere leges,
Induperatores pugnare ac proelia obire,
Nautæ contractum cum ventis degere bellum,
Nos agere hoc autem et naturam quærere rerum
Semper et inventam patriis exponere chartis,"

and *infra,* 1011 *et seq.* :—

"Porro hominum mentes, magnis qui mentibus edunt
Magna, itidem sæpe in somnis faciuntque geruntque ;
Reges expugnant, capiuntur,'proelia miscent,
Tollunt clamorem, quasi si jugulentur ibidem," &c.

Hamlet. Why, look you now, how unworthy a thing you make of me! You would play upon me; you would seem to know my stops; you would pluck out the heart of my mystery; you would sound me from my lowest note to the top of my compass; and there is much music, excellent voice in this little organ; yet cannot you make it speak. 'S blood! do you think I am easier to be played on than a pipe? Call me what instrument you will, though you can fret me, yet you cannot play upon me."

And also with what he says to Horatio—

"Blest are those
Whose blood and judgment are so well commingled,
That they are not a pipe for fortune's finger
To sound what stop she please."

Compare, *ibid.*,—

"For love shal me yeve strengthe and hardynesse,
To make my wounde large ynogh, I gesse,"

with Mercutio, of his own fatal hurt—

"No, 'tis not so deep as a well, nor so wide as a church door; but 'tis enough; 'twill serve. Ask for me to-morrow, and you shall find me a grave man."

The only Canterbury pilgrims, perhaps, that have been present to Shakespeare's mind, on its days of creation, are the Host and the Sompnour. The resemblance between mine host of the "Tabard" and mine host of the "Garter" has often been pointed out, as also that between the physique of the Sompnour and "one Bardolph, if your majesty know the man: his face is all bubukles, and whelks, and knobs, and flames of fire." That there should not be other personal parallels besides that between the landlords arises partly from the different principles on which the two geniuses worked. Shakespeare did not attempt to reproduce the society of his time fully and exactly as did Chaucer. It would be easier to find counterparts to Chaucer's characters in Ben Jonson, the great collector and preserver of "humours." That difference in "*personæ*" arises also from the immense change that passed over English life between the fourteenth and the sixteenth century. The social world has its deluges no less than the material—

"O earth! what changes hast thou seen!"

and the interval between those centuries was a "diluvial period." The old forms of life had been swept away. The "wanton and merry" friar, the "full fat" lordly monk, the smooth-tongued pardoner, and many another, had all gone hence, and were no more seen; and a race had succeeded that knew not St. Thomas or his fellow-saints.

Of Shakespeare's knowledge of the *Knight's Tale* there are several indications in the *Midsummer Night's Dream*.[1] In both pieces the presiding figures are those of "Duke" Theseus and Hippolyta; the scenes are Athens and woods near Athens. The name Philostrate is common to both— in the older work as the name worn by Arcite when he returns disguised to the court of Theseus, in the later as that of the Master of the Revels to Theseus. The poem begins just after the marriage of Theseus. The conqueror of "the regne of Femynge" is just bringing his bride

"hoom with him in his contre,
With moche glorie and gret solempnite."

In the play he has just brought her home, to be wedded there

"With pomp, with triumph, and with revelling."

It is impossible when, later on in the tale, we see Theseus and Hippolyta, out a hunting in the May time, come upon Palamon and Arcite, madly fighting for love in a forest glade, not

---

[1] See some excellent remarks on this point in Hippesley's *Chapters on Early English Literature*, pp. 60-62.

to remember how in the play the same noble pair, "hearing the music" of the hounds, discover a group of lovers strangely reposing on the woodland grass, having risen up early, as the Duke thinks, " to observe the rite of May," all rivalry, as the event proves, now appeased and ended. In both pieces we have two lovers devoted to one lady. In the play this position is repeated twice. But still closer is the contact between Shakespeare and the *Knight's Tale*, if, as is stated in the edition of the *Two Noble Kinsmen*, published in 1634, that work is indeed " by the memorable worthies of their own time, Mr. John Fletcher and Mr. William Shakspeare ;" for the *Two Noble Kinsmen* is, in fact, a dramatization of the *Knight's Tale*. The statement of the title-page might go for little, if it were not supplemented by internal evidence. For our part we are inclined to agree with those critics who recognize the direct work of Shakespeare in certain passages of the drama and imitations of him in other parts. The subsidiary plot of the gaoler's daughter and her furious passion for Palamon is certainly not by the hand of the master. The madness scene would appear to have been suggested by Ophelia's frenzy. Gerrold and his rustic merrymakers seem a faint reflection of the incomparable Bottom and his company. The scenes which are assuredly Shakespeare's, if any are, are those which confine themselves to the story as rendered by Chaucer, expanding or contracting it as is required by dramatic necessity and the judgment of the reproducer. They are, without controversy, the work of one who held his original in no mean honour. The warmly admiring and reverent mention of its author, made in the Prologue, has already been quoted.

But the work of Chaucer's whose traces are most frequently perceptible in Shakespeare's writings, is unquestionably *Troilus and Cressida*. *Troilus and Cressida* was the most popular love-poem of our literature, from the time of its composition, or free and vigorous reproduction from Boccaccio. In the fifteenth century a Scotch poet, by name Henryson, wrote a continuation of it.[1] Sixteenth-century praises of it abound. "Chaucer," says Sidney, in his *Apologie for Poetrie*,[2] "undoubtedly did excellently in hys Troylus and Cressid; of whom truly I know not whether to mervaile more either that he in that mistie time could see so clearely, or that wee in this cleare age walke so stumblingly after him."

Shakespeare's acquaintance with this general favourite is, in our opinion, exhibited, as we have said, most strikingly in his play of the same name, in *Romeo and Juliet*, in *Tarquin and Lucrece*, and in *Venus and Adonis;* but in others of his works also there may perhaps be discerned symptoms of it. Compare—

"For hit is seyd men makyn oft a yerd
With which the maker is himself ybeten
In sundry maner as thes wise men tretyn,"

with *King Lear:*—

"The gods are just, and of our pleasant vices
Make instruments to scourge us."

Compare—

"What know I of the queene Niobe?
Let be thin old ensaumplis, I the pray."

with Hamlet's—

"What is Hecuba to him, or he to Hecuba?"

---

[1] From the "Cressida was a beggar" of *Twelfth Night* (iii. 1), it would appear that Shakespeare knew this continuation.

[2] See p. 62 of Mr. Arber's reprint. Is Mr. Arber's excellent series of reprints generally known to our readers? It is not easy to commend them too warmly for their accuracy and their cheapness.

In the *Merchant of Venice*, in that famous "out-nighting" scene, Lorenzo says how—

> "in such a night
> Troilus, methinks, mounted the Trojan walls,
> And sigh'd his soul toward the Grecian tents,
> Where Cressid lay that night."

This is straight from Chaucer, who describes the poor forlorn lover, how—

> "Upon the walles fast ek wolde he walke,
> And on the Grekes oost he wolde see;
> And to hymself right thus he wolde talke:
> So yonder is myn owene lady free,
> Or elles yonder, ther the tentes be,
> And thennes cometh this eyre that is so soote,
> That in my soule I feele it doth me boote.
>
> "And hardyly this wynd that moore and moore
> Thus stoundemele encressith in my face,
> Is of my lady depe sykes sore;
> I preve it thus, for in noon other place
> Of all this town, save oonly'in this space,
> Feel I no wynde that souneth so lyke peyne,
> It'seith 'Allas! why twynned be we tweyne?'"

But, to turn to the pieces above mentioned as more especially reflecting the knowledge of Chaucer's poem: it is in *Venus and Adonis*, "the first heir of my invention," as might be expected, that the influence of Chaucer's manner is most visible. We venture to think that Chaucer is the master of Shakespeare in undramatic as Marlowe in dramatic poetry. In both poetries the style of the teacher has left its mark at least upon the earlier productions of the pupil. The leading features of Chaucer's *Troylus and Cryseyde* are, an extreme minuteness and fulness of description, an over-brimming abundance of imagery and illustration, an almost excessive display of poetical richness and power. In all these respects the *Venus and Adonis* of Shakespeare corre-

sponds. There are signs of youthfulness in both works—
the youthfulness of singularly deep and fertile natures. In
each poem there is but little action. Each writer is encumbered, so to speak, by the wealth of his genius, so that
movement is almost impossible. The exuberant growths of
fancy cling around them trammellingly. The poems consist
for the most part of long conversations, or else monologues
reported at the fullest length. They are the thinkings aloud
of minds of the utmost conceivable fulness and efflorescence.
The passion depicted in both pieces is of the same sensuous
order. The likeness in this respect is extremely noticeable.
Something of what has been said applies also to *Tarquin
and Lucrece*, but not all. The style of that work is severer
than that of *Venus and Adonis*, though there is the same inexhaustible plenitude and lavishness of power. In one point
of view it affords a remarkable contrast to the poem published in the preceding year. The chaste-souled Lucrece
seems to rebuke the self-abandoning passion of Venus, as
also that of the old Trojan paramours. The structure of the
poem does not differ from that of *Venus and Adonis*, which,
as we have pointed out, is that of the Chaucerian work. It
is not perhaps so important to notice that the metre of it is
the same as that of Chaucer's poem—the seven-lined stanza
or "rime royal," as it is called (which we in England
might rather call the Chaucerian stanza; for it is to Chaucer
we owe as well its introduction into our country as its most
successful cultivation)—inasmuch as it is the metre of the
Mirrour of Magistrates and other Tudor works; but yet the
fact should not be forgotten.

In the great love-play, *Romeo and Juliet*, there are to be
observed many reminiscences of the great love-tale, *Troylus
and Cryseyde*. Mercutio,[1] the love-mocker, recalls to the

[1] Compare also Benedick in *Much Ado about Nothing*.

mind of the reader what Troilus was before the hour of his sweet captivity came upon him. Pandarus reminds the smitten knight, how—

> "thou were wont to chace
> At Love in scorne, and for despyt hym calle
> Seynt Idiote, Lord of thes folis alle.
>
> "How oft hast thou made thy nice japis
> And seyd that Loves servauntis everichon
> Of nycete ben verrey goddis apys;
> And some wold monche her brede alone,
> Lying in bed, and make hem for to grone;
> And some thow seydist had a blaunch fevere,
> And preydist God he shold never kevere.
>
> "And some of hem toke on hem for the cold,
> More than ynow, so seydist thow ful oft;
> And some have feynid oft tyme and told
> How they wake, whan her love slepe soft.
> And thus have broght hem self a loft,
> And natheles were undere at the last;
> Thus seydist thow, and japedist ful fast."

Compare Mercutio's name of "the ape" for Romeo, and his other lively wit-flights at the expense of the "tender passion." Compare Cryseyde's

> "Ful sharp bygynnyng brekith oft at ende,"

with Friar Laurence's sage—

> "These violent delights have violent ends,
> And in their triumph die."

Compare the partings of the lovers as the day breaks (book iii. of *Troilus and Cressida*; act iii. scene 5, of *Romeo and Juliet*).[1] Compare Troilus's presentiment—

---

[1] This parallel is pointed out by Godwin in his *Life of Geoffrey Chaucer*.

"Alas! thow saist right soth, quoth Troylus;
But, hardely, it is not al for nought,
That in myn herte I now rejoysse thus;
It is ayenis some good, I have a thought;
Not I not how, but sen that I was wrought,
Ne felt I swich a comfort, dar I seye;
She comth to nyght, my life that dorste I leye,"

with Romeo's—

"If I may trust the flattering truth of sleep,
My dreams presage some joyful news at hand;
My bosom's lord sits lightly in his throne,
And all this day an unaccustom'd spirit
Lifts me above the ground with cheerful thoughts."

But it is most natural to look for signs of Shakespeare's knowledge of Chaucer's *Troylus and Cryseyde* in his play of the same name; and certainly signs are there, but they are signs of a dissentient knowledge rather than of a sympathetic. It can scarcely, we think, be necessary for us, after what has already been said, to insist that the commentators are imperfectly informed who tell us that Shakespeare knew nothing of Chaucer's poem, and that his only sources were Caxton's *Recuyell of the Historyes of Troye* and Lydgate's *Historye, Sege, and Dystruccyon of Troye*. That he drew from those works of Caxton and Lydgate, we do not deny; for his play covers a much wider field than that of Chaucer's poem, and indeed the best parts of it have nothing to do with the lovers; but there can be no doubt that for those scenes in which the eponyms do figure the older celebrator of them was his chief authority. Chaucer is the one original in English for the story of *Troilus and Cressida*. His own debt to Boccaccio is unquestionable; who "Lollius" was, to whom he acknowledges such perpetual obligations, is a yet unsolved mystery; but for English readers he is the one original. Thus Lydgate, in his Troy book, when he comes to *Troilus and Cressida*, at once cites Chaucer's poem as the source of all he has to tell, and, after those sincere expressions of reverence and love, to which we have referred above, proceeds to reproduce it. And so Gascoigne,[1] who died a few years before Shakespeare left Stratford for London, when he alludes to the story, names Lollius and Chaucer as the great relaters of it.

But Shakespeare does not accept the story in the spirit in which Chaucer recounts it. Shakespeare's play by no means belongs to his " apprenticeship," as Dryden makes bold to state in the Preface to his own queer version of it; it is, in fact, one of his later plays. We should incline to hold that Chaucer's poem belongs to about the same period of his life as that to which *Romeo and Juliet* belongs in the life of Shakespeare: it is the work of his genius when yet comparatively nascent, in no wise mellow fruit. Hence the difference of treatment. Shakespeare's fully ripened judgment rejects altogether a certain unreality that marks Chaucer's poem. The fact is that the heroine, as the older poet paints her, is a mere fancy-creature. Chaucer's heart was very soft towards women, and he could not harden it enough to represent Cressida faithfully. 'He could not bring himself to call her by her right name; he is always yearning to excuse her; even for what he does say he is afterwards ready to make amends, and endeavours to make amends in the *Legend of Good Women*. With all her frailty he loved her tenderly, and would fain have been blind to her terrible treason. He was like some executioner paralyzed by the exceeding fairness of the head laid on the block before him.

"Ne me ne list this sely womman chyde
Ferthere thanne the storie wol devyse;

[1] See Gascoigne's *Dan Bartholomew of Bathe.*

> Hire name, allas! is published so wyde,
> That for hire gilte it ought ynough suffise;
> And if I myght excuse hire any wyse,
> For she so sory was for her untrouthe
> *Ywis I wold excuse hire yet for routhe.*"

Shakespeare, on the other hand, more keen-sighted at all times, and writing at a season of life when the eyes of the wise, at least, are not so easily caught, and mere outward beauty is rated and valued with a truer discrimination, does justice inflexibly; and when Nestor praises her, equivocally perhaps as "a woman of quick sense," Ulysses cries aloud and spares not:—

> "Fie, fie upon her!
> There's a language in her eye, her cheek, her lip,
> Nay, her foot speaks; her wanton spirits look out
> At every joint and motive of her body."

Quite different, too, are the representations of Pandarus. Chaucer, though not perhaps without misgivings, ascribes his wonderful assiduity in his friend's behalf to the bond of "sworn brotherhood," by which he and Troilus, just as Palamon and Arcite, were so closely united; Shakespeare does not deign to notice any such plea. He is persistently plain-spoken; he lets black be black. It is then perhaps in his pointed disagreements with Chaucer's poem that Shakespeare's knowledge of it is manifested rather than in any concordance of incident or expression, though most certainly there is this concordance also.

Our space has not permitted us to attempt an exhaustive list of the Chaucerian traces to be observed in the works of Shakespeare. Perhaps of those we have quoted, some may seem fanciful; it is not essential to maintain our proposition that all should be admitted; but assuredly they cannot all be dismissed as unsubstantial or fortuitous.

There is, then, good ground for indulging the belief that the works of the great narrative poet of our literature were not absent from the studies of the supreme dramatist, who alone, perhaps, of all greatest geniuses, was in certain gifts of the imagination ever to surpass him.

IV.

SHAKESPEARE'S GREEK NAMES.

(From the *Cornhill Magazine*, February, 1876.)

THE critics of the last century found a curious pleasure in proving that Shakespeare was a dunce. It could not be denied that there was something in him; but there was a general reluctance to allow that he knew anything of books. That he could write was demonstrable, and that he could read was beyond doubting; but not much more was allowed him in the way of accomplishments. Persons who were not themselves acquainted with Italian, as was amply proved by the blunders they committed in discussing the matter, easily convinced themselves and their disciples that Shakespeare was quite innocent of that language. And so with regard to French, it was thought absurd to believe that he had any knowledge of French; though to be sure there is in several of his plays an appearance of some knowledge of it. Of all symptoms of such a knowledge it was not difficult to dispose by the theory that he had a friend who had enjoyed superior advantages, and could readily inform him what was the equivalent for "finger" and "hand" and so forth. As to Latin, the University men rather resented the notion that he could read his Ovid in the original. Shakespeare might have studied and interpreted nature with remarkable success; but art and the great works of art were out of his line. Certainly there were endless signs in his writing that their author was possessed of some Latinity: but what arguments are considerable when the case is prejudged? To entertain for a moment the idea that he was in the slightest possible degree a Greek scholar would have been held the mere wildness of phantasy. It was even maintained that his knowledge of his native tongue was unsound and blundering. In all these respects the views of Shakespearian criticism have materially changed. An unbiassed inspection of the facts has produced a tendency to believe that Shakespeare was not after all such an utter ignoramus. Scholars of note have found reasons for concluding that he had some acquaintance with both Italian and French, and that Ben Jonson's famous line—

"And though thou hadst small Latin and less Greek—"

is entirely decisive evidence that his attainments in what are specially called the classical tongues were of an appreciable amount, considering how high was the learned Ben's standard, and what therefore his "small" would represent. As to English, it has been made now fairly clear that if Shakespeare knew nothing of that tongue, the whole Elizabethan age was in a like condition; as what were noted as the signs of his ignorance are found to be not peculiarities of Shakespeare's style, but common characteristics of our language in the Tudor times.

We do not propose to enter here upon the general question. All that we wish now to do is to point out two or three possible or probable instances of Shakespeare's knowledge of Greek; though indeed to set forth anything new regarding our great master is a rare achievement, and it may perhaps turn out that some lynx-eyed commentator has anticipated every observation we propose to make. We wish to consider certain Greek names that are used by Shakespeare.

We may remark, in passing, that Shakespeare's nomenclature presents a subject for study that has by no means

yet received the attention it deserves. He is never merely
servile in following his originals in this particular; but exercises a remarkable independence, sometimes simply adopting, sometimes slightly varying, sometimes wholly rejecting
the names he found in them. It is difficult to imagine that
this conduct was merely arbitrary and careless. Euphony
must of course have had its influence; often there must
have occurred other considerations of no trifling interest, if
only we could discover and understand them. A singular
instance of a complete re-christening is to be found in *The
Winter's Tale.* The material of this play is, as is well
known, Robert Greene's *Dorastus and Faunia.* Here are
the two name-lists:—

The Novel.		The Play.	The Novel.		The Play.
Pandosto	=	Polixenes.	Gavinter	=	Mamillius.
Egistus	=	Leontes.	Dorastus	=	Florizel.
Bellaria	=	Hermione.	Faunia	=	Perdita.
Franion	=	Camillo.			

In the older *Hamlet*—in the 1603 4to.—Polonius is called
Corambis, Corambus in the German Play printed by Mr.
Albert Cohn; Claudius in the German Play is Erico. Comparing *As You Like It* with its original—Lodge's *Euphues'
Golden Legacie*—in this respect, we find no trace of Jaques
and Touchstone either in name or personality; the Orlando
we know so well is the development of a certain Rosader;
Oliver, Orlando's brother, is Saladyne; Celia is Alinda; but
the names Aliena, Phœbe, Ganymede, Adam, are taken
from Lodge without alteration But we cannot here attempt
the investigation of this question. We will only say that
we believe that from a thorough scrutiny of it some valuable
light might be cast upon Shakespeare and his art.

To turn to our special business in this paper: some of

the most noticeable Greek names used by Shakespeare are Apemantus, Sycorax, Autolycus, Desdemona—through the Italian, possibly Ophelia. Every one of these names, except perhaps Sycorax, was adopted by Shakespeare from some older work; but what we wish to point out is the full intelligence and mastery of their sense and associations with which he uses them.

Of the name Ophelia Mr. Ruskin has spoken with much ingenuity. He considers it to be the Greek ὠφελία, "help," and in its application to Polonius's daughter to have an ironical force. In one point of view Ophelia was the cause of the terrible tragedy, in whose wild current she herself too was swept away. She by her weakness, as Lady Macbeth by her strength, spread destruction round about her. Not that one is to blame her; she acts according to her nature and capacity, and she can do no more. But it is piteous and dreadful to see how vainly her lover turns towards her for sympathy and succour. More than once, with his faith in humanity well nigh prostrate and all his powers unstrung by suspicion and doubt and despair, he would fain find in her some high restorative of belief and confidence—some divine elixir to make life livable; he would fain find help, but help for him there is none. The name she bears then may contain in it an awful irony. And this Shakespeare may have perceived and felt and acknowledged,—*Hamlet* was certainly written in a period of his life when for some reason or another his soul was vexed and embittered within him,—although he did not create the name. It was his characteristic to see the significance of things just as they were put before him, instead of re-arranging them in order to express some meaning he might wish to give them. That he found the name in the older play—the play referred to by Nash in his Preface to Greene's *Menaphon* in 1587, and mentioned in Henslowe's Diary in 1594—we can scarcely doubt. It does not occur in *The Hystorie of Hamblet*, the translation from Belleforest's *Histoires Tragiques*, which itself derived the story from the *Historia Danica* of Saxo Grammaticus, though there is a curious mention in it of a lady employed to corrupt Hamlet, who, however, informed him of the treason, "as being one that from her infancy loved and favoured him." In the 1603 4to. it appears as Ofelia; the German play has it in the shape that is familiar to us.

A play, remarkable for its Greek nomenclature, is the *Winter's Tale*, already mentioned on another account—remarkable because there is little in the original to suggest or encourage such Hellenism; see the list given above. To the Greek names there recorded may be added, Antigonus, Cleomenes, Archidamus, Dion, Autolycus, and Dorcas. We may observe that all these names, except perhaps Dorcas and Leontes, are found in Plutarch's *Lives*. We will say a few words about Autolycus.

Both the character and the name are entirely of Shakespeare's invention. Whence came this prince of pedlars and of pickpockets? No doubt the man had in some sort been espied and watched by him who has painted him for all time—at some Stratford wake, when Mr. Shakespeare of New Place was taking Mistress Susanna and her sister Judith to see what was to be seen; or at Bartholomew Fair, as he strolled through it perchance with Mr. Benjamin Jonson; but what a name to give him! Yet it was carefully chosen. There was an ancient thief of famous memory called Autolycus. His name probably is significant of his nature. It should mean All-wolf, Very-wolf, Wolf's-self. See Hom. *Od.* xix. 392-8, where the old nurse Eurukleia is bathing the feet of the not yet identified Odusseus:

Νίζε δ' ἄρ' ἆσσον ἰοῦσα ἄναχθ' ἑόν· αὐτίκα δ' ἔγνω
οὐλήν· τήν ποτέ μιν σῦς ἤλασε λευκῷ ὀδόντι
Παρνησόνδ' ἐλθόντα μετ' Αὐτόλυκόν τε καὶ υἱας,
μητρὸς ἑῆς πατέρ' ἐσθλὸν, ὃς ἀνθρώπους ἐκέκαστο
κλεπτοσύνῃ θ', ὅρκῳ τε· θεὸς δέ οἱ αὐτὸς ἔδωκεν
Ἑρμείας· τῷ γὰρ κεχαρισμένα μηρία καῖεν
ἀρνῶν ἠδ' ἐρίφων· ὁ δέ οἱ πρόφρων ἅμ' ὀπήδει.

Here is Chapman's rendering of the passage, published in 1616, but, probably enough, read and known in a certain circle some years before. As the old servant bathes her sovereign's feet she observes the scar—

      "Which witness'd by her eye
Was straight approv'd. He first received this sore
As in Parnassus' tops a white-tooth'd boar
He stood in chase withal, who strook him there
At such time as he lived a sojourner
With his grandsire Autolycus; who th' art
Of theft and swearing (not out of the heart
But by equivocation) first adorn'd
Your witty man withal, and was suborn'd
By Jove's descent, ingenious Mercury,
Who did bestow it, since so many a thigh
Of lambs and kids he had on him bestow'd
In sacred flames; who therefore when he vow'd
Was ever with him."

Let us notice, by the way, that curious addition Chapman makes—"not out of the heart, but by equivocation"—which there is nothing whatever in the Greek to justify. Evidently the Englishman with his ideas of truth telling, did not appreciate, or understand, the Greek δεινότης, "awful cleverness," "sharpness," "subtlety." Again, ἐκέκαστο does not mean "adorn'd," but "surpassed." In the following lines the "descent" seems to mean descendant, son: "Jove's descent" is Chapman's equivalent for θεὸς αὐτός. Turn from the *Odyssey* to the *Winter's Tale*. "My traffic is, sheets," says the worthy prig-pedlar; "when the kite builds, look to lesser linen. My father named me Autolycus, who being, as I am, litter'd under Mercury, was likewise a snapper up of unconsidered trifles." We will add that the statement made in the latter sentence about his father, must surely be connected with what Autolycus is said by Ovid to have been —*patriæ non degener artis;* see the eleventh book of the *Metamorphoses*, where is narrated the birth of our light-fingered friend—*furtum ingeniosus ad omne.* Another point of contact between Shakespeare's rogue and the ancient one, is that both have a ready gift of self-transformation. The ancient is said to have had the power of metamorphosis. And so, in the *Winter's Tale*, the rogue often changes his part. He appears as a shabby, *ci-devant* valet—which he is, as the denuded victim of thieves, as a most successful pedlar, as a courtier, and lastly as a fawning and servile dependent.

The name Desdemona claims a few words. In the narrative upon which *Othello* is certainly founded (*Hecatommithi*, Decad. III. Nov. 7),—whether Shakespeare read it in the original or a translation must remain an open question, the more probable answer at present being that he read it in the Italian—that, as Mr. Collier points out, is the only name introduced by Cinthio. In Cinthio's novel Othello is "the Moor," Cassio "the lieutenant" (il capo di squadrone), Iago "the ensign" or "ancient" (l'alfiero). There can be little doubt, we presume, that the name Desdemona is from the Greek δυσδαίμων, "ill-starred," and its singular fitness for the unfortunate woman who bears it will need no assertion for those who really know the play. Amongst all Shakespeare's heroines she is emphatically ἡ δυσδαίμων, "the ill-starred one." So lovely, so loving, so accomplished, and true and pure, yet perishing so miserably! "Oh, the world hath not a sweeter creature; she might lie by an emperor's side and command him tasks. . . . An admirable musician; oh, she will sing the savageness out of a bear; of so high and plenteous wit and invention. . . . And, then, of so gentle a condition!" "Ay, too gentle," says Evil incarnate in the shape of Iago. "Nay, that's certain," replies the poor victim; "but yet *the pity of it, Iago! O Iago, the pity of it, Iago!*" For the most part Shakespeare delights in tracing the action of the great moral laws of the world, and showing how fearful is the penalty of transgression—how, as Æschylus has it—

$$\text{ἤ τις Ἀπόλλων}$$
$$\text{ἢ Πὰν ἢ Ζεὺς} \ldots$$
$$\ldots$$
$$\text{ὑστερόποινον}$$
$$\text{πέμπει παραβᾶσιν Ἐρινύν.}$$

But sometimes he exhibits a yet more dreadful spectacle—a spectacle mysterious, inscrutable, soul-prostrating. It is Fate blind, inexorable, rapacious. Desdemona is one of Fate's choicest victims. Her "graces serve" her "but as enemies." Her very virtues bring on her ruin. What is most innocent is construed into evidence against her. In obeying the best instincts of her clear spirit she excites the evilest suspicions and secures the bitterest condemnation. The truth from her lips is turned into a lie. In the last Act, when Othello charges her with unfaithfulness, her answers, by an almost incredible infelicity, are, through the very purity of her nature, just such as to confirm his detestable impeachment. "Let him confess the truth," she says of Cassio and the handkerchief.

"*Oth.* He hath confess'd.
Des. What, my lord?
Oth. That he hath—us'd thee.
Des. How? unlawfully?
Oth. Ay.

Des. He will not say so.
Oth. No, his mouth is stopp'd ;
Honest Iago hath ta'en order for't.
Des. O ! my fear interprets ; what, is he dead?
Oth. Had all his hairs been lives, my great revenge
Had stomach for them all.
Des. Alas ! he is betray'd, and I undone.
Oth. Out, strumpet ! weep'st thou for him to my face ?
Des. O, banish me, my lord, but kill me not !"

Could replies be more unfortunate ? She lies in the toils of Fate, and there is no escape for her. "But yet the pity of it, Iago ! O Iago, the pity of it, Iago !" We said that this name is from the Greek δυσδαίμων, "ill-starred ; " but we may go further and say it is merely a variation of δυσδαιμονία, "ill-starredness." She is not only unhappy, she is unhappiness itself. It should be remembered that in the Italian the name is Desdémona, not Desdemóna.

Let us now turn to a name of a very different interest—to Sycorax. The name Caliban is, it is fairly certain, a mere metathesis of Cannibal, which is itself a corruption of Caribale, of which the English form is Caribbee. The name of " my dam's God " is found in Eden's *History of Travayle*, in an account of the capture of two Patagonians : " When they felt the shackles fast about their legs, they began to doubt ; but the captain did put them in comfort and bade them stand still. In fine, when they saw how they were deceived, they roared like bulls, and cried upon their great devil Setebos to help them." Ariel—in the first folio the words " an ayrie spirit " stand opposite the name in the list of characters—is an old title used in a new sense. In Heywood's *Hierarchie of the Blessed Angels*, Ariel is the " Earth's great Lord ; " and the word, as Hunter suggested, may be the same as occurs in Isaiah xxiv. 1, 2, and 7, where Jerusalem is so called. Sycorax is, we believe, of Shakespeare's own formation. At all events this name has not yet been found occurrent elsewhere. And we think the conjecture that it is compounded of the Greek σῦς (ὗς is a variant) and κόραξ, and is therefore a contraction of Syokorax, can scarcely be despised. As both sows and ravens are associated with witchcraft and such superstitions, the compound might serve not ill to denominate that "foul witch" (*Tempest*, I. iii. 258), "damned witch" (*Ib.* 263), "blue-eyed hag" (*Ib.* 268), of whose "mischiefs manifold and sorceries terrible to enter human hearing," and "earthly and abhorred commands," and "most unmitigable rage," Prospero speaks with such genuine loathing. Notice Caliban's opening curse:—

> "As wicked dew as e'er my mother brush'd
> With *raven's* feather from unwholesome fen
> Drop on you both!"

In other plays we find such phrases as "the hateful raven," "the fatal raven," "the croaking raven doth bellow for revenge" (*Hamlet*, III. ii. 265):

> "O it comes o'er my memory
> As doth the raven o'er the infected house
> Boding to all." *Othello*, IV. i. 20.

> "The raven himself is hoarse
> That croaks the fatal entrance of Duncan
> Under my battlements." *Macbeth*, I. v. 39.

Other illustrations old and new might easily be given. Poe's description of this bird in his well-known poem will occur to every reader:—

"Ghastly, grim, and ancient Raven, wandering from the nightly shore."

"This grim, ungainly, ghastly, gaunt, and ominous bird of yore."

"'Prophet!' said I, 'thing of evil! prophet still, if bird or devil.'"

For the sow, it is not mentioned, indeed, by Caliban

among his mother's "charms,"—" toads, beetles, bats,"—
but into that foul caldron, whose ingredients are catalogued
in *Macbeth*, the first witch bids also—

"Pour in *sow's* blood, that hath eaten
Her nine farrow."

Or the mere grossness of the one animal and the supposed
malignity of the other may be referred to; and so the name
Sycorax be designed to express a horrid mixture of those
two characteristics—something bestial and fiendish withal.
"With age and envy" she "was grown into a hoop." She
had almost lost what human form she once had, and approached in semblance the brute whose nature she shared.
Prospero speaks of—

"The son that she did *litter* here,
A freckled whelp hag-born, not honour'd with
A human shape."

The last name we shall notice is Apemantus in *Timon of
Athens*. This name is not found in Barckley's *Discourse of
the Felicity of Man*, but is so in the novel in Painter's *Palace
of Pleasure*, which treats "of the straunge and beastlie nature
of Timon of Athens, enemie to mankinde, with his death,
buriall, and epitaph." It was no doubt also observed in
North's translation of Amyot's translation of *Plutarch's Life
of Antonine*. All that Plutarch says of Apemantus is com-
prised in these sentences, here quoted from North's version:—

"Apemantus, wondering at it [his shunning 'all other
men's companies but the company of young Alcibiades, a
bold and insolent youth, whom he would greatly feast, and
make much of, and kissed him very gladly'—ἠσπάζετο καὶ
κατεφίλει προθύμως], asked him the cause and what he meant,
to make so much of that young man alone, and to hate all

others. Timon answered him, 'I do it,' said he, 'because I know that one day he shall do great mischief unto the Athenians.' This Timon sometimes would have Apemantus in his company, because he was much like of his nature and his conditions, and also followed him in manner of life. On a time when they solemnly celebrated the feasts called Choæ of Athens (to wit, the feasts of the dead, when they make sprinklings and sacrifices for the dead), and that they two then feasted together by themselves, Apemantus said unto the other: 'O here is a trim banquet, Timon.' Timon answered again, 'yea,' said he, 'so thou wert not here.' (Τοῦ δ' Ἀπημάντου φήσαντος ' ὡς καλόν, ὦ Τίμων, τὸ συμπόσιον ἡμῶν,' ' εἴγε σύ,' ἔφη, ' μὴ παρῆς.')"

It will be allowed that there is little here to suggest the characterization we find in Shakespeare's play. It may justly be said that that characterization is in accordance with that rule of contrast which the great dramatist so commonly observes. It was obvious to develop Apemantus into the affected, self-conscious, egotistic cynic whose bitterness should by its very shallowness make the unfathomed indignation of the genuine misanthrope more effectively felt. Apemantus is an impostor. He professes to loathe his kind, and yet is always intruding himself into its society. He cannot understand the genuine feeling of which his spitefulness is a mere simulation—the "sæva indignatio" quæ cor lacerat. When he hears of Timon's withdrawal into the cave near the seashore, he thinks that Timon too is acting a part. He has not sensibility enough to be a good hater—a thorough man-hater. "Men report," he says to one whom he regards as a sort of would-be rival in his line of ferocity—

"Men report
Thou dost affect my manners, and dost use them."

The grand distinction between the two characters springs

from the fact, that the one is a man of noble nature whose
trust in humanity has been rudely dethroned; the other, a
man of an inferior breed, that has not ever known anything
of sympathy and affection. Timon's hate is so pathetic and
so terrible, because he has loved, if not wisely, yet too well.
There is no denying that he is "more sinned against than
sinning"—that he is dreadfully wronged; and one cannot
wonder, if with his ill-balanced temperament he rushes into
the furthest extremes of acrimony and loathing. But Apemantus has no such right to be savage; he can bring no
such justifying accusation against the world; he is more
sinning than sinned against.

>   "Fie, thou art a churl: ye've got a humour there
>   Does not become a man: 'tis much to blame."

Now, what we have specially to point out, is the curious
way in which his very name is indication of the fact that, as
compared with Timon and whatever license to curse Timon
may claim, he is without a grievance,—is an unwronged man.
This is exactly what his name means. It is the Greek
ἀπήμαντος, meaning literally "un-hurt"—a word, as we learn
from Liddell and Scott, used by Homer, *Od.* xix. 282; by
Pindar, *Ol.* viii. end.:

>   ἀλλ' ἀπήμαντον ἄγων βίοτον
>   αὐτούς τ' ἀέξοι καὶ πόλιν—

and Æschylus, *Agam.* 378. A noticeable coincidence, and
of use for the comprehension of the play, if indeed it is not
something more. Let us now read Timon's own analysis of
Apemantus:—

>   "Thou art a slave, whom Fortune's tender arm
>   With favour never clasp'd, but bred a dog.
>   Hadst thou, like us, from the first swath, proceeded

> The sweet degrees that this brief world affords
> To such as may the passive drugs of it
> Freely command, thou wouldst have plunged thyself
> In general riot; melted down thy youth
> In different beds of lust; and never learn'd
> The icy precepts of respect, but follow'd
> The sugar'd game before thee. But myself,
> Who had the world as my confectionary—
> The mouths, the tongues, the eyes and hearts of men
> At duty, more than I could frame employment;
> That numberless upon me stuck, as leaves
> Do on the oak, have with one winter's brush
> Fell from their boughs, and left me open, bare
> For every storm that blows;—I, to bear this,
> That never knew but better, is some burden.
> Thy nature did commence in sufferance; time
> Hath made thee hard in it. *Why shouldst thou hate men?*
> *They never flatter'd thee: what hast thou given?*"

In *Macbeth* the "second murderer" describes himself thus:—

> "I am one, my liege,
> Whom the vile blows and buffets of the world
> Have so incensed that I am reckless what
> I do to spite the world."

We might call him Pemantus, if there were such a word in the Greek language, which there is not. At all events, he makes exactly intelligible what the name Apemantus may mean.

To conclude these remarks, we think it would be rash indeed to infer from such considerations as we have laid before our readers that Shakespeare was a Greek scholar of any great pretensions. There is nowadays so much wild theorizing about Shakespeare—gentlemen who seem scarcely to have read his works through are so ready with their inestimable decisions—that we wish to keep well within the limits of our facts. It cannot be demonstratively shown that

Shakespeare was conscious of the curious significancies we have discussed. "Beware instinct. . . . Instinct is a great matter." All we wish to suggest is a probability in some cases that he may have been so. But, even if so much cannot be conceded us, we venture to hope that the few remarks we have made may be not useless for the better understanding of the masterpieces they concern.

V.

HAZLITT'S SHAKESPEARE'S LIBRARY.

(From the *Athenæum*, Aug. 21, 1875.)

MR. HAZLITT, whose name is conspicuous by its absence from the title-pages of the work before us, but appears on the label attached to the back of each volume, can only be described as an editor by some oxymoron. Some such interdiscordant phrase as the Greek tragedians so frequently employ naturally rises to one's lips as one thinks of him, or sees a fresh exhibition of his workmanship. He is an "editor that is no editor." To every lover of old books he is dear, and at the same time detestable; always welcome, and as often ill-come; not to be done without, and yet to be perpetually grumbled at. The critic, in judging of this gentleman, can take his stand, so to speak, neither on the mountain of blessing nor that of cursing—neither on Gerizim nor Ebal; but, if this is anyhow possible, must plant a foot on either eminence, and smile and scowl alternately. Mr. Hazlitt has, indeed, done for all students of English literature excellent service in bringing back within reach works that have become inaccessible, and we sincerely hope he will not desist from his labours. On the other hand, how greatly the value of this service would be increased by a little more editorial care! We would rather, if we may say so, he would do less for us, and do what he does better. If he would once permit us to take up one of his reprints with unmixed satisfaction! The work before us exactly illustrates what we have just said. It is a "boon," but a "boon" we shall never enjoy without some regret and annoyance. We think every genuine student of Shakespeare should possess himself of it; and yet,

"Medio de fonte leporum,
Surgit amari aliquid."

Let us first notice the "amari aliquid," and then the "lepores." The first volume opens in this wise: it begins with a list of the plays whose sources, or supposed sources, are presented in it; then comes Mr. Collier's preface to the first edition (1844), then a preface by Mr. Hazlitt himself, which is principally curious as showing his own incertitude as to what should and what should not be added to his predecessor's collection; then a "synthetical table of contents" of the entire work; and then we come to the main body—to the play-sources arranged, or thrown together in an "admired disorder." The best order, surely, in such a work as this would have been the alphabetical; at all events, some order should have been observed. The succession Mr. Hazlitt professes "in the main" to follow, he "in the main" disregards. These opening pages, especially the editor's preface, have their significance. There was some truth in the old superstition about stumbling on the threshold. We are prepared for what is the fact—a compilation of an uncertain kind. We do not know what we may find in it, and what we may not find. The first extract—it is from Johnes's *Monstrelet*—given in "pursuance of a suggestion found in Dyce's edition of Shakespeare"—language somewhat misleading—is supposed to illustrate *Love's Labour's Lost*, but how it does so one cannot readily see. To be sure it mentions a sum of money to be paid by a king of France to a king of Navarre; and in the play there is mention of a money transaction between kings of those countries; but all the details are quite different. "There is a river in Macedon, and there is also, moreover, a river in Monmouth; it is called Wye at Monmouth, but it is out of my prains what is the name of the other river; but 'tis all one, 'tis alike as my fingers is to my fingers, and there is salmons in both." In connection with the *Midsummer Night's Dream*, we are favoured with the Life of Theseus from North's *Plutarch*, though certainly Shakespeare derived the Theseus of that play mainly from Chaucer's *Knight's Tale*. For the *Comedy of Errors* is given " W. W.'s "—Warner's—translation of the *Menæchmi*, printed in 1595, though Shakespeare's play, if not produced so early as 1589, as some good scholars hold, yet unquestionably came out before 1595, and no one has shown any reason for supposing that Shakespeare had the benefit of perusing Warner's version before its publication. One might think, to listen to some people, that the Elizabethan age had its Mudie, with a circulating library of new and entertaining MSS.; moreover, there is that important entry in the *Gesta Grayorum*, 1594 :—

"After such sports, a *Comedy of Errors* (like to Plautus his Menechmus) was played by the players; so that night was begun and continued to the end in nothing but confusion and errors; whereupon it was ever afterwards called the Night of Errors."

After the *Menæchmi*, which Shakespeare may have read in the original Latin, Mr. Hazlitt presents us with *The Story of the Two Brothers of Avignon*, from Goulart's *Admirable and Memorable Histories*. These histories were published in 1607! "Possibly the story, which is printed from Goulart here, may have been seen by him in some earlier publication." Such a meagre possibility scarcely justifies Mr. Hazlitt in giving Goulart a place on Shakespeare's shelves. At this rate Shakespeare's library must have been of quite extraordinary dimensions. That he had read the *Amphitruo* seems to us really more probable. Under the head of *Merchant of Venice* is printed a ballad called *The Northern Lord*, which the editor allows was in all likelihood never beheld by Shakespeare, and " was even (almost to a certainty) later· than his day"! In the same way, under another head, he bestows upon us the ballad of *Lear and his Three Daughters.* Whether *Gernutus* has any right to be · included in these volumes is uncertain,.and Mr. Hazlitt may have the benefit of the doubt. As to the various tales printed in the section devoted to *The Merry Wives of Windsor*, they would all be rightly placed in a work designed to illustrate Shakespeare ; but it is another thing to print them as his originals. At the close of the list we have " The first Sketch of the Play," *i.e.* a reprint of the quarto of 1602. *Que diable allait-il faire dans cette galère ?* Why have we not, then, the 1603 *Hamlet*, or the 1597 *Richard III.?* It will be noticed that Mr. Hazlitt adheres to Mr. Halliwell's view as to the 1602 edition of the *Merry Wives.* The 1603 *Hamlet*, on the other hand, he regards as a pirated copy; but this by the way. To glance at other parts of these volumes, the *Measure for Measure* section contains a story from the histories of Goulart, already mentioned as published in 1607. *Troilus and Cressida* has no originals quoted for it, though if Mr. Hazlitt was at all consistent he should have quoted Chaucer's *Troilus and Cressida,* inasmuch as he quotes the *Knight's Tale* in connection with the *Two Noble Kinsmen !* For *Cymbeline* we are supplied with a copy of the *Story of the Fishwife of Standon-the-Green* from *Westward for Smelts,* 1620 ! But signal as are other of Mr. Hazlitt's achievements in this direction, his crowning exploit, we think, is quoting the Life of Pericles from North's *Plutarch* to illustrate the play of *Pericles.* Tyre is as Athens to Mr. Hazlitt. After this remarkable feat, we really do not see why he has stopped anywhere. Why not reprint all *Plutarch?* Why not Elizabethan literature as a whole? Why not all literature?

It will be by this time abundantly clear to our readers that the title of this work is by no means particularly accurate. In fact, Mr. Hazlitt rather reminds us of Juvenal:

> "Quicquid agunt homines . . . .
> nostri est farrago libelli."

Nor can we say that the details of the editing are eminently praiseworthy. The texts given can, indeed, boast of an accuracy superior to that displayed in Mr. Collier's volumes. Mr. Collier speaks frankly enough on the subject in his preface:

" The editor has had time to do little more than to afford a general superintendence, and to preface the introductory notices: the intelligent publisher, who has devoted so much time and study to Shakespearian literature, has often saved him the trouble of searching materials in public and private depositories, and of collating the reprints with the originals. For this part of the task, therefore, Mr. Rodd is responsible."

Similarly, Mr. Hazlitt had to thank Mr. B. J. Jeffery, of the Department of Manuscripts, British Museum. " Mr. Jeffery verified for me a large proportion of the texts introduced here, and the volumes owe to him the correction of innumerable errors in the former edition." . In a note to the *Tale of the Fishwife of Brentford* it is said that "the text exhibited by Mr. Halliwell is not true to the original"— words that leave an impression somewhat unjust to Mr. Halliwell. But beyond this textual carefulness—which, however, is a great matter—little or nothing is done. Mr. Hazlitt's notes are "few and far between," but they cannot on that account be likened to "angels' visits." The metrical arrangement is not always exact—*e.g.*, we find these lines printed as prose (Part II., vol. i., p. 312)—

> " Pleaseth your Grace the Earle of Salsbury,
> Penbroke, Essex, Clare, and Arundell,
> With all the Barons that did fight for thee,
> Are on a sodeine fled with all their powers
> To joyne with John to drive thee back againe."

If this is prose, what then is "metre" or "measure"?

The Taming of the Shrew is mentioned as the *Taming of a Shrew*. Surely Mr. Hazlitt knows the importance of the article here? In another place he speaks of "*The Life of Timon* by North."

Having pointed out some of the shortcomings and redundances of this misnamed work—why not call it Mr. Hazlitt's Library, or, indefinitely, Somebody's Library, or, better, Nobody's Library?—we may dwell with pleasure on its merits. We may remove the foot from Ebal—the attitude we described is something fatiguing,—and stand at ease on the cheerfuller height.

We think it is a very great advantage to have so much of Shakespeare's undoubted material placed within general reach. Mr. Hazlitt here combines, with additions, two books of extreme value to the student—Mr. Collier's work, already several times mentioned, and Steevens's *Six Old Plays*. It is nearly a century since the latter compilation was issued—more than a generation since the former appeared—and both are very rare. Now to those who really care to study Shakespeare, and not merely to talk and dogmatize about him, while they know little or nothing of the subject—we are overrun with such persons—the reprinting of two such compilations is no small blessing. Obviously one of the very best ways of estimating Shakespeare is furnished by an acquaintance with the material that he had to use and used. Common enough clay this was, and yet starting up at his wondrous touch into the most exquisite, various, substantial forms of life. Two things are noticeable : (1) the fidelity with which at times he followed his originals, and (2) the subtlety with which, even as he follows them with such humble faithfulness, they are transformed and ennobled. What inscrutable magic! The words seem all the same, and yet a new life breathes out of them. The voice is Shakespeare's voice; but the hands are the hands of Plutarch, or Greene, or Lodge. It has often been remarked how closely Shakespeare follows North in *Julius Cæsar* and in *Antony and Cleopatra*, especially in the famous passage describing the "gypsey's" progress along the Cydnus. A not less memorable instance is to be found in *Coriolanus*. Here is North's version of a part of Volumnia's speech, when the mother kneels before the son, whose pride and obstinacy, amazing as they are to her, are yet fruit she has herself planted and nurtured :—

"Then she spake in this sort: If we held our peace (my sonne) and determined not to speake, the state of our poor bodies, and present sight of our raiment would easily bewray to thee what life we have led at home, since thy exile and abode abroad; but think now with thyselfe, how much more unfortunately then all the women living, we are come hither, considering that the sight which should be most pleasant to all other to behold, spitefull fortune hath made most fearefull to us : making my selfe to see my sonne, and my daughter here, her husband, besieging the walles of his native countrey: so as that which is the onely comfort to all other in their adversitie and miserie, to pray unto the Gods and to call to them for aide is the onely thing which plungeth us into most deep perplexitie," &c. (Part I., vol. iii., p. 304).

One cannot wonder that a speech, spoken so simply, so truly, so pathetically, should have had attractions for Shakespeare. He appropriates it not only in substance, but often *verbatim*, yet with such changes as make it a new thing. A minute study of such appropriations, of the rejections, the expansions, the additions—a study not yet made as far as we know—could not fail to cast light upon the secrecies of his art. Of course, in the instance we are considering, the metrification, if we may use the word—"metrify" is used—accounts for something of the new effect, but by no means for all of it. The mere rhetoric is improved and refined; but what is most remarkable is the transference of the whole scene into a new air; we are insensibly borne away into that strange, delightful, inexplicable land, the land of "poetry." Here is the passage as it rises from the hands of the master :—

> "Should we be silent and not speak, our raiment
> And state of bodies would bewray what life
> We have led since thy exile. Think with thyself
> How more unfortunate than all living women
> Are we come hither, since that thy sight, which should
> Make our eyes flow with joy, hearts dance with comforts,
> Constrains them weep, and shake with fear and sorrow ;
> Making the mother, wife, and child to see
> The son, the husband, and the father tearing
> His country's bowels out. And to poor we
> Thine enmity's most capital ; thou barr'st
> Our prayers to the gods, which is a comfort
> That all but we enjoy," &c.

What Dryden says of Ben Jonson might better be said of Shakespeare : "He invades authors like a monarch, and what would be theft in other poets is only victory in him." Assuredly, the extent of such invasions is at first sight surprising. In this respect, the second part of Mr. Hazlitt's collection is the more interesting, though we must not forget

Euphues' Golden Legacy, in the second volume of Part I. The second part contains, besides other pieces, *The True Tragedie of Richard the Third, The Troublesome Raigne of John King of England, The Famous Victories of Henry Fifth, The First Part of the Contention of the Two Famous Houses of York and Lancaster, The True Tragedie of Richard Duke of York, The Historie of Promos and Cassandra, The True Chronicle Historie of King Leir and his Three Daughters, The Taming of a Shrew.* To appreciate adequately the splendour of Shakespeare's genius, these specimens of the drama as he found it should be carefully read and compared with the drama which he created. Justly might he have adapted and adopted Augustus's boast as to the city he had renewed and beautified. "Urbem," writes Suetonius, "neque pro majestate imperii ornatam et inundationibus incendiisque obnoxiam, excoluit adeo ut jure sit gloriatus *marmoream se relinquere quam latericiam accepissit.*"

VI.

THE SHAKESPEARE KEY.[1]

(From the *Athenæum*, July 12, 1879.)

THIS is a very different key from that with which, according to Wordsworth, Shakespeare "unlocked his heart." It is described on the title-page as "Unlocking the treasures of his style, elucidating the peculiarities of his construction, and displaying the beauties of his expression, forming a companion to 'The Complete Concordance to Shakespeare.'"

These bold promises are fairly justified by the volume. It is a worthy addition to the many useful labours for which the world is indebted to its veteran authors, only one of whom, alas, has lived to see its publication. It does not profess to give any new discoveries or bring out any new principle of interpretation. There is little or nothing in it that has not been suggested or said before in some sort somewhere. It is a compilation, but a compilation made with much intelligence and showing wide reading and various information.

"A peculiar advantage possessed by the present work," says the preface, "is that it places *collectively* before the eye comparative evidence heretofore scattered in notes, glossaries, and other forms of animadversion on Shakespeare's style; so that it may be seen *at one view* how he uses the same word or form of expression, and thus frequently becomes an

---

[1] By Charles and Mary Cowden Clarke. (Sampson Low and Co.)

interpreter to himself. Consequently 'The Shakespeare Key' will aid in determining various disputed readings and readings suspected of error, by showing *assembled together* several similar passages to the one in question; thus affording proof of its being in accordance with Shakespeare's peculiar style."

But is not this, the reader will say, just what is already done for us by Dr. Alexander Schmidt in his *Complete Dictionary of all the English Words, Phrases, and Constructions in the Works of the Poet?* And it must be allowed that in this department of their work Dr. Schmidt is a formidable rival, and one already in possession of the field. Indeed, but for his volumes the present would have been considerably larger. "While it lay in manuscript," says Mrs. Cowden Clarke, "an extremely comprehensive lexicon was brought out which included many verbal points, amounting to no fewer than 639 pages of written labour." Mrs. Clarke certainly did right in cutting out those pages, and a yet further excision might have been made. But it remains true that her volume is a valuable help to Shakespearian study.

It consists of upwards of a hundred articles of various length and importance. Amongst the subjects are: " Affected Use of Words," " Alliteration," " Dramatic Time," " Emphasis," " Idioms," " Legal Phrases," " Pronunciation," " Similes," " Spelling of Foreign Words," " Technicalities ; " and on each of these and the other subjects, if no one is treated exhaustively, something of interest is noted or recorded. The cardinal defect of the compilation is the absence of an index, the only clue provided being a table of contents, many of the terms of which are not easily intelligible, or are not altogether differential. Who would feel quite sure as to what is meant by " Crossing Speeches,"

"Perfection by Marriage," "Physical Indications," "Power in Writing Silence and Perfect Impression through Imperfect Expression," "Sentences Spoken as to what might be Said"? What distinction would one expect to be meant between "Iterated Words" and "Repeated Words"? Other headings are "Bitter Puns and Plays on Words: Conceits," "Ironical Phrases," "Sarcasms," "Peculiar Replies," "Peculiar Use of Words," "Verbs peculiarly Used." Who is sufficient for these things? The age of the Schoolmen is gone, and it is no longer a common faculty to

> "Distinguish and divide
> A hair 'twixt south and south-west side."

It may be doubted whether Touchstone himself, subtle discriminator as he was between retort and quip and reply and reproof and the rest with their proper adjectives, could readily decide to which section to turn for some particular matter.

The great defect of this compilation, then, is the inaccessibility of its details. A key is wanted to the key. In fact, there is here a valuable collection of material rather than a well-ordered book. It is therefore not likely to be useful in the way in which it should be and might be, that is, as a work of reference: it rather forms an interesting assemblage of Shakespearian notes. In this way it is really valuable, and worthy of high recommendation. But the other kind of value might so easily have been added. It is to be hoped that in a future edition it will be, and so the reader's gratitude may be doubled. Good indexes are becoming, in the immense increase of literature, more and more essential; and for this sort of work the importance of an index can scarcely be exaggerated.

Not the least interesting of the many interesting sections

is that on dramatic time, which works out the theory first put forward by the Rev. N. J. Halpin and Prof. Wilson, that Shakespeare in some of his plays observes two times, both "long" and "short"—represents a considerable period as having elapsed during the proceeding of the action, and also confines it to the course of a few hours or a day. He leaves the impression of a prolonged space, and yet crowds his events into the smallest. Thus, in the first three acts of *Julius Cæsar* there are many passages which speak as if some appreciable interval had passed between the conversation in which Cassius first tampers with Brutus and the soliloquy in which Brutus makes up his mind to join the conspirators; there are others from which we learn that that soliloquy is uttered during the very night that followed that conversation. And the like is noticeable in many other plays. Even in the *Tempest*, where the time is limited to two or three hours ("Your eld'st acquaintance cannot be three hours," says Alonso to Ferdinand when at last they are reunited), the impression is left of a much longer period. Ferdinand is wrecked, wanders over the island searching for his father, falls in love, is "austerely punish'd," *i.e.* is thoroughly tested and tried, is betrothed, has a masque performed for his pleasure, and plays chess, all in one wonderful afternoon. A strange rush and throng of experiences! What are the fewest minutes in which one could fall in love and propose, or be proposed to, and arrange everything satisfactorily? Of course, we have heard of people loving at first sight, but what of proposing at first sight? This question of Shakespeare's dramatic time deserves the attention it is receiving from Shakespearian scholars, and the section on it in *The Shakespeare Key* is well worth reading. That his use of two times should be merely accidental and careless is an idea scouted, and we think justly, by Mr. and Mrs. Clarke; and an intelligent study of it may cast some light on an art which, after all that has been said about it, is yet most imperfectly appreciated or understood.

Another extremely interesting section is that headed "Technicalities." It gives a capital list, with plentiful illustrations from the plays, of the various sports, fashions, arts, and sciences whose terminology the poet deigns occasionally to borrow. Here are recorded Shakespeare's debts to falconry, hunting, archery, war, riding, duelling, tilting, seamanship, tennis, heraldry, painting, &c. These pages may be worth the perusal of those brilliant critics who, because they find Shakespeare familiar with the terms of an art or a trade, are so ready to insist that he was, or had been, a professor or follower of the said art or trade. He uses baking terms, therefore he was a baker. On the strength of this section it may be maintained by one of these gentlemen that he was a Jack-of-all-trades. Perhaps this is what Greene meant by calling him Joannes Factotum. We respectfully submit this view to the moths who are always hovering around the Shakespearian candle, and are never happy till they have scorched themselves in it.

VII.

ELZE'S ESSAYS ON SHAKESPEARE.

"TRANSLATED, WITH THE AUTHOR'S SANCTION, BY L. DORA SCHMITZ."

(From the *Academy* for Oct. 9, 1875.)

GERMANY is so highly distinguished for its Shakespeare studies, and Dr. Elze's name is so well known in connection with the German Shakespeare Society, that we opened this volume with considerable interest and hope; and we have not been disappointed. It consists of nine articles, five discussing certain plays—*The Tempest, A Midsummer Night's Dream, The Merchant of Venice, All's Well that Ends Well*, and *Henry VIII.*—in certain aspects, chronological or material or æsthetic, and three treating respectively of "The Supposed Travels of Shakespeare," "Sir William Davenant," and "The Orthography of Shakespeare's Name." On the whole we can recommend the volume, if not to all readers, yet to all students of Shakespeare. That wonderful being "the general reader" would probably rise from its perusal confused and clouded. The interminable controversies and seemingly distinctionless differences which it indicates or contains would reduce him to a pitiable condition of utter bewilderment. Chaos would be come again. But one more familiar with the subject discussed, and resolved not to be lost in the mists that will arise in the treatment of questions so subtle and delicate, but to hold his way right on through them, may derive much advantage from Dr. Elze's essays. To our thinking Dr. Elze is by no means always right in his conclusions. We think he is quite wrong as to the date of *The Tempest*, which, mainly on the strength of a passage in Ben Jonson's *Volpone*, he holds to be 1604; and so as to the date of *Henry VIII.*, which he supposes to have appeared before the death of Queen Elizabeth. In cases where he cannot be said to be certainly wrong, he can as little be pronounced certainly right. Throughout the book there is a want of solidity, so far as demonstration is concerned. The evidence, indeed, that is occasionally advanced is so slight as to be scarcely tangible. But yet the book is worth reading. It has been said, libellously or not, of women and of certain judges, that it would be well if they would give their conclusions without stating their reasons. Now just the opposite may be said of Dr. Elze: we value his reasons, but not his conclusions. The information in which he abounds is so various and so valuable that we are glad to have the benefit of it, though often we sympathize not at all with the purpose to which it is applied. So to speak, it is pleasant to wander with Dr. Elze in the byways and meadows of the Elizabethan age; however we may differ from him as to the destination of any particular path. He has so much to say about the scenery through which we pass, that we willingly follow for a while. But when after an agreeable lecture, our guide proclaims that he has conducted to such and such a spot, we can only say: "Thank you much, Doctor, for your good company; but really we think we have not arrived at the place you name, but at quite a different spot, if, indeed, we have arrived anywhere. And why should we be always arriving? Pray, talk on, and do not trouble yourself and us as to our whereabouts!" Let us mention one or two of the points on which Dr. Elze is well worth hearing, quite apart from "argal" expressed or understood in his consideration of them. We are happy to find him confirming two notions we have ourselves long entertained,—that our great poet's obligations to Montaigne and to Marlowe have not yet been adequately recognized. Of course everybody has noticed the direct quotation from the famous Essays—from Chap. XXX. "Of Cannibals," made by Gonzalo to amuse the sorrow-stricken king in *The Tempest* (act ii. sc. 1, 144-172); but other signs of acquaintance with Montaigne, though that quotation might well have prepared us to expect them, have, we believe, been scarcely at all perceived. In his essay on *The Tempest* Dr. Elze makes these remarks:— "Hamlet's views about the uncertainty of death, his persuasion that 'the readiness is all,' his thoughts about suicide, have their prototype in Essai XIX. of the first book of Montaigne ('Que philosopher, c'est apprendre à mourir'), and in Essai III. of the second book ('Coustume de l'Isle de Cea'). The idea that nothing in itself is either good or bad, but that our thinking makes it so, which is expressed not only in *Hamlet* II. ii., but in other passages of Shakespeare as well, might recall Essai XL. of the first book ('Que le goust des biens et des maux despend en bonne partie de l'opinion que nous en avons'); this is, however, only a specious resemblance, for Montaigne speaks of physical, Shakespeare of moral good and evil. The description of the music of the spheres in *The Merchant of Venice* (V. i.) seems likewise taken from Montaigne (Book i. Essai XXII.), which at the same time proves that Shakespeare must have read the French philosopher in the original, for at the time of the composition of *The Merchant of Venice* (1594), Florio's translation can scarcely have been in existence, or it must have literally followed the maxim *nonum prematur in annum.*" Dr. Elze does not insist on Shakespeare's indebtedness in these passages. "All these passages," he writes, "treat of views and ideas which no doubt were widely spread, and the similarity is too little palpable to justify the reproach of 'stealing.'" (*Volpone*, III. 2.)

In any case, he has given us some valuable illustrations, and if, as to the points just mentioned, we do not believe in the actual contact of the greatest French mind with the greatest English of the sixteenth century, yet—and this is of higher interest—we are led to discern a certain native alliance and sympathy between these supreme geniuses. We think ourselves that there are many more indications of that direct contact than have yet been collected; but we cannot now stay to particularize. We should confidently point to the fact that a copy of Florio's Montaigne has come down to us with Shakespeare's autograph in it, but that the genuineness of the inscription has been seriously doubted.

The influence of Marlowe upon Shakespeare is more patent and certain. If the great master ever had himself a master it was Marlowe. Many a "saw" of that shepherd he found "of might." It is true that as he grew to artistic maturity, he saw in his predecessor's work much that was provocative of ridicule, and that he ridiculed it. To make Pistol talk in Tamberlaine's vein was significant of a keen sense of Tamberlaine's excesses. But in his not unkindly laughter at such fantastic bombast, he never ceased to admire what was to be admired. If he derides in *Henry IV.*, he quotes approvingly in *As You Like It*. In the *Merry Wives of Windsor* the derision and the acceptance appear together. In his wrath—it was only comical wrath—he remembered mercy; nay, he remembered affection. Perhaps only now are we beginning really to appreciate the power of the first in time of the great Elizabethans. Certainly no formal tribute has ever before been paid him comparable with that lately offered by a poet of our own day, who is also a critic of no mean order. But the highest tribute of all was paid him by Shakespeare's attention and study. Of this connection, as seen in at least one play, Dr. Elze speaks very positively. He says that, "the prototype of Shylock" ... clearly lies in Marlowe's *Jew of Malta*, without which the *Merchant of Venice* would, in all probability, never have been written. It is strange that, so far as we know, no German commentator has yet compared Marlowe's tragedy; other English critics deny, or at all events do not sufficiently apprize (*sic*) the relations existing between the two plays. In Hallam's eyes, Marlowe's Barabas is unworthy to be regarded as the prototype of Shylock, though the *Jew of Malta* may possibly have furnished Shakespeare with a few hints. Dyce despatches the subject with equal brevity. He admits, indeed, that Shakespeare was intimately acquainted with Marlowe's play, "but," he continues, "no one who has carefully compared the character of Barabas with that of Shylock will allow that he received more than unimportant hints from it." The collection of so-called parallel passages from both plays in the appendix of Waldron's edition and continuation of Jonson's *Sad Shepherd*, he says, "proves nothing." And Dr. Elze proceeds to "see what is meant by a few and unimportant hints." A good deal of what he proceeds to say is somewhat overstrained; but something, we think, holds firm.

"'To such a searcher of hearts as Shakespeare it was an irresistible temptation to transform this Barabas into a genuine Jewish usurer, and to change the bombastic and impossible criminal into a real man, with human motives, passions, and actions. Barabas, if any, was the man suited to be made the claimant in the law-suit in regard to the pound of flesh; while at the same time his daughter afforded the poet a handle to bring him into connections of a different kind with the Christian world."

And in all the Essays, whether we go with their leading tenets or not, there is much that "tends to edification." Thus in another part of that on the *Merchant* may be found some remarks on the question, often raised, whether Shylock is a tragic or a comic character. How greatly public opinion has changed in certain respects is very curiously indicated by the very existence of such a question. It is certain that to an Elizabethan audience there could be nothing tragic in the presentment of Shylock, if the idea of tragedy involves, as it certainly does, an element of pity. Shylock might well say, "Sufferance is the badge of all our tribe." Dr. Elze quotes from Hebler this quotation from Luther :—" Know thou, dear Christian, that next to the devil, thou canst have no more bitter or eager enemy than a downright Jew, one who seriously means to be the Jew. I will give thee mine honest advice : set fire to their synagogues, and that which will not burn, load and cover it with earth, so that man shall see neither a stone nor a vestige of it everlastingly."

When such crying bigotry possessed the leaders of the people, what could be hoped? When the blind lead the blind they both, we are told, fall into the ditch.

Marlowe's Barabas was got up in a purely comic fashion. He was equipped with a big red nose. "O, mistress," says Ithamar, "I have the bravest, gravest, secret, subtle, *bottle-nosed* knave to my master that ever gentleman had." How merciless is Gratiano's banter in Shakespeare's play! How supreme the gentle Antonio's scorn ! What a terrible impeachment it is that Shylock can bring against

> "The kindest man,
> The best condition'd and unwearied spirit
> In doing courtesies."

"He hath disgraced me, and hindered me half a million, laughed at my losses, mocked at my gains, scorned my nation, thwarted my bargains, cooled my friends, heated mine enemies; and what's his reason? I am a Jew!" What a revolution of sentiment has taken place! "However grievously Shylock may have offended, however heartily we may despise and condemn his character, yet we cannot avoid a momentary feeling of sympathy with him when he staggers out of the court, crushed by the pardon which the Doge has granted him. Nay, we feel inclined to agree with the young lady who, according to H. Heine, at the conclusion of the fourth act, exclaimed, 'The poor man is wronged!'"

Certainly there is no more impressive proof of Shakespeare's splendid humanity than the manner in which, without shocking the prejudices of his age by any pedantic sermonizings, he has brought the outcast of society within the range of our sympathy. Marlowe's Jew is a monster; the Jew of Shakespeare is, after all, a man, with a heart once capable of tenderness, but at length petrified by ill uses and ill usage, God-made, like the rest of us, man-marred, like so many.

There is much interesting matter in the chapter on Shakespeare's supposed travels. Dr. Elze does not see any reason for agreeing with Knight as to his having visited Scotland. He thinks that the "Laurence Fletcher, Comediane to his Majestie," of the Aberdeen records of 1601, was not a member of a strolling company of players, but was "lent" by the King to Sir Francis Hospitall, of Haulszie, a French nobleman, upon whom the freedom of the borough was conferred. "The king lent him his court comedian, who in so far, may be regarded as a pendant to 'my lord of Leicester's jesting player.'" Surely a very gratuitous assumption. His court comedian? The phrase seems to carry us back to pre-Thespian days, when a *corps dramatique* consisted of one. We do not think it could mean "a fool." Besides, we happen to know the name of King James's fool, and it was not Fletcher. We do not think Knight's argument decisive, far from it; but really, as Shakespearian arguments go, it is not so bad.

Dr. Elze may be said to add something to the probability of Shakespeare's having visited Italy. It is indeed difficult to believe that the poet never himself saw those fair blue skies beneath which so many of his creations move as beneath their native and proper canopy. The very air of Italy seems blowing through so many of his scenes. Does any non-Italian work transport us into the bright, careless, star-clear South, as the last act of *The Merchant of Venice* transports us? The most striking fresh suggestions Dr. Elze makes, relate to the mention of Julio Romano in *The Winter's Tale*:—

"To the question why he should have selected this artist before all others, some critics might be inclined to answer that he picked up the name at random, if we may use the expression. But such an answer would be quite unsatisfactory, in the face of the fact that the poet most correctly estimates Romano's merits as an artist, and praises him not only in eloquent but the most appropriate words." Dr. Elze's answer is "that he obtained his knowledge of Romano's works by personal inspection." The Palazzo del T in Mantua, built by Romano, and filled with his paintings and drawings, was one of the wonders of the age. But Shakespeare makes him a sculptor! Here Dr. Elze's answer is really notable. It is given by the quotation of two epitaphs found in Vasari.

"Videbat Jupiter corpora *sculpta* pictaque
Spirare, aedes mortalium aequarier coelo,
Julii virtute Romani ; tunc iratus
Concilio divorum omnium vocato,
Illum aeteriis (*sic*) sustulit ; quod pati nequiret
Vinci aut aequari ab homine terrigena."

And,

"Romanus moriens secum tres Julius arteis
Abstulit ; haud mirum, quatuor unus erat."

"Tres artes! Corpora sculpta!" exclaims Dr. Elze, with pardonable exultation. "It is true that Vasari makes no further mention of Romano's sculptures, neither do his German translators, nor, as far as we know, any recent art-historian, say a word about them. But Shakespeare is nevertheless right ; he has made no blunder; he has not abused the poetical licence by introducing Romano as a sculptor. And more than this, his praise of Romano wonderfully agrees with the epitaph in which truth to nature and life is likewise praised as being Julio's chief excellence (if he could put breath into his work—' videbat Jupiter corpora spirare'). Is this chance?"

Dr. Elze's conclusion is that Shakespeare had been at Mantua, and had there seen Romano's works, and read his epitaphs. As we have said, we think he has, by this and other considerations, certainly increased the probability of the Italian travels.

Our readers may by this time be able to judge for themselves of the possible profit to be derived from the volume before us. We will only now, in conclusion, briefly mention what seems to us Dr. Elze's chief deficiency, and his chief misapprehension.

He seems unable to appreciate adequately the importance of the consideration of style—we use the term in its most comprehensive sense—in deciding or discussing Shakespearian chronology, and other Shakespearian questions. We submit, for instance, that no critic duly competent in this respect, would dream of assigning *The Tempest* to about the same date as *King Lear*. It is in this respect that German criticism has so often failed disastrously. How else could Schlegel and other countrymen of his give such remarkable verdicts on what we English call, and persist in calling, the "spurious plays?" Think of this dictum of Schlegel's: *Thomas Lord Cromwell, Sir John Oldcastle* (First Part), *A Yorkshire Tragedy*, "are not only unquestionably Shakespeare's, but in my opinion, they deserve to be classed among his best and maturest works!"

Again, Dr. Elze, in our opinion, lays a great deal too much stress on Shakespeare's early maturity. The facts, all that are well substantiated, do not make for this view; but Dr. Elze will have it so. What encourages him is what may be called comparative biography. He is always ready with a list of achievements performed at an early age—Raphael's painting the *Sposalizio* in his twenty-first year, the *Entombment*, in the Borghese Gallery, and the *Belle Jardinière*, in his twenty-fourth, and beginning the *Stanze* in his twenty-fifth; Mozart's composing his *Mithridates* in his fourteenth year, his *Idomeneo* in his twenty-fifth, his *Entführung aus dem Serail* in his twenty-sixth. But, putting aside the questions of antecedents—the question whether Shakespeare's early advantages equalled those enjoyed by other great spirits—comparative biography tells also a quite different tale. It tells us of great geniuses who were slow in putting forth fruit. In England, for instance, Dryden, Richardson, Scott all ripened slowly. If all these three men had died even when they were upwards of forty, their names would well-nigh have passed away with them; at the best, but a dim glory would have been theirs. Of

Shakespeare, we know for certain that he wrote his *Rape of Lucrece* in 1593 and the following year. We know it for certain, because, dedicating *Venus and Adonis* to the Earl of Southampton, in 1593, and apologizing for his "unpolished lines," he vows "to take advantage of all idle hours till I have honoured you with some graver labour." And, in 1594, the *Rape of Lucrece*—"the graver labour promised"—appears, dedicated, of course, to the same nobleman. We have, then, a sure representative of Shakespeare's development in 1593-4, when he was just thirty years old. Now, what does it show us? Not the great playwright, but the great poet, in the full lavish enjoyment of a yet unpruned exuberant youthful fancy, his powers not yet reduced to obey dramatic restraints, the greatest heir of the world, filled with the delighted consciousness of his magnificent dower, but not yet wholly submitting himself to artistic discipline and economy.

VIII.

SOME CONDITIONS OF THE ELIZABETHAN DRAMA.

(From the *Saturday Review* for July 31, 1875.)

A QUESTION debated in many minds just now is the possible revival of the drama. When one of the chief poets of the day, who has previously written nothing of the kind, appears as a playwright, hope naturally awakes. Such was the brilliancy of our Elizabethan era that we can never cease to be dazzled by it—never cease to think of it as the golden age of our literature, and, therefore, as an age, the forms and modes of which are always to be aspired after. It is true that since those palmy days the decline and fall of our drama has been steady and complete; but yet we cannot help hoping it may rise again. We cannot reconcile ourselves to the extinction of the glory of our literature. We know that there are "flaming ministers," whose former light can be restored, and we are eager to believe this to be one of them. And yet for that "cunning'st pattern of excelling nature," as we may well call the Elizabethan drama, when its flame is put out, who knows " where is that Promethean heat that can " its " light relume " ?

It may be worth while considering for a moment two of the conditions under which our drama throve so splendidly at the close of the sixteenth century. Let us notice, first, the active intellectuality of the Elizabethan age; and, secondly, that it was not a time when books were abundant, or the study of them a common habit. Out of many circumstances that must co-exist, if a drama is to prosper, there are certainly two of them most important. There must be a thirsty nation, and it must slake its thirst, not at books, but at plays. The demand will create the supply. If a people, roused by keen intellectual impulses, turns to the stage for the satisfaction of its wants, the stage will be found responsive. The " drink divine " which is asked for by " the thirst which from the soul doth rise " will assuredly be provided. It is only at certain junctures that a people will so turn; but at them it will not turn in vain. Both at Athens and in London, when the nation crowded to the theatre, the theatre gave it a royal welcome.

It is hardly necessary to point out how various and how intense was the mental activity of the Elizabethan age. Life in England has never been broader and deeper than it was then. It was morning with us, so to speak. We were waking to a fresh consciousness of ourselves, and of the world around us. The old things had passed away, and, behold, all things were become new.

" Bliss was it in that dawn to be alive ;
But to be young was very heaven !"

A strange sense of power thrilled us, and the revelation of unsuspected opportunities for exertion and enterprise transformed our inmost being. The very earth widened around us ; and where but yesterday there rose forbidding. barriers, there now spread far away an endless expanse of unexplored regions, mysterious, fascinating, delightful ; and as with material confinements, so it was with spiritual. In the universe of thought the mind wandered free. For good and for evil, it defied the restraints of previous dogmatisms, and stepped boldly within the precincts from which it had been rigorously interdicted. Was there ever in England such another age of movement?—an age so eager, so fearless, so sanguine, so exultant in its liberty, so swift to do or die? Never, perhaps, was the national imagination so quickened and so vigorous. Every day produced its poet:

> "The isle is full of noises,
> Sounds and sweet airs that give delight and hurt not."

Nor could it be otherwise. A land so bright-hearted could not but break forth into singing. Joy, even as sorrow, must have words given it—the joy

> "That does not speak
> Whispers the o'erfraught heart, and bids it break."

There is no more striking recognition of the keen intelligence of the Elizabethans, and the readiness and facility of their imaginations, than is afforded by Shakespeare himself in the choruses of his *Henry V.* Reading them, one sees how a Shakespeare was possible. They show us how he could rely upon his audience. Conscious of the grotesque contrast between the "unworthy scaffold" of the Globe and the "so great an object" brought forth upon it—

> "Can this cockpit hold
> The vasty fields of France? or may we cram
> Within this wooden O the very casques
> That did affright the air at Agincourt?"

He can appeal to the spectators to make up all the deficiencies. "Let us," he says,

> "On your imaginary forces work.
> *   *   *   *   *
> Piece out our imperfections with your thoughts;
> Into a thousand parts divide one man,
> And make imaginary puissance;
> Think, when we talk of horses, that you see them
> Printing their proud hoofs i' the receiving earth:
> For 'tis your thoughts that now must deck our kings,

> Carry them here and there ; jumping o'er times,
> Turning the accomplishment of many years
> Into an hour-glass."

In another prologue he bids them

> "Play with your fancies, and in them behold
> Upon the hempen tackle ship-boys climbing—
> * * * *
> O, do but think,
> You stand upon the rivage, and behold
> A city on the inconstant billows dancing.
> * * * * *
> Follow, follow !
> Grapple your minds to sternage of this navy.
> * * * * *
> Work, work your thoughts, and therein see a siege ;
> * * * * *
> 'Still be kind,
> And eke out our performance with your mind."

In the prologue of the last act there is a very noticeable phrase :

> "But now behold,
> In the quick forge and working-house of thought,
> How London doth pour out her citizens."

The fires in the forge of thought burnt brightly in the Elizabethan age, and the hands wrought busily in its working house.

"When the cheerfulness of the people is so sprightly up, as that it has not only wherewith to guard well its own freedom, but to spare, and to bestow upon the solidest and sublimest points of controversy and new inventions," a great literature may be reasonably expected, but the form will not be always the same. In the Elizabethan age, with its social habits, with its gaiety of spirit, its delight in action, the form could not but be dramatic. The particular consideration we have here to entertain is that it was not an age given to books and to book-study. It was the age of

L'Allegro, rather than of Il Penseroso. It found its pleasure in an oral literature. The stage exactly answered to its necessities, and so all of a sudden it sprang up to its perfection. It is strange to think that one of the writers of *Gorboduc*—the play that is known as our first tragedy—lived to see *Hamlet* and *Macbeth*. Just so in Greece, under highly similar conditions, the drama leapt to its maturity. Æschylus might have seen Thespis perform; Sophocles was nearly twenty years old when Phrynichus exhibited his *Phœnissæ*.

It ought to be carefully remembered that the Elizabethan plays were written to be acted, not to be read. This characteristic is stamped upon them. They are the result of immediate contact between the people and the author. In this connection between the dramatist and his audience there is something not to be found in other kinds of literature. Criticism is not distant and, possibly, powerless, but instant and decisive. Every genuine dramatic literature may be said, in a very special sense, to be the creation of the circle to which it belongs. The Elizabethan drama was the creation of its circle, and that circle was the nation. The people did not play at plays, as we do now-a-days. With us books are real things; with them the theatre was a real thing. They believed in it. It is true there were certain religionists—well-meaning, but rudely-cultivated men—who stood aloof from it; but the nation as a whole rejoiced in it ardently. Let us thoroughly realize this signal fact, that in the absence of books and newspapers, and other now most common means of information and culture, the drama was then the one literature of the day. It was everything to that age. To such an extent was it so as to be in danger of degradation in artistic respects. It was in danger of being used for political and controversial purposes, a danger not always escaped. In several extant plays one may see how the drama was made to perform the function of the pamphlet, or of the modern newspaper—a function which the old comedy at Athens performed freely. In this respect the jealousy with which the drama was watched by authority, was of real service to its true development. It saved it from a thousand snares to which it was exposed by its very popularity. The very existence of that jealousy is highly significant of the influence and power of the drama that excited it. In short, the theatre was at that time the great centre of English art and thought. It drew to itself the highest intellects of the time; it dealt with the highest and gravest questions; it portrayed with incomparable power the deepest and intensest passions.

> "All thoughts, all passions, all delights,
> Whatever stirs this mortal frame"—

all were but ministers of the Elizabethan drama, and fed its "sacred flame."

A time came when the intellect of the nation looked elsewhere for its sustenance, and it was then that the drama decayed. Books gradually came within everybody's reach and to everybody's liking; and in delighted communion with master minds, through such media, men no longer flocked to the play-houses, once resonant with the life and the joy of the nation. With less gregarious habits, the quiet and calm of the study charmed more than the excitement and noise of the theatre. Fascinated, as we must ever be, by the dramatic form, modern days may, perhaps, successfully develop for themselves a new species of drama—the reading drama, as we may call it, as distinguished from the acting; and into this new species an immortal life may be breathed by another race of geniuses, who may find in it the fittest embodiment for thoughts that wake to perish never; but that the theatre, however it may be improved, can ever again be what it once was, seems merely impossible.[1] Our voices change as we grow older, and so the voice of literature changes, and the old tones cannot be brought back, charm we never so wisely.

[1] See also the paper on *Shakespeare and Chaucer*.

IX.

HALLIWELL'S [NOW HALLIWELL-PHILLIPPS] PAPERS REFERRING TO SHAKESPEARE.

(From the *Athenæum* for Feb. 21, 1874.)

IT is a common lament—and by many eager spirits it is felt to be a real grievance—that we are so scantily informed as to the lives of our noblest poets—that, in a certain sense,

"The world knows nothing of its greatest men."

True it is that they pass before our wistful eyes like Virgil and his guide in their nether journey,

"Obscuri sub luce maligna."

That this vexatious darkness will ever be wholly dissipated, and that we shall see in perfect clearness the forms and the movements whose present dimness, or invisibility, so troubles us, is certainly not to be expected; but there is good reason for hoping that the obscurity may be in some degree at least diminished, the shrouding clouds pierced by some few rays of light, and those coveted outlines discerned, if not distinctly, yet somewhat less hazily. With regard to Chaucer, the discoveries lately made, and now making at the Record Office—of which accounts have appeared from time to time in our columns—this hope is in the very act of realization. The mists that surrounded him are growing thinner, and so he seems nearer to us and better knowable. Still more cheering is it to have grounds for believing that as to Shakespeare, too, fresh facts may be forthcoming. It is certain that all the sources of information about him are not exhausted. The statement of Steevens is no longer true, if, indeed, it was ever true. "All that is known with any degree of certainty concerning Shakespeare," wrote that peremptory commentator, "is that he was born at Stratford-upon-Avon; married, and had children there; went to London, where he commenced actor, and wrote poems and plays; returned to Stratford, made his will, died, and was buried." The ceaseless industry of Malone and his fellows has added fact to fact, till what has been gained from oblivion is of no contemptible amount. It is possible that yet greater additions may be made. There may be lurking in the corner of some library, public or private, or in some not yet finally sifted repository of national documents, still fuller illustrations of what may well be a central interest with all English-speaking peoples. If ever—to echo words of Malone's—if ever the office books of Tilney and Sir George Buc should be found! Tilney and Sir George Buc were Masters of the Revels before Sir Henry Herbert; and if ever their official records should be discovered, it is probable the dates of Shakespeare's plays would be conclusively settled, and we should know for a certainty what was the progress of his art, and could study at our leisure his splendid growth. And it is easy to conjecture other fountains of information that may sooner or later be opened. Of some, indeed, there are already rumours, of which we hope in due time to give good account. Of course these investigations as to the biography of the supreme dramatist are not to be regarded as the final and highest Shakespearian work. They are only means to an end. But they are means of very considerable value, and every genuine student of Shakespeare will be thoroughly grateful for any enlargement of them.

This line of Shakespearian study is not likely to be neglected or ill followed whilst we have amongst us one so ardent and so able to pursue it as Mr. Halliwell. What we have specially to announce in this paper is a fresh discovery made by him, which, partly at the instance of Mr. Furnivall, the director of the "New Shakspere Society," as we gather from the "note" prefixed to the copy now, thanks to Mr. Halliwell's courtesy, before us, he has considerately decided to place at once within the reach of those who may care for it.

And who will not care for it? The mere occurrence of Shakespeare's name is enough to make any Elizabethan document or book interesting; and here we have a series of papers concerning the theatrical company to which he belonged, and in one of them an account of his first belonging to it.

"Nearly four years," says the "note," "have elapsed since the day on which in search of materials for a work on the Life of Shakespeare, it was my good fortune to discover a remarkable series of documents respecting the Globe and Blackfriars, in which the nature of the poet's connection with those two theatres was for the first time satisfactorily ascertained. It was my intention to have published these manuscripts long since, and in fact some progress in the composition of my new work had been made, when circumstances enforced almost exclusive attention to other matters. . . . . In the summer of 1870, by the kind permission of the authorities of the Lord Chamberlain's Office, I was enabled to examine all the books therein preserved, with liberty to copy any documents relating to the early English stage. . . . . Amongst the miscellaneous records was a small thin folio manuscript, bearing the title of *Presentations and Warrants in the years* 1631, 1632, &c. Upon looking it over, I could hardly believe my eyes when coming across a list of shareholders in the Blackfriars and Globe theatres, with information respecting their management that no amount of reading could have elicited from a million of scattered notices. Although the papers were of a somewhat late date, they emanated from persons well acquainted with the stage of Shakespeare's time. The last petition contains the evidence of Cuthbert and Winifred Burbage, the great actor's brother and wife, one of whom at least was unquestionably familiar with all that related to Shakspeare's connection with the stage."

We think our readers will sympathize with Mr. Halliwell's surprise and satisfaction. He could hardly believe his eyes when coming across those familiar names, Burbage and Lowen, and Taylor, and Condell or Cundall, and Heming. He fairly reminds us of Keats "on first looking into Chapman's *Homer.*" He had travelled much in the realms of black letter and of manuscript; through many registers and records had he been: yet this was an ecstatic moment.

> "Then felt he like some watcher of the skies
> When a new planet swims into his view;
> Or like stout Cortez, when with eagle eyes
> He stared at the Pacific."

May Mr. Halliwell's generous zeal be often so rewarded!

These papers are of the year 1635, nearly twenty years after Shakespeare's death, but they take us into the midst of the circle where he was once so well known amongst those he called "fellows." The circle, it is true, is not unbroken: the place that knew Richard Burbage, the famous actor of Richard III., of King John, of Richard the Second, of Henry the Fifth, of Lear, and Othello, and Macbeth, knows him no more. Heming and Cundell, the Editors of the *Folio* of 1623 (to whom with Richard Burbage, the poet gave and bequeathed "xxvis. viiid. a peece to buy them rings,") are gone; Kempe, the Launcelot and Touchstone of his day, has joined his famous comrade in the other world; but there yet survive many with whom Shakespeare was once intimate, and those who had departed are still represented. There is Cuthbert Burbage, the great actor's brother; and the great actor's wife Winifred (now married to the actor Robinson), and his son William; Mrs. Cundall, widow of the Henry of the Will; William, son of John Heming; and besides these relics, there is Lowen, one of the chief of the King's players after Heming and Burbage had passed away; and Taylor, a famous actor in his time, the original performer of Hamlet; and Swanston and Shanks, who had probably many a time trod the boards along with the author, whose association with them is a warrant for their immortality.

These papers, six in number, with a closing note by the original receiver of them, all relate to one and the same matter. Five of them are petitions and counter-petitions, addressed to the Lord Chamberlain of His Majesty's household, viz., Philip, Earl of Pembroke and Montgomery, brother of the William whom some critics have identified with the "W. H." of the Sonnets; two are the rescripts, or memoranda, of his Lordship.

The series opens with the petition of three of the King's Players—this company was under the government of the Lord Chamberlain—that they might be admitted sharers or "housekeepers"—shareholders, as we should say—in the playhouses of the Globe and Blackfriars. The complainants are Robert Benfield ("Benefield"), Heliard (also Eyloerdt, and also Eyllardt; elsewhere Elyard and Eliard), Swanston, and Thomas Pollard, all names of more or less note. Their grievance is that they do not get their fair share of the profits. It seems that those "interested in the house," or the "housekeepers," received for themselves half the receipts for the galleries and boxes, and at the Globe half the money taken at the tiring-room (*i.e.*, the green-room) door; the remaining half and the money received at the "outer doors," that is, it would seem, the receipts for the pit, was divided amongst the actors; so that those who were both shareholders and actors received a greatly superior dividend to those who were actors only. It is against this inequality that the above-mentioned trio make their murmur. The actors, it appears, had to defray the working expenses. They had to pay the "hired men," the supernumeraries wanted on occasion; to provide apparel, *poets*, lights, and other charges of the houses whatsoever. A strange conjunction, "apparell, *poetes*, lights," &c. Falstaff's trunk-hose, Falstaff's *creator*, and the candles to see them by! They judiciously omit to mention that the shareholders paid the rent. Then comes an account of the shares as then held. Of the sixteen Globe shares:—

Cuthbert Burbidge holds	$3\frac{1}{2}$
Winifred (now Mrs. Robinson)	$3\frac{1}{2}$
Mrs. Cundall	2
"Shanks" who had purchased from "Hemings"	3
Taylor	2
Lowen	2

The eight Blackfriars stand thus:—

Shanks	2
Burbage	1
Mrs. Robinson	1
Taylor	1
Lowen	1
Mrs. Cundall	1
Underwood	1

The petition is to the effect that the Burbages may be directed to sell two of their Globe shares, and Shanks one of his Globe shares and one of his Blackfriars to the complainants: " for which your petitioners shall have just cause to blesse your Lordship, as, however they are dayly bound to doe, with the devotions of most humble and obliged beadsmen."

Next comes his Lordship's reply, dated " Court at Theoballes, 12 July, 1635," that " haveing considered this petition, and the severall answeres and replyes of the parties, the merites of the petitioners, the disproportion of their shares, and the interest of his Majesties service," he thinks fit and does order that the complainants shall be admitted to the purchase of the shares they desire; and he desires "the housekeepers, and all others whome it may concerne, to take notice and to conforme themselves therein accordingly," and then follow threats in case of disobedience. .

But the order and the threats were in vain. The shareholders clung to their possessions. And so in the 3rd Document, Messrs. Benfield, Swanston, and Pollard, as importunate as the defendants were tenacious, address the Lord Chamberlain once more. In this second petition they gave more minute details; they state that the working expenses amount to " 900 or 1000*li.* or thereabouts, per annum, being 3*li.* a day, one day with another, besides the extraordinary charge which the said actors are wholly at for apparell and *poets*, &c.; Whereas the said houskeepers out of all their gaines have not till our Lady Day last payd above 65*li.* per annum rent for both houses, towardes which they rayse between 20 and 30*li.* per annum from the tap houses, and a tenement and a garden belonging to the premises, &c., and are at noe other charge whatsoever, excepting the ordinary reparations of the houses. So that upon a medium made of the gaynes of the howskeepers and those of the actors, one day with another throughout the yeere, the petitioners will make it apparent that when some of the houskeepers share 12*s.* a day at the Globe, the actors share not above 3*s.*"

They pray that the matter may be settled in the way previously urged, or otherwise, that his Lordship may be pleased to consider "whether it bee not reasonable and equitable that the actors in general may injoy the benefitt of both houses to themselves, paying the said howskeepers such a valuable rent for the same as your Lordship shall thinke just arid indifferent."

And now come two counter-petitions, one from Shanks, the other from the Burbages.

Shanks in document (*d*) relates how he bought the shares he holds, and what he paid for them, which came to more than £350. William Heming (Hemings of Christ Church), was clearly not the man of business his father was. It was he who sold the shares to Shanks, and received help from him "since hee was in prison." To return, this petitioner refers to his long dramatic service; he is an old man in this quality (compare *Hamlet*, II. ii. 363), and has yet made no provision "for himselfe in his age, nor for his wife, children and grandchild." Moreover, his profits "are thinges very casuall and subject to bee discontinued and lost by sicknes [*i.e.*, through the plague, for during such visitations the theatres were closed; see the licence "Pro Jacobo Burbage et aliis, 1574," &c.], and diverse other ways and to yield noe profit at all." Further, he urges that the applicants are well enough paid: they each received £180 "this yeere last past," besides which Mr. Swanston, one of them who is most violent in this business, "had and receaved this last yeer above 34*li.* for the profitt of a third part of one part in the

Blackfriers, which he bought for 20*li.* and yet hath injoyed two or three yeeres allready, and hath still as long time in the same as your suppliant hath in his, who for soe much as Mr. Swanston bought for 20*li.* your suppliant payd 60*li.*" &c. The amount of the rent he says is £100, "besides reparacions, which is dayly very chargeable unto them." He further states, "that he hath still of his owne purse supplyed the company for the service of his Majesty with boyes, as Thomas Pollard [now it may be presumed one of the three would be shareholders], John Thompson deceased (for whom he paid 40 *li.*), your suppliant having payd his part of 200*li.* for other boyes since his comming to the company, John Honiman, Thomas Holcombe, and diverse others, and at this time maintaines three more for the sayd service," and that he is not in a position to sell his shares, for he has made them over "for security of moneys taken up . . . . of Robert Morecroft of Lincolne his wifes uncle for the purchase of the sayd partes." Lastly, he hopes his Lordship will not encourage demands of such a kind, or there will be no peace; young men "shall alwayes refuse to doe his Majesty service unlesse they may have whatsoever they will, though it bee other men's estates."

Next comes the most important document of the collection, the counter-petition of the Burbages—"Cutbert Burbage, and Winnifred his brother's wife [Robinson, who had married her, is quietly ignored], and William his sonne."

The general drift of this paper coincides with that of the preceding. It is urged that the complainants ought to be content with their present havings, &c.; but the tone of the documents is such as befits a family of such theatrical eminence as that of the writers. They are "the old family of the stage." "The father of us . . . . was the first builder of playhouses:" They speak of the complainants as "men soe soone shot up," and as "these new men that were never bred from children in the King's service" (was not Pollard so? see above); and grow genuinely indignant at the thought of the proposed outrage. The passage of the utmost interest in their paper, and in the whole collection, is that in which they sketch the history of the theatres and of the company.

"The father of us, Cutbert and Richard Burbage, was the first builder of playhouses, and was himselfe in his younger yeeres a player. The Theater he built with many hundred poundes taken up at interest. The players that livd in those first times had only the profitts arising from the dores, but now the players receave all the comings in at the dores to themselves, and halfe the galleries from the houskeepers. Hee built this house upon leased ground by which means the landlord and hee had a great suite in law, and by his death the like troubles fell on us his sonnes. Wee then bethought us of altering from thence, and at like expense built the Globe, with more summes of money taken up at interest which lay heavy on us many yeeres: and to ourselves we joyned those deserveing men, Shakspere, Hemings, Condall, Phillips, and others, partners in the profittes of that they call the House, but makeing the leases for twenty-one yeeres hath beene the destruction of ourselves and others, for they dying at the expiration of three or four yeeres of their lease, the subsequent yeeres became dissolved to strangers as by marrying with their widdowes and the like by their children. Thus Right Honorable as concerning the Globe, where wee ourselves are but lessees. Now for the Blackfriers that is our inheritance; our father purchasèd it at extreame rates and made it into a playhouse with great charge and troble, which after was leased out to one Evans, that first sett up the boyes commonly called the Queene's Majesties Children of the Chappell. In processe of time, the boyes growing up to bee men, which were Underwood, Field, Ostler, and were taken to strengthen the King's service, and the more to strengthen the service, the boyes dayly wearing out, it was considered that house would be as fitt for ourselves, and soe purchased the lease remaining from Evans with our money, and placed men players which were Hemings, Condall, Shakspeare, &c. And Richard Burbage who for thirty-five yeeres paines, cost and labour, made meanes to leave his wife and children some estate, and out of whose estate soe many of other players and their families have beene mayntaned, these new men, that were never bred from children in the King's service would take away, with oathes and menaces, that we shall bee forced, and that they will not thanke us for it; soe that it seemes they would not pay us for what they would have or wee can spare, which more to satisfie your honor than their threatening pride, we are for ourselves willing to part with a part betweene us, they paying according as ever hath beene the custome and the number of yeeres the lease is made for."

It is not too much to say that this is one of the most important passages regarding Shakespeare that has yet been discovered. As to his connection with the stage, it is the most important.

We cannot do more now than point out the leading features of it. We are sure that, for exposition and illustration, it is in good hands with Mr. Halliwell. And we hope that he will let as little time as is consistent with sound workmanship elapse before he makes the result of his researches generally accessible.

For the first time we have a direct and trustworthy account of Shakespeare's first connection with the Lord Chamberlain's players and the Globe Theatre. It would appear that it was after the building of the Bankside Theatre that "those deserving men Shakspeare, Hemings, Condall, Phillips and others" were made "partners in the profittes of that they call the House." Now that house was erected about 1594; so that a certain list, purporting to give the names of the Blackfriars shareholders in 1589, or rather the views it represents, for the list itself has now for some years been accepted as spurious, are finally negatived. Again we see that those biographers are mistaken who have represented the building of the Globe as undertaken by Shakespeare himself. Further, it was not, it would seem, till the time when Evans's lease of the Blackfriars Theatre was purchased back from him that the said "deserving men" acted in that theatre. Now this re-purchase was made when the Children of the Chapel whom Evans had "set up" there grew to be men. Of these children, Underwood, Field, and Ostler are specially named; and we know that these three acted as boys in Ben Jonson's *Poetaster* in 1601, and that Ostler and Underwood acted as men in *The Alchemist* in 1610. If they were taken to strengthen the King's service, the transference did not take place till after May, 1603, obviously, and also because not till the accession of James the First was Burbage's company specially retained by the King, and entitled the "King's Players." Thus we learn that Shakespeare's connection with the Blackfriars Theatre began at a much later date than is commonly supposed. Also, does it not seem probable that he continued to act later than the general opinion allows? On various other matters of interest suggested by this passage, we cannot now enter.

The sixth document reports how Shanks had attempted to make an arrangement with this discontented three; "but they not onely refused to give satisfaccion, but restrained him from the stage."

The series concludes with a memorandum by the Lord Chamberlain:—

"I desire Sir H. Herbert and Sir John Finett, and my solicitor Daniell Bedingfield, to take this petition and the several papers heerunto annexed into their serious considerations, and to speake with the severall parties interested, and therupon and upon the whole matter tò sett downe a proportionable and equitable summe of money to bee payd unto Shankes for the two partes which hee is to passe unto Benfield, Swanston, and Pollard, and to cause a finall agreement and convayances to be settled accordingly, and to give mee an account of their whole proceedinges in writing."[1]

Aug. 1, 1635.

[1] A copy of these documents is now to be found in the Appendix to Part I. of Mr. Halliwell-Phillipps' *Illustrations of the Life of Shakespeare*. Longmans, 1874.

X.

A CONCORDANCE TO SHAKESPEARE'S POEMS.[1]

(From the *Academy* for Oct. 17, 1874.)

IT is not likely that there will soon be an end of Shakespearian controversies. For more than a century war has raged over the remains of the great dramatist, and the *odium Shakespearianum* has scarcely been surpassed by that which characterizes rival theologians. There have arisen from time to time noisy sciolists, who have settled everything to their own satisfaction with an overbearing dogmatism varying inversely with their fitness for the work; and a glance at the criticism of our own day suffices to show that this breed is not extinct, or on the verge of extinction. Literary quackery has in fact displayed itself with peculiar brilliancy in connection with Shakespeare. The mountebank has come forward with his nostrum, and audacious and blatant after the manner of his kind, professed to cure every disorder; and for an hour or so foolish people have listened. But presently this gentleman and his goods have disappeared, and some new doctor has taken his place and bawled out the virtues of some fresh panacea. The Commentators have become proverbial, not for wisdom. Not that there have not been amongst them men of infinite

---

[1] *A Concordance to Shakespeare's Poems: An Index to every Word therein contained.* By Mrs. Horace Howard Furness. (Philadelphia: J. B. Lippincott and Co., 1874.)

merit, and men who have done for their special study imperishable service ; but it is certain that as a class they are not considered models of sagacity. Too often they have resigned their judgment to some queer fancy, or superstition, or fatally narrow creed. They have insisted that Shakespeare was all this, and all that, and not seen that he was both this and that. They have attempted to arrange all difficulties by some single test that can only, at the best, serve as the humble ally of better methods. A strange motley group they form, if one pictures them all together on one field. In the midst there stands the colossal figure of the great poet, his head rising out of sight into the clouds. Around his feet his interpreters disport themselves like so many preternaturally grave boys—young heads on old shoulders. One of exceptional vigour has managed to climb up as far as the knee of the statue, which he is convinced is its shoulder, and this conviction he is proclaiming with wild gesticulations to an enthusiastic mob below. Others are amazingly busy with its clothes and the general costume. To hear them orate on Shakespeare's boots, you would think those integuments were of more moment than the feet inside them ; and that anything might possibly be said of his cap, or the head it covered, would seem a quite irrelevant notion. Then the volumes on his doublet and hose! Ah! what a theme! Whose heart would not leap up at it? But it is too vast for one mind to comprehend. So men tell themselves off for special investigations. Who does not know the great authority on Shakespeare's buttons? Then his "points"—what a marvellous work that is on that thrilling theme! And his gloves—how that luminous treatise on his gloves astonished everybody with its learning, acumen, imagination! For many people it is not too much to say that the chapter on the thumb of the right hand made an epoch in their lives. Meanwhile, as we have said, the clouds enfold the upper part of this huge form. It may be noticed that the greater part of the multitude below have been conveyed to the spot on hobby-horses of the stoutest build.

There are happily other critics of a far different race. These stand afar off, and yet see more. They shrink from the dictatorial ignorance of that remarkable crowd, as also from the fatuous misdirection of its idolatry. They are content to study, not to dogmatize. They are thoroughly conscious of the immensity of the subject, and would as soon be guilty of the arrogance of finally estimating it by their own puny standards as of measuring the heavens with a two-foot rule.

These latter critics will rejoice in the invaluable contribution to Shakespearian study that has just reached us from the United States. And for those others, with their crude theories and ever-ready dogmatisms, let them bethink themselves, if that is possible, for no more fatal enemy to their race has ever yet appeared.

The *Concordance to Shakespeare's Poems* is a worthy companion to *The Complete Concordance to Shakespeare, being a Verbal Index to all the Passages in the Dramatic Works of the Poet.* It too is the work of a lady, the wife of one whose *Variorum Shakespeare* is making him everywhere known and distinguished. We do not think we exaggerate when we say that no two more effective and inestimable helps to real Shakespearian criticism exist than the volumes for which we are so deeply indebted to Mrs. Cowden Clarke and Mrs. Horace Howard Furness. We welcome the newly-arrived one with the utmost heartiness. It is like the coming of a fresh breeze that will never cease to blow, to blow away the foolish phantasies that are perpetually issuing from the brains of ill-informed guess-mongers, to blow strength and vigour into all criticisms that are genuine births of knowledge and judgment, and of a sound and healthful nature.

We are bound to notice specially that it is to two women that we owe these treasuries of classified fact. The ordinary conception of "the sex." may justly be disturbed by this phenomenon. The masculine exploit of Cruden has been equalled by feminine industry. Why may not a lady Liddell-and-Scott, or a Johnsoness, be looked for in the process of the ages? "The perfecter sex," as Milton is pleased to call the male kind, may well look to itself; or, more wisely, rejoice that fresh workers have come into the field. For new lines of Shakespearian study are perpetually opening, and fresh help is perpetually wanted for the exploration of them.

> "Well may we labour still to dress
> This garden, still to tend plant, herb, and flower,
> Our pleasant task enjoined; but, till more hands
> Aid us, the work under our labour grows."

Mrs. Furness has executed her task with unsparing diligence. She has recorded every word that occurs in the Poems. Even *a* has been tabulated. In this respect her work is more complete than that of her predecessor, though, as she remarks with kindly considerateness, no "imperfection is hereby imputed to Mrs. Clarke's invaluable Concordance of the Dramas. The bulk of that work was a sufficient bar to the plan I have been enabled to follow in the lesser task before me." In another matter the new Concordance is the exacter: Mrs. Furness gives the number of the line in which each word occurs. Those who have spent precious minutes in hunting through long scenes in the plays, will be grateful for this definiteness. Of course it can scarcely be hoped that the references are absolutely accurate.

"As the pages are stereotyped," says Mrs. Furness, "corrections can be made at any time of misprints, against which it seems no human vigilance can guard, and I shall be grateful to the kindness that will notify me of them." A quite faultlessly printed book is said never yet to have been issued from any press. *Humanum est errare.* Errata will happen. So much must be allowed; but we must say that, so far as our own use of the volume is concerned, and it has already been considerable, we have detected no flaw in the figures.

It is just possible a word or two may have been accidentally omitted; but in this respect, too, the work, so far as we have tested it, seems to us a wonder of completeness. We will venture to extend Mrs. Furness' appeal, and hope that any of our readers who find any fault whatever in this minute directory will favour her with the information.

By the *Poems* are to be understood all the non-dramatic works that are usually connected with Shakespeare's name. Mrs. Furness follows the text of the Cambridge edition, from which " with the exception of some trifling deviations in punctuation," she reprints the poems at the end of her volume, for the sake of convenient reference. And in so using the title *Poems* in this sense, she has acted wisely, though by so doing she includes several pieces that are almost certainly not by Shakespeare. It was not her business in this cataloguing to settle or to entertain questions of authenticity. It would be as unwarrantable to complain of her having admitted into her index " Live with me and be my love," as to accuse Mrs. Cowden Clarke of negligence for having excluded *The Two Noble Kinsmen*.

(From the *Athenæum* for Sept. 12th, 1874.)

This work supplies an undoubted want, and, we are happy to add, supplies it in an admirable manner. To those who know little or nothing of Shakespearian difficulties—of the vexed and vexatious questions of authenticity that beset the thorough student, or of the perpetual troubles that are connected with the great dramatist's vocabulary—it may, perhaps, seem a waste of labour to have chronicled with all possible pains and accuracy every word that occurs in his poems. The sole use that a Concordance serves for such persons is that it enables them to find a quotation. Mrs. Cowden Clarke's famous compilation is valuable in their eyes on this account only; and such an end may well seem to fail in justifying the means, seeing that the means involve weariness, and painfulness, and watchings. But far other is the estimate of such productions that is made by the student. Familiar as he is with the wild assertions incessantly volunteered as to what is Shakespeare's and what is not, he is profoundly grateful for any help in analyzing the genuine work of the poet. The existence of Concordances, and the judicious use of them, might have stifled half the follies of which many a criticaster has been proudly guilty. And the age of criticasters is not past; perhaps, indeed, it is only now fully come. The effrontery of these gentlemen is amazing. They "have no bands" in their statements. Conscience never makes a coward of them. Now, against such persons what is the antidote? How are we to disinfect ourselves and get rid of them? The unfailing antiseptic is *facts*. They cannot away with facts; only let facts be laid about everywhere, and they will soon be extirpated. For them and their kind it is difficult to conceive a more deadly book than a Concordance. It is mere hemlock. "By my troth," they "cannot abide the smell of it." The appearance, therefore, of a companion volume to that of Mrs. Clarke is really a memorable event.

The new volume is in shape uniform with the valuable "Variorum Shakespeare" now issuing by the husband of the compiler. In point of topography there is nothing to be desired.

It contains a short record of every word occurring in the Poems, even of prepositions and conjunctions; in short, of every word without exception. The tabulation of *the*, for instance, occupies no less than twenty columns.

"As it is impossible," runs the preface, "to limit the purposes for which the language of Shakespeare may be studied, or to say that the time will not come, if it has not already, when his use of every part of speech, down to the humblest conjunction, will be criticized with as much nicety as has been bestowed upon Greek and Latin authors, it seems to me that in the selection of words to be recorded no discretionary powers should be granted to the 'harmless drudge' compiling a Concordance.

"Within a year or two a German scholar has published a pamphlet of some fifty pages on Shakespeare's use of the auxiliary verb *to do*, and Abbott's Grammar shows with what success the study of Shakespeare's language in its minutest particulars may be pursued. I have therefore cited in the following pages every word in his Poems."

Also the number of the line, not only the number of the poem, in which each word occurs is given, a detail which will save the explorer many a minute. In these two respects, Mrs. Furness's work is more exact than that of Mrs. Cowden Clarke. In one way it is less complete; but no one will grudge the difference.

"Having adopted," says Mrs. Furness, "the rule of recording every word, I thought it needless expenditure of space to insert in every instance the entire line in which a word occurs. I have given the clause in which the word stands, and the number of the line, and then, that nothing may be wanting to the convenience of the student, the Poems themselves are reprinted at the end. If in any case the citations appear meagre, the original is instantly accessible."

Mrs. Furness's design is most satisfactory; happily the execution is no less so. Of course it is improbable that there are not some few errors, both of omission and commission. Mrs. Furness is as conscious of this possibility as her "dearest foe."—only there cannot be any such monster —could be. "As the pages are stereotyped," she writes, "corrections can be made at any time of misprints, against which it seems no human vigilance can guard, and I shall be grateful to the kindness that will notify me of them." It would indeed be a marvel if every entry was faultless, or if no claimant for enrolment had been overlooked; for there are some thirty-three thousand entries, each one consisting of several words, and from one to five figures. Surely the most "hanging" judge in the world would be lenient in such a case, and wink with the utmost readiness at an occasional slip of the pen or the compositor's fingers.

> "Ubi plura nitent in carmina, non ego paucis
> Offendar maculis quas aut incuria fudit,
> Aut humana parum cavit natura."

We say that everybody would be willing to show indulgence towards such a minute register. Mrs. Cowden Clarke, with all her excellence, is not independent of indulgence. But we must not speak as if Mrs. Furness stood in special need of consideration. So far as we have at present used her work, we have only found reason to be astonished at the accuracy with which it is executed.

We may just add, that by the "Poems," Mrs. Furness means the pieces usually printed along with Shakespeare's plays. Some of them are not by Shakespeare; but Mrs. Furness has done well, we think, in following the popular attribution. Those to whom her Concordance will be most useful are in no danger of being misguided.

We heartily thank Mrs. Furness for her work. It is a credit to herself, to her sex, and to her nation. Properly considered, it is a most valuable contribution to true Shakespearian study, by the side of which much of what passes for Shakespearian lore is shown in its full worthlessness.

XI.

SHAKESPEARE-LEXICON.[1]

(From the *Academy* for March 20, 1875.)

THE time has long gone by when it was the fashion to speak of a German as some inferior being. With us of to-day to say that "Hermann" was "a German" would rather exalt than lower the claims of the said Hermann to be listened to with all attention and respect. With regard to Shakespeare particularly, to whose highest interpretation Germans have already contributed so nobly, one cannot but receive with especial interest any fresh offering of German scholarship. It is easy to laugh at certain features in their criticism, and occasionally to wish for an explanation of their explanations; but it is not easy to over-estimate our obligations to them for raising the general tone of Shakespearian study, and helping to rescue us from a danger that seems ever imminent in England of forgetting the spirit in the letter. Textualism, and verbiage, and archæology are pursuits whose importance none would deny; but we want continually reminding that for the real comprehension of Shakespeare these, taken altogether, do not constitute the end, but are only the means, or rather some of the means, to the end. Certainly, whatever mistakes the German may

---

[1] *Shakespeare-Lexicon. A complete Dictionary of all the English Words, Phrases, and Constructions in Works of the Poet.* By Dr. Alexander Schmidt. Vol. I. A—L. (Berlin: Georg Reimer. London: Williams and Norgate, 1874 and 1875.)

make concerning our great poet, in whatever mists he may seem to enfold him—

"ἐκάλυψε δ' ἄρ' ἠέρι πολλῇ,"

as the bewildered Briton so commonly cries—however impossible may be his exegeses in the vulgar opinion, he does not commit the fatal blunder of treating the plays as mere *mortua corpora*, and ignoring the living soul that burns with greater or less intensity in every one of them. And this fact is at last gaining a full recognition. Also we are beginning to see that the German school is not antagonistic to the English, but supplementary to it, and to value more fairly efforts and achievements in a line of investigation we have ourselves too much neglected.

The more these two great schools understand each other, the better must be the result. Undoubtedly each has something to learn from the other. Perhaps the work, or instalment of the work, whose appearance we have to notice in this paper may be taken as a sign that Germany is purposed not to neglect the methods hitherto more particularly followed in this country and the United States. Dr. Schmidt's work in the first place aims at being a complete concordance. But it does more than the excellent works of Mrs. Cowden Clarke and Mrs. Howard Furness : it classifies the occurrences of each word according to the sense, so that it is, in short, a concordance and a glossary combined. Assuredly no work could be less liable to the charge of nebulosity. It may be well or ill executed ; but there is no mysticism about it. It is as matter of fact as the multiplication table.

We are glad to say that the work is executed with great care and accuracy. It is no wonder if the English is not always quite faultless—*e.g.*, s.v. *Catercousins*, Dr. Schmidt speaks of "persons who peaceably *feed together*"—but even in this respect one cannot complain, but may rather admire. The definitions are expressed with clearness and without pretence. The arrangement is satisfactory. The type is all that could be wished. On the whole, the work is a very valuable help to thorough Shakespearian study.

We quote one or two specimens, that our readers may judge for themselves :—

"*Cockney*, as it seems, a person who knows only the life and manners of the town, and is consequently well-acquainted with affected phrases, but a stranger to what every child else knows : *this great lubber, the world, will prove a c.*, Tw. IV. 1, 15. *Cry to it, as the c. did to the eels when she put 'em i' the paste alive*, Lr. II. 4, 123."

"*Eke*, adv. also (used only by Pistol, the Host, and Flute), Wiv. I. 3, 105 ; II. 3, 77 ; Mids. III. 1, 97."

"*Eysell*, vinegar : *I will drink potions of e. 'gainst my strong infection*, Sonn. 111, 10 (vinegar being esteemed efficacious in preventing the communication of the plague and other contagious distempers). *Woo't weep? woo't fight? woo't fast? woo't tear thyself? Woot drink up e.? eat a crocodile?* Hml. V. 1, 299 (Qq. *esill*, Ff. *esile* in italics ; Keightley *Yssel*, Hanmer *Nile*, Capell *Nilus*. About *to drink up* = to drink ; see *Drink* and *Up*. Hamlet's questions are apparently ludicrous, and drinking vinegar, in order to exhibit deep grief by a wry face, seems much more to the purpose than drinking up rivers. As for the crocodile, it must perhaps be remembered that it is a *mournful* animal; cf. H6B III., 1, 226, and Oth. IV. 1, 257)."

The idea that the feats Hamlet volunteers should be pertinent to the occasion has, perhaps, not been considered enough by those who have dealt with this vexed passage.

Such is the general character of this work. Anything of the kind so exhaustive has never before been attempted. The labour involved is obviously prodigious; but Dr. Schmidt has faced it boldly. *Sudavit et alsit*. He has certainly won the honour to which he aspires. " Der Verfasser hat keiner grössern Ehrgeiz—wenn es einem Lexicographen erlaubt ist Ehrgeiz zu hegen—als den, auch eingebornen

Engländern nützlich sein zu können." Having thus expressed our high opinion of this work, we may now, without any danger of misleading, point out respects in which we think it improvable.

To turn to a few details, out of several that present themselves:—

"*Catercousin*, quatre cousin, remote relation, misapplied by Gobbo to persons who peaceably feed together : *his master and he are scarce —s* Merch. II. 2, 139."

No doubt *cater* suggests *quatre*, and editors have perpetually yielded to the suggestion; but, as there is no such phrase in French as *quatre cousin*, so far as is known, the result is not of much value. It is a case of " ignotum per ignotius ; " for, whatever be the derivation there was, and is, such a phrase as *cater cousin* in English ; it is still in use in the provinces ; see Halliwell's *Dict. of Prov. and Archaic Words*. Is it impossible that the *cater* is connected with *cate* or *cake*, *cater*, *acater*, *caterer*, &c., and that the word means simply *messfellow?* This explanation has been offered before ; it still requires confirmation.

In the valuable article on *it* we are told in section 4, that it is "used for the def. article in the language of little children : *go to it grandam, child ; it grandam will give it a plum*, John II. i. 160, 161." What exactly is meant? Surely *it* here is either simply the archaic form, which was in Shakespeare's age in the course of supersession by *its;* or else, the context considered, it is meant to be a piece of broken language—of nursery English—of child's talk.

We are told that *interest* in *Macbeth* i. 2, 64:—

> " No more that thane of Cawdor shall deceive
> Our bosom interest."

That *interest* means "concern, advantage," as in *Lear*, v. 3. 85. We commend to Dr. Schmidt's notice, the interpretation given by the editors of the edition of *Macbeth* published by the Clarendon Press. "*Bosom interest,* close and intimate affection;" and then follow some well-chosen quotations to illustrate the senses of both *bosom* and *interest.* In *King Lear,* i. 1, 87 :—

> "to whose young love .
> The wines of France and milk of Burgundy
> Strive to be *interess'd.*"

Dr. Schmidt, it seems, prefers to read *interested,* and gives as an equivalent "to found a claim!" "M. Edd.," *i.e.* Modern Editors, "preposterously *interess'd.*" Why "preposterously?"

(From the *Athenæum* for March 25, 1876.)

Many glossarists and concordance-makers have done good service, but Dr. Alexander Schmidt excels them all. It is really difficult to over-estimate the usefulness and value of his performance. Germany has long been famous for its services to the study of our great poet; but they have for the most part—we do not forget Dr. Delius and his admirable labours—been services in the way of what is called æsthetic criticism and interpretation. In the volumes now before us Germany makes a splendid contribution to quite another line of exploration. The indefatigable industry for which that country is famous has produced a compilation hitherto unattempted, and has produced it, we think, with singular accuracy and success.

The speciality of Dr. Schmidt's lexicon is this—it is both a concordance and a glossary. Moreover, as a concordance, it includes the words, not only of the plays, but of the poems. It may be briefly described as a concordance, in which the words are provided with definitions, and where in the case of words used in various senses these uses are arranged in groups. It is not a mere catalogue, but a *catalogue raisonné*. But even this account scarcely does the work justice, for, incidentally, much other information or suggestion is given, besides the bare signification or significations, and the occurrences of every vocable. Lastly, there are appendices containing "grammatical observations," "provincialisms," "words and sentences taken from foreign languages," "list of the words forming the latter part in compositions." To use the stereotyped phrase, this is an aid to the study of our great dramatist that no scholar should be without.

As to the plays, the words of which are registered, Dr. Schmidt has not fallen into the error, or at least has not acted upon it, committed with enthusiasm, of some of his countrymen, of recognizing all the additional plays found in the two later folios as genuine. He deals with the thirty-six plays of the first two folios—" the two first folios," as he has it,—together with *Pericles*. For thus limiting his collection, it is not likely that any competent critic in England will quarrel with him. He has also shown, in our opinion, a wise discretion in leaving out both *Edward III.* and *The Two Noble Kinsmen*. With regard to Shakespeare's connection with both these plays, the question must be pronounced still open. Indeed, few really capable critics have yet spoken upon it; and such is the nature of the evidence by which it must be decided, that critics worthy to be heard upon it are, and must always be, extremely rare. In fact it is a question not likely ever to be settled beyond controversy. "The stage directions, too, even those of the earliest editions, have been left unnoticed, as it appeared more than

doubtful whether they were written by Shakspeare himself."
Another praiseworthy feature in these volumes is that they
record the readings of both the folios and the quartos, where
quarto editions are extant. They exclude, however, "those
quartos which the editors of the first folio meant when
speaking of stolen and surreptitious copies, maimed and deformed by the frauds and stealths of injurious impostors,"
namely, the quartos of *The Merry Wives* and *Henry V.*, the
first part of *The Contention*, *The True Tragedy*, and the
earliest impressions of *Romeo and Juliet* (1597), and of
Hamlet (1603). "Their variations," adds Dr. Schmidt, "are
at the best, of the same weight as the conjectures of modern
emendators." Dr. Schmidt says he excludes these quartos,
"of course." We confess we see no "of course" in the
matter, or at least in some parts of it, as in the case of the
1603 *Hamlet;* but here, too, we are brought face to face
with one of the most difficult Shakespearian questions that
there are. We do not say Dr. Schmidt is mistaken in acting
as he does, but the question is not one to be disposed of
with an "of course." But it would be wrong to use hard
words to one who deserves so well of us as Dr. Schmidt.

"To make the poet his own interpreter, by discarding all
preconceived opinions, and subordinating all adventitious
means of information to those offered by himself, was
throughout the principle of the work. What Aristarchus
did for Homer, and Galen for Hippocrates, was yet to be
done for Shakespeare." And then follows a highly pertinent
quotation from Galen, which is too long to re-quote here. A
Shakesperian student may certainly share Galen's wonder:
ὅθεν, he concludes, after describing what a proper exegesis
should comprehend,—ἔμοιγε καὶ θαυμάζειν ἐπῆλθε τῶν ἅπασαν
ἐξηγεῖσθη τὴν Ἱπποκράτους λέξω ἐπαγγειλαμένων εἰ μὴ συνί-
σασιν ὅτι πλείω παραλείπουσιν ὧν διδάσκουσιν.

That the principle Dr. Schmidt announces in the words just quoted is sound and laudable there can be no dispute. But it may be pressed too far. And once or twice Dr. Schmidt is in danger of so pressing it. It is certainly not enough in discussing any special sense of a word, to say that it does not occur elsewhere in Shakespeare in that sense. At times what Dr. Schmidt terms "adventitious means of information" must undoubtedly be called in; for, as is well known, Shakespeare's vocabulary is of immense range and variety. It is always ramifying, and extending, and expanding. There is nothing more remarkable about our great poet than his unceasing movement. He is never as one that has already attained perfection, or is already perfect; but he "follows after." His artistic form is perpetually changing. He is ever essaying new methods, conquering new worlds; ever striving to hold the mirror up to nature with a firmer hand, so as to secure a more steady and faithful image. Hence, to return to his language, there is in his writings a vast number of ἅπαξ λεγόμενα—of words that occur only once, and of word senses that occur only once. To take an example, Dr. Schmidt objects to "smote" in *Hamlet*, I. i. 63:

"When in an angry parle,
He smote the sledded pollax (*or* poleaxe) on the ice."

(we give the reading given in the lexicon) being interpreted "he beat or defeated;" he says it can only mean, "he struck them." But the use of "smote" in the sense of defeated is common enough in other Elizabethan writings, notably in the Bible, as in Judges xv. 8: "And he [Samson] smote them [the Philistines] hip and thigh, with a great slaughter." Cranmer's Bible has "smote" here; and it is worth noticing in this connection that there are several "scripturisms" in *Hamlet*. Again, one of Dr. Schmidt's objections to "putter out," in *Tempest*, III. iii. 48, meaning one that lays out money, is that "put out" is not used by Shakespeare in this sense; and he holds that "putter out" means a traveller, one that puts out to sea! Now it may well be that Shakespeare does not happen to use "put out" elsewhere in the sense of Horace's *ponere* in Epod. ii. 70; but the phrase is most usual in our language at all times. Thus, to quote from Johnson, Psalm xv.: "Lord, who shall abide in thy tabernacle? ... He that *putteth* not *out* his money to usury." Dryden translates the lines of Horace referred to:—

> "To live retired upon his own,
> He called—his money in;
> But the prevailing love of pelf
> Soon split him on the former shelf,
> He *put* it *out* again."

It is clear, we hope, that the design of these volumes, though there may be slight imperfections, is truly excellent. Obviously the most essential point in the execution of such a design is accuracy. It is obvious, too, that one cannot bestow this praise upon such a work till after long and frequent use. All we can say is that, so far as we have at present used it, we have found it deserve the very highest commendation in this respect. The use of "these" in "O dear Ophelia, I am ill at *these* numbers," is not noted, but similar uses are so. With regard to other matters, one is reminded sometimes that it is a foreigner's English one sees before one, as when a *Threshold* (misprinted Treshold) is defined to be "the plank that lies at the bottom of a door;" but even in this respect there is little to complain of. One redundancy catches our eye, s. v. *Square*, where the well-known *King Lear* phrase is quoted, both under (1) and also under (3); but this may possibly be intentional. If so, however, the two references should have been connected by a see (3) and a see (1). It is somewhat bold to define *pilcher* (*Romeo and Juliet*, III. i. 84) as a scabbard, although "in contempt" is added. It means some sort of garment. We venture to suggest that its use by Mercutio might serve to illustrate the "breeched"—"their daggers unmannerly *breeched* with gore"—of *Macbeth*. "The ears" in *Romeo and Juliet*, which has tempted "emendators" to read "pitcher" is intelligible enough, if we remember what *pilcher* means. Dr? Schmidt thinks that *subtlety* in *The Tempest*, v. 124, has no culinary reference, but does not *taste* support Steevens's note?

> "You yet do *taste*,
> Some subtilties of the isle that will not let you
> Believe things certain."

As to *three-suited* in *Lear* II. ii. 16, Dr. Schmidt objects to the ordinary interpretation, and suggests that "perhaps we have here a trace of a custom once reigning among the peasantry of Germany, to put on their whole wardrobe on festival occasions, one suit above another;" but surely Ben Jonson's expression in *The Silent Woman*, quoted by Singer, "Wert a pitiful fellow ... and having nothing but *three suits of apparel*," &c., is against him. See also in that same play (Act iii. sc. 1), where Mistress Otter addresses her captain, just entered "with his cups": "Who gives you your maintenance; and, pray you, who allows you your horse meat and man's meat? your *three suits of apparel a year*, your four pair of stockings—one silk, three worsted?" &c. The phrase is explained by the fact that Elizabethan wardrobes were of prodigious extent. "I know the man as well as you," is an ambiguous rendering of "Novi hominem tanquam te." With regard to the dialectic speeches in *King Lear*, Steevens, writes Dr. Schmidt, "pleads for Somersetshire, in the dialect of which rustics were commonly introduced by ancient writers."

Steevens did not know, but we now do, that the so-called "Somersetshire" dialect spread once all over the south of the island. In Kent and Surrey once f's and s's were flattened, a fact pointed out years ago by Dr. Guest; see his *History of English Rhythms*, ii. 188. Is it not rather comical to treat "a" in "and merrily hent the stile a," and such uses, as a remnant of Anglo-Saxon suffixes?

Criticisms of this sort might be considerably extended, but it is not necessary. They will suggest themselves to all intelligent persons who consult Dr. Schmidt's work; and they are not of a kind seriously to impair the value of this excellent lexicon, for which we beg to thank its compiler heartily.

XII.

SHAKESPEARE SCENES AND CHARACTERS.[1]

(From the *Academy* for June 16, 1877.)

THE good Shakespearian service that Germany has done by its verbal criticisms is so well known that we turn with interest to a volume in which it attempts interpretation of another kind. Not that we have in it Germany's first attempts in the pictorial illustration of the supreme Teutonic —the supreme human—poet. Retzsch and Kaulbach are no strange names to us. But this volume is in a special sense representative, as it contains the designs of no less than six distinguished German artists; and as these are living artists, "it may be considered," as Prof. Dowden justly remarks, "in a measure to represent the contemporary art-movement of that country. Munich must be regarded as the centre around which the artists whose work appears in this volume are grouped; but each has his own distinctive traits, and they have been brought under the influence— one in Rome, another in Paris, a third in the Dresden galleries—of various art-methods, ideas, and traditions."

Certainly, in England, our comprehension of Shakespeare

[1] *Shakespeare Scenes and Characters.* A Series of Illustrations designed by Adams, Hofmann, Makart, Pecht, Schwoerer, and Spiess; engraved on steel by Barkel, Bauer, Goldberg, Raab, and Schmidt; with Explanatory Text selected and arranged by Prof. E. Dowden, LL.D., Author of "Shakspere; a Study of his Mind and Art." (London: Macmillan and Co., 1876.)

is not very seriously indebted to the painter's art. Occasional caricatures appear on the walls of the Royal Academy which we find connected in the catalogue with scenes from the plays. And there are in the National Gallery one or two pictures that deserve to be spoken of in a more respectful manner. But, on the whole, we have not much in this line to thank our painters for. What shall be said of the volume before us? Do we find in Hofmann, or any one of his fellows, any adequate intelligence and power? In many ways these designs merit very high praise. They evidence abundantly careful, conscientious, scholarly, accurate, refined workmanship. They are the fruits of no superficial or devotionless study. Few Shakespearian students may not derive help from them in conceiving the mere externals of the lives they exhibit; and, what is more, few will rise from the inspection of them without a deepened, if an unsatisfied, interest in those lives. A thoughtful picture, however far it may be from correspondence with our own ideal, may yet be stimulating and serviceable; and these may be described as thoughtful, as well as learned, pictures. Whether in other important respects they can be pronounced successful may be doubted. They seem to us deficient, or inclined to be deficient, in humour, in sprightliness, in passion, and at times in grace; and we turn from them to the originals as we see them, with a wonder at the difference.

> "And that's your Venus!—whence we turn
> To yonder girl that fords the burn."

Take Adams's Falstaff in his illustration of the famous scene at the Boar's Head, where the fat Knight recounts his adventures at Gadshill. The other figures are satisfactory enough—Poins and Peto grinning delightedly at the lies that flow so readily, and Bardolph gazing at their author with the admiration that afterwards made him say: "Would I were with him, wheresome'er he is, either in heaven or in hell." But can that be Falstaff? Could that face, which might serve with slight modification for Chaucer's Franklin, belong to the immortal wit? The "gross fat man" might have looked so respectable once perhaps—in that golden age when he was "virtuous enough, swore little, diced not above seven times a week." But it would be insulting, not "chaff," to call such a personage "that old whitebearded Satan." (His beard is, in fact, denied him.) Quite different, but not more successful, we think, is Makart's portrait in his illustration of the *Merry Wives*. It is, indeed, something repulsive, and such as to make the whole affair incredible. (Mrs. Ford's left foot in this design seems to stand in a very odd relation to her body.) As to sprightliness, take Adam's Beatrice. It is a somewhat solid figure, with lack-sparkle eyes so far as can be seen, "sober, steadfast, and demure," "la pensierosa," not "l'allegra." And so Schwörer's Puck, that "shrewd and knavish sprite"—that "merry wanderer of the night," who "jests to Oberon and makes him smile," appears as a sad-faced youth, who might be placing a flower on Titania's death-chilled brow instead of playing some wild trick as she sleeps. As to intensity and passion, we must often cry "not content." Take, for instance, the two illustrations of *King John*, both by Adams. His Constance does not wildly abandon herself to her sorrow. She seems looking round to see what others are doing—perhaps to see whether the kings are coming to bow to her throne—instead of lying

> "At random, carelessly diffused,
> With languished head unpropt,
> As one past hope abandoned,
> And by himself given over."

As for the scene between Hubert and Arthur, it is for all the world like an interview between a small patient and a somewhat grim dentist. Hubert, a most resolute-looking Teuton, has placed his left hand on the boy's head, to hold it back and to incline it; in his right he holds an instrument of a curious shape—really, we suppose, an eye-gouge, but which at the first glance may well pass for something much more familiar. For gracefulness, what a plentiful lack of it in Pecht's illustration of 2 *Henry IV.* iv. 5, when the dying king gives his son "the very latest counsel that ever he will breathe." Hal, negligently yet awkwardly leaning on the table where rests the crown, with his left hand upon his hip, by no means allures us. We wish the hinges of his knees, also those of his back, were more "pregnant." We doubt whether he is listening to those last paternal advices. His heart must be with his eyes—far away, not perhaps at the Boar's Head, but across the seas perchance, in France. But surely it ought to be in the chamber with that poor "shaken," care-worn, conscience-pricked figure, which is rapidly going "into the earth." So in Spiess' tomb-scene from *Romeo and Juliet*, there is something grotesque in the form of Tybalt—or is it Paris?—with his head propped up against the marble whereon Juliet has been laid; nor do we think Romeo will attract many admirers. He was, it seems, a very "plain" young man, with thick matted hair.

As to the letterpress that accompanies the illustrations, its selection and arrangement could scarcely have been entrusted to fitter hands than Prof. Dowden's, so wide is his acquaintance with Shakespearian literature both abroad and at home, and so tolerant and at the same time discriminating is his judgment. In this respect certainly the volume is eminently representative not of England only, or of Germany only, but of both these countries, and America and France to boot. Such a critical *florilegium* was well worth making, and we thank Prof. Dowden for making it.

XIII.

THE DRAMATIC WORKS OF WILLIAM SHAKESPEARE.[1]

(From the *Academy* for April 8, 1876.)

IT may seem at first an idle paradox to say that there is a great want of a readable edition of Shakespeare, and also of the Bible, if without offence we may mention together works of such different interest and position. And yet is it not so? Commonly the form is double-columned, and the type small. Probably no two volumes have so much to answer for in respect of the weak eyesight which is said to be becoming more and more prevalent. A fine result of Biblical and of dramatic studies, if they are to make us blind! Why should it always be thought of such importance to compress such writings into the smallest space possible? Of the Bible, is there any readable edition—one in good type, not double-columned, not divided into chapters and verses? Surely this is what is called a Desideratum. And for Shakespeare things are better perhaps; but yet far

---

[1] *The Dramatic Works of William Shakespeare.* With Biographical Introduction. By Henry Glassford Bell. Six Volumes. (London and Glasgow: William Collins, Sons and Co., 1875.)

The Dramatic Works of William Shakespeare. The Text carefully revised with Notes. By S. W. Singer, F.S.A. With a Life by W. Watkiss Lloyd. Ten Volumes. (London: George Bell and Sons, 1875.)

Critical Essays on the Plays of Shakespeare. By William Watkiss Lloyd. (London: George Bell and Sons, 1875.)

from well. Shakespeare, Shakespeare everywhere; but seldom, if ever, a good edition to read.

Of the reprints now before us, neither supplies this want, though both have merits. That published by Messrs. Collins would go far to satisfy us, if only it were issued in twelve volumes instead of six, and the type were a little larger, and the text, about which no information is given, carefully revised! Even as it is, we welcome it. What specially recommends it from our present point of view is that there are no notes. It is certainly true of Shakespeare, as of the Bible, that the text is not enough studied by itself. We are so beset with commentators that it is difficult to get at the work itself. All along the various approaches to the shrine they are posted in dense array, with their handbooks and guides and keys. It is a great blessing occasionally to be delivered from these busy gentlemen—to be left alone with Shakespeare himself. It is like going round the chapels at Westminster, as happily, thanks to Dr. Stanley, one can now do, without a cicerone to spoil everything with his intrusive information or ignorance.

"Let him," says Dr. Johnson (and Mr. H. Glassford Bell pertinently reminds us of his words), "that is yet unacquainted with the powers of Shakespeare, and who desires to feel the highest pleasure that the drama can give, read every play, from the first scene to the last, with utter negligence of all his commentators. When his fancy is once on the wing, let it not stoop to correction or explanation. When his attention is strongly engaged, let it disdain alike to turn aside to the name of Theobald and of Pope. Let him read on, through brightness and obscurity, through integrity and corruption; let him preserve his comprehension of the dialogue and his interest in the fable. And when the pleasures of novelty have ceased, let him attempt exactness, and read the commentators. Particular passages are cleared by notes, but the general effect of the work is weakened. The mind is refrigerated by interruption; the thoughts are diverted from the principal subject; the reader is weary, he suspects not why; and at last throws away the book which he has too diligently studied. Parts are not to be examined till the whole has been surveyed; there is a kind of intellectual remoteness necessary for the comprehension of any great work in its full design and in its true proportions; a close approach shows the smaller niceties, but the beauty of the whole is discerned no longer. It is not very grateful," he adds, " to consider how little the succession of editors has added to this author's power of pleasing. He was read, admired, studied and imitated, while he was yet deformed with all the improprieties which ignorance and neglect could accumulate upon him, while the reading was yet not rectified, nor his allusions understood."

These words are well worth weighing at a time when, perhaps, there is some danger of treating Shakespeare as a mere platform for the display of antiquarian lore, of critical ingenuity, of super-subtle exegesis. Shakespeare is sore of many another besides Theobald. To some persons he would seem to be merely an immense tangle, which it is their high vocation to unravel and arrange. Because they find a thread or two loose here and there, they are unable to see the magnificence and the perfection of the pattern that lies before them, worked with immortal skill and unfading brilliancy.

This reprint of the late Mr. H. Glassford Bell's edition is welcome, then, for its absolute notelessness, there being at the present time a " plentiful lack " of noteless editions in a readable form. The only pages not occupied by the plays are devoted to a " Biographical Introduction," which, indeed, might be dispensed with, but in its kind is written both with knowledge and taste. It should in any case have been revised before its reproduction. It relies upon those "New Facts" which have turned out to be New Fictions; see especially pp. xiv., xlviii., lxxxiii. And some curious statements occur. Is it not quite a wild thing to say that "high literature and high art rarely or never reflect their own age"? What do they reflect, then? What can Hamlet mean when he says that the "purpose of playing," "both at the first and now, was and is to hold, as 'twere, the mirror up to nature, to show virtue her own feature, scorn her own image, *and the very age and body of the time his form and pressure*"? *King Lear* was not printed in 1603, and for certain reasons could not possibly have been so. The statement on p. lxxi. is inaccurate, as *Othello* was published in 1622. Richard was the son, not the brother, of James Burbage (p. xlv.). It was not on the boards of the Blackfriars Theatre that Shakespeare "first appeared" (p. xlv.). It should not be asserted as a fact that Shakespeare came to London the year Sir Philip Sidney died (p. xxiv.). What is "the Greek peplon" (p. lxxiv.)? There is in late Greek a plural πέπλα, and there is in Latin a form *peplum* as well as *peplus*; but *peplon* can scarcely be defended. Again, *Pericles*, "though an early production, is entirely Shakespearian." What an extraordinary announcement! On the whole, however, this Biographical Introduction deserves reading.

The other reprint before us is annotated. It must by no means be understood from what we have said that notes are always to be despised. What we have been protesting against is their omnipresence and omnipotence. In their place they are highly desirable. The late Mr. Singer's notes are of well-known excellence, learned but not pedantic, suggestive and informing without becoming trivial or intrusive. To note in Latin means to brand, and it is in this sense that some editors "note" their authors. Pope has lately been "noted" in this sense, and Shakespeare often enough. In the last century, and since, the censors were for ever scoring their intelligent marks against his name. But it is not in this manner that Mr. Singer proceeds. When he criticises, he does so with proper humility. He is no rash or lavish corrector of the text, though on occasion he is not found wanting. His chief service is his illustrations, and the charm of these is their freshness and variety. He draws water for himself straight from Elizabethan fountains—does not borrow it from a neighbour's cistern or tub. Each play has its "Preliminary Remarks," dealing with the date and the material, and like matters. The type of the text is of merciful size. Altogether, this is a capital edition of its sort.

Of course offences will come; but we will by no means on that account cry "Woe to Mr. Singer." Here are a few offences: his note on "Sandblind" (*Merchant of Venice*, ii. 2) is a quotation from Holyoke's *Dictionary:* "Having an imperfect sight, as if there was sand in the eye Myops;" which looks odd enough through a "full stop" having dropped out after the word "eye," and is surely a piece of but feeble etymology. Probably the *sand*, as has been suggested, is as the Anglo-Saxon *sám* (the Latin *semi*, Greek ἡμι), as in *sám-cwic*, *sám-wís*, &c. Again: "We learn from the account of the Revels at Court that it [the *Merry Wives of Windsor*] was acted before James I. on the Sunday following the 1st November, 1604." Do we? Or should it not rather be written, "We do not learn, &c."? Again, is there not a want of humour in saying, *apropos* of "I paid nothing for it neither, but was paid for my learning," "to *pay* in Shakespeare's time signified to beat; in which sense it is still not uncommon in familiar language. 'Seven of the eleven I *paid*,' says Falstaff in *Henry IV.*, Part I." Again in *Richard II.*, i. 1:—

"Upon remainder of a dear account,"

is "dear," or "deere," "an evident press error for 'cleere'"? *Dear* in a well-known Elizabethan usage makes excellent sense. Mr. Singer makes no alteration in *Romeo and Juliet*, i. 5:—

"O dear account! my life is my foe's debt;"

nor in *Much Ado about Nothing*, iv. 1:—

"By this hand Claudio shall render me a dear account"—

passages aptly quoted by the Clarendon Press editors. As to the date of *Macbeth*, there is no mention made of the passage in the *Puritan* first noticed, we think, by Farmer, which one can scarcely doubt refers to Banquo's Ghost:—

"Come, my inestimable bullies," says Sir Godfrey, "we'll talk of your noble acts in sparkling charnico; and instead of a jester we'll have the ghost in the white sheet sit at the upper end of the table."

It is curious how commonly this passage is overlooked; yet it is very important, as the *Puritan* was printed in 1607. For ourselves the more we study the question the more convinced we are that those are in the right who advocate an earlier date for *Macbeth* than 1610. As this play attracts so much attention just now, we may just remind our readers that there is another allusion to Banquo's Ghost in Beaumont and Fletcher's *Knight of the Burning Pestle*, produced in 1611, when Jasper, entering "with his face mealed," thus addresses Venturewell:—

"When thou art at thy table with thy friends,
Merry in heart, and filled with swelling wine,

> I'll come in midst of all thy pride and mirth,
> Invisible to all men but thyself."

It should not be forgotten that Mr. Collier has found a Ballad of Macdobeth entered in the Stationers' Company Registers, Aug. 27, 1596. Singer does refer to the passage in Kemp's *Nine Daies Wonder*, printed 1600, where this ballad is mentioned. The words, which he might have quoted, are these :—

"I met a proper upright youth, onely for a little stooping in the shoulders, all hart to the heele, a penny Poet, whose first making was the miserable Stolne story of Macdoel, or Macdobeth, or Macsomewhat, for I am sure a Mac it was, though I never had the maw to see it."

Of whom or how was the story stolen, we wonder. See Mr. Furness's encyclopædic edition of *Macbeth*, p. 387. In Act i. sc. 3, Singer rightly reads "weird sisters" in spite of Hunter's protest. "The old copy," he notes, "has 'wayward,' probably to indicate the pronunciation; it is also used by Heywood."

The "Life" which occupies some hundred pages of the first volume of this reissue is written by Mr. W. Watkiss Lloyd. The critical essays by the same author, which appeared in the original edition, are now reprinted in a separate volume, uniform with the plays. Mr. Lloyd is a well-known worker in various fields—in the Periklean no less than the Elizabethan. What he does is always well done—is always done freshly, thoughtfully, in a scholarly spirit. His style, it must be observed, is often unfortunate, so that one does not always quite understand what he means to say; and there are lines of criticism which he scarcely recognizes; but, on the whole, his volume of *Essays* is to be cordially recommended—if only the print were not so cruelly small. On the whole, they are really remarkable for their learning, breadth, and general soundness. In discussing the dates of the plays, for instance, though we by no means always agree with his conclusions, yet we cannot but admire the comprehensive intelligence of his method. His culture delivers him from the vigorous one-sidedness that deforms so much Shakespearian criticism. He sees the necessity of entertaining several considerations instead of blindly abandoning himself to a single one. With such a volume within reach, and with such another as Professor Dowden's recent work, Shakespearian study may be fairly hoped to make some better progress.

For its size, there is, perhaps, no Life of Shakespeare that gives more information. We think a more minute investigation would convince Mr. Lloyd that "Willy" in Spenser's *Tears of the Muses* can scarcely be Shakespeare; that he is not justified in giving 1594 as the date of the Aetion lines in *Colin Clouts Come Home Again ;* that the composition of the Roman plays does not belong to the latter years of the poet's life—he is speaking of the years 1614-15—for *Julius Cæsar* is referred to, as Mr. Halliwell-Phillipps has discovered, in 1601, and *Antony and Cleopatra* is entered in the books of the Stationers' Company in 1608 ; (but it must be mentioned that Mr. Lloyd in his Essay on the play disputes the latter fact, we think ineffectually, though he allows it in his *Julius Cæsar* essay;) and there are other such matters ; yet, on the whole, the Life is conspicuously well-informed and complete.

We will end with one or two notes on the *Essays:*—
"'Ariel' is without capacity of sympathetic affection in any form ; can recognize the compassionable as an object of intellect, but knows no touch of the appropriate sentiment; and for aught that can be inferred, would be equally incapable of personal hatred." Is this estimate quite compa-

tible with the spirit's wistful cry "Do you love me, master? no?" (*Tempest*, iv. 1, 48)? Mr. Lloyd considers the name Sycorax to be a softened form of Psychorrhex (ψυχορρήξ), heartbreaker; but rather, we think, it is contracted from συοκοραξ, derived from σῦς and κόραξ.[1] In his remarks on the *Two Gentlemen of Verona* Mr. Lloyd accounts for "the alacrity of" Valentine's "renunciation of all previous rights in the blushing damsel who has no word of recognition or gratitude to greet him with" by casting reflections on the character of poor Silvia! The scene is strange, no doubt; but there are other ways of treating it; we really do not think Silvia is meant to be sacrificed. In what sense would readers take these words in the *Measure for Measure* essay?—

"Applying the canon of sequence approved in the examination of the parallelisms of the *Two Gentlemen of Verona*, I would deduce the necessary posteriority of *Measure for Measure* to *Much Ado about Nothing*, and to *King Henry IV.*, on the ground that it contains the germs of characters and scenes which appear in those plays in perfect and entire development."

As it appears from the context, either Mr. Lloyd uses the word "posteriority" in a quite unusual way, or it is a mere slip for "priority." Anyhow, we think his date for *Measure for Measure* can hardly be accepted.

[1] See page 114.

XIV.

SHAKESPEARE AND SATIRE.

(From the *Antiquary* for Nov., 1881.)

GASCOIGNE'S *Steel Glass* may be called the first formal English satire. But, with all its merits as a first effort, it is but a crude performance. The first notable satires published, which may deserve to be ranked in the series to which the masterpieces of Dryden and of Pope belong, are those of Hall, afterwards Bishop of Exeter, and then of Norwich.

The satirical spirit may be, and has been, variously embodied. In the Middle Ages it frequently used the form of a tale or a fable; its most trenchant expression in the Elizabethan period was the dramatic; as, for instance, in the plays of Ben Jonson, who is nothing if not satirical; it has frequently taken a lyrical shape. No wonder if, in the age of the Renascence, under the example and influence of Juvenal and Persius, it assumed a form of its own, and there began to be a literature, not only satirical in spirit, but satirical in form, according to the great Roman models.

Satire is the expression of scorn and disgust and hate, rather than of admiration and praise and love. Therefore, it is an evil thing for an age when its literature is mainly satirical. Only in ages debased and fallen, as in that of the Restoration, can it be so. Happily, in the Elizabethan, nobler sentiments could prevail, and prevailed; the time was not out of joint; at all events, if there was then, as at all times, some cause for discontent and indignation, there was yet more for satisfaction and pride; and the greatest geniuses did not surrender themselves to merely satirical impulses; they were minded to bless rather than to curse. In several of Shakespeare's plays a satirical element is perceptible—is obvious; but it never becomes supreme. When Jaques, in *As You Like It*, longs for the liberty of the satirist—longs for leave

> " To speak my mind, and I will through and through
> Cleanse the foul body of th' infected world,
> If they will patiently receive my medicine,"

the Duke administers to that witty pessimist a rebuke most worthy of the consideration of all persons who conceive they have a right to scourge their neighbours.

> "*Duke.* Fie on thee! I can tell what thou wouldst do.
> *Jaques.* What, for a counter, would I do, but good?
> *Duke.* Most mischievous foul sin, in chiding sin;
> For thou thyself hast been a libertine,
> As sensual as the brutish sting itself;
> And all th' embossed sores, and headed evils,
> That thou with licence of free foot hast caught,
> Wouldst thou disgorge into the general world."

It is surely interesting to note that the Duke's words were first uttered just about the time when satirical literature, in the technical sense, was beginning. At about the same date as *As You Like It*—not to mention that Ben Jonson's plays were just then coming out—appeared the satires of Hall and of Marston.

Hall's first three books of satire, " poetical, academical, moral,"—" toothless satyrs," as he called them—(*satire* and *satyr* were identified by Elizabethan scholarship), were published in 1597; and in the prologue he claims to be the first practiser of the art :—

> "I first adventure, with fool-hardy might,
> To tread the steps of perilous despite.

> I first adventure, follow me who list,
> And be the second English satirist."

In the following year appeared three more books; those called "biting satires." The general title of the whole series was *Virgidemiæ*, from Plautus' *Virgidemia* (a canage), a comical analogue of *Vindemia* (a vintage). In the same year (1598), appeared Marston's *Scourge of Villany*, and also his *Metamorphosis of Pigmalions's Image and certaine Satyres*. But when Hall, whom Marston so closely followed, satirizing the satirist, boasted of leading the way, some at least of Donne's satires had been written, though not published, for at least four years. Thus, both Donne and Hall conceived independently the satirical idea, Donne before Hall; but to Hall belongs the honour of prior publication.

Hall writes with skill and with spirit. It can scarcely be said of him: *Facit indignatio versum*. He finds a pleasure in imitating, and in some sort reproducing, his Latin models; and this is rather his inspiration than any moral fervour. And the chief value of his work is its vigorous picture of Elizabethan ways and manners. Whatever the old comedy did for Athens in the way of illustrating the old Athenian life, that satire did for Rome, and with inferior, but yet no mean force, Hall did for Elizabethan London. It is no contemptible service to have helped to keep alive for us an age so fascinating, so glorious, so momentous. Whoever would picture to himself the very town in the midst of which Shakespeare moved, its lights and shadows, its whims and phantasies and follies—"a mad world, my masters"—see "the very age and body of the time, his form and pressure," and learn what were its daily thoughts, interests, cares, credulities, passions—will find truly valuable aid in Hall's satires.

XV.

MILTON'S FAMILIARITY WITH SHAKESPEARE'S PLAYS.

MILTON'S lines on "that admirable dramatic poet, Mr. William Shakespeare," and a few other of his allusions to him, are well known; but it may be doubted whether his appreciation of his great predecessor has yet been adequately recognized. We do not now propose to go into the general question, but only to take a particular instance, and to illustrate the keen receptive delight with which Milton when young studied the *Midsummer Night's Dream*. Other plays that might be especially named are *Romeo and Juliet, As You Like It, King Lear*, and *Macbeth;* but we will confine ourselves now to the *Midsummer Night's Dream*, and among Milton's works to the famous pendants *L'Allegro* and *Il Penseroso;* and as we read the younger poet, listen for echoes of the elder.

1. The chief note of *L'Allegro* and its twin is, in fact, struck in the *Midsummer Night's Dream*, though amongst all the suggested "sources" of Milton's two poems, Shakespeare's play has, so far as we remember, scarcely been mentioned.

"Go, Philostrate,"

says Theseus:

> "Stir up the Athenian youth to merriments;
> Awake the pert and nimble spirit of mirth;
> Turn melancholy forth to funerals;
> The pale companion is not for our pomp."

       "'Come, thou goddess fair and free,
In heav'n yclept Euphrosyne,
And by men heart-easing mirth."

and

     "Hence, loathed Melancholy," &c.

2. "Jest and youthful *Jollity*."
    "Nightly revels and new *jollity*."

3. "*Nods* and Becks."
    "*Nod* to him, elves, and do him courtesies."

4. "Laughter holding both his sides."
    "And then the whole quire hold their hips and laugh."

5. "Come and trip it as you go."
    "And this ditty after me
Sing and dance it trippingly."

and

    "Then, my queen, in silence sad
Trip we after the night's shade."

6. "Through the sweetbriar and the vine,
Or the twisted eglantine."
    "Quite over-canopied with luscious woodbine,
With sweet musk-roses and with eglantine."

7.   "How the hounds and horn
Cheerly rouse the slumbering morn,"

in "the vaward of the day," when Theseus is out a hunting.

8. "Right against *the eastern gate*,
When the great sun begins his state,
Robed in flames, and amber light."
    "Even till *the eastern gate, all fiery red*,
Opening on Neptune with fair blessed beams,
Turns into yellow gold his salt green streams."

9. Observe the fairy lore common to both poets.

10. "The *lubber* fiend."
    "Thou *lob* of spirits."

11. "There let Hymen oft appear
In Saffron robe, with taper clear,

> And Pomp, and Feast, and Revelry,
> With Mask and antique Pageantry."

> "But I will wed thee in another key,
> With Pomp, with triumph, and with revelling."

12. "Such sights as *youthful poets dream*
    On summer eves by haunted stream."

Is it impossible that this is a direct allusion to the *Midsummer Night's Dream?* Notice the immediately preceding words; and also the mention of Shakespeare in those that immediately follow.

13. "Or sweetest Shakespeare, Fancy's child,
    Warble his native wood-notes wild."

Surely this way of speaking of the great dramatist is suggested by a vivid memory of a certain "wood near Athens," as also of Arden?

14. "That Orpheus self," &c.

In the *Midsummer Night's Dream* we hear of

> "The Thracian singer."

15. To pass on to *Il Penseroso*:—

> "How little you bested,
> Or fill the fixed mind with all your *toys?*"

> "I never may believe
> These antique fables, nor these fairy *toys.*"

16. "The fickle *pensioners* of Morpheus' train."

    "The cowslips tall her *pensioners* be."

17. "The rugged brow of Night."

    "Black-browed Night."

18. "While Cynthia checks her dragon yoke."

    "The triple Hecate's team."

and

> "Night's swift dragons."

19. "When glowing embers through the room
Teach light to counterfeit a gloom."

"Now the wasted brands do glow."

and

"Through the house give glimmering light
By the dead and drowsy fire."

20. "Not trickt and frounc't as she was wont
With the Attic boy to hunt."

"I with the morning's love have oft made sport."

The meaning of Shakespeare's words has been disputed. How Milton took them is clear.

21. "Th' unseen Genius of the Wood."

Is he not thinking of Oberon?

"—— the 'invisible' Oberon?"

Notice also these words as common to the poems before us: frolic (as an adj.), grain (of a dye), buskin'd, virtuous (power-possessing potent), triumphs (shows), antique (= antic), &c.

From other plays other illustrations might easily be drawn; *e.g.* cf. "Day's garish eye" and "the garish sun" in *Romeo and Juliet*, &c. But, taking together all the coincidences we have mentioned, not laying stress on any single one, though indeed there are several that might well have stress laid upon them, surely we have already sufficient evidence to show with what worship and joy the young Milton sat at the feet of Shakespeare—sufficient evidence not that he consciously imitated or borrowed from him, or was in any sense untrue to his own originality, but that Shakespeare's works had become, so to speak, part of his mental garniture.

XVI.

RICHARD II.

(From the *Academy* for Nov. 20, 1875.)

THERE is, as is well known, great variety of opinion as to whether the play of *Richard II.*, acted by the request of Sir Gilly Merrick the day before Essex's rising, was Shakespeare's or some other. The probabilities are, on the whole, perhaps in favour of its being Shakespeare's. As Shakespeare was intimately acquainted with Southampton, who was one of Essex's leading partisans, it is probable that those partisans would apply for any dramatic help they might want, or fancy they wanted, to the company to which Shakespeare belonged. Again, the omission of the Deposition Scene from the quartos of 1597 and 1598, though there can be little doubt it was then written, cannot but be regarded as significant of the use to which that scene might be turned. The publisher of those quartos evidently saw in it something that might be construed into a sense unfavourable to the Queen, and so welcome to her enemies. Nor, I think, can the fact of the play's being called an old play, and one that it would not pay to act, be said to counterweigh these probabilities. Others, however, and critics of judgment, may decide for themselves differently. But what I wish now to do is to recall attention to a piece of evidence brought forward years ago, but which seems to have been oddly overlooked or ignored by some recent editors—a piece of evidence which greatly increases the probability that the play was really Shakespeare's.

In a report of Attorney-General Bacon's speech in the *State Trials*, there is given the name of the actor with whom Sir Gilly Merrick negotiated. It is Phillips: and unless good reason is shown to the contrary, we can scarcely doubt that this is the Augustine Phillips who was a member of the famous Globe company, *i.e.*, one of Shakespeare's "fellows." In the licence of 1603 the names run: Lawrence Fletcher, William Shakespeare, Richard Burbage, Augustine Phillips, &c. A notice of him may be found in the *Historical Account of the English Stage*, and elsewhere.

The report is that described as "a fuller account of the Trial of Sir Christopher Blunt, Sir Charles Davers, Sir John Davis, Sir Gilly Merrick and Henry Cuffe, from a MS. purchased at a sale of the MSS. of Peter Le Neve, Esq., Norroy King-at-Arms;" and the passage that concerns us occurs on p. 1445 of the 1809 edition of *State Trials* :—

"And the story of Henry the Fourth being set forth in a play, and in that play there being set forth the killing of the King upon a stage, the Friday before, Sir Gilly and some others of the Earl's train having a humour to see a play, they must needs have the play of ' Henry the Fourth.' The players told them that was stale, they should get nothing by playing of that; but no play else would serve, and Sir Gilly gives forty shillings to Phillips the player to play this, besides whatever he could get."

The play's being called *Henry IV.* surely cannot cause any difficulty, seeing what is said of its contents. But if any one should think otherwise, there is abundant other evidence to show that the play was also called, or rather commonly called *Richard II.* See, for instance, Bacon's " Declaration of the Practices and Treasons attempted, and committed by Robert, Earl of Essex, and his complices, against her Majesty and her kingdoms," where we are told that, "it was given in evidence . . . . that the afternoon before the rebellion, Merick, with a great company of others that afterwards were all in the action, had procured to be played before them the *play of deposing Richard the Second*. Neither was it casual, but a play bespoken by Merick."

But if there could be any doubt on this point, or as to who that Phillips was, it must be all dissipated by the document of which a facsimile is given by Mr. J. O. Halliwell-Phillipps, in that vast storehouse of learning his Folio Shakespeare, now to be found also in the *Calendar of State Papers*, Domestic Series, 1591-1601, p. 578—a document surely not so much noticed and considered as it deserves. It is headed: " Examination of Augustine Phillips, servant to the Lord Chamberlain and one of his Players, before Lord Chief Justice Popham and Edward Fenner," and runs thus :—

"On Thursday or Friday sevennight Sir Charles Percy, Sir Josceline Percy, Lord Monteagle, and several others spoke to some of our players to play the deposing and killing of Richard ii., and promised to give them 40*s*. more than their ordinary to do so. Examinate and his fellows had determined to play some other play, holding that of King Richard as being so old, and so long out of use that they should have a small company of it ; but at this request they were content to play it." We may just ask whether the above names do not suggest that some of Essex's accomplices may have nursed designs very different from his own, or at all events from those he professed? But this by the way. What is noticeable for us is that "the deposing and killing of Richard II." is exactly the subject of Shakespeare's play.

Considering now the general probabilities, and the facts that the company employed by the Essexians was that to which Shakespeare belonged, and that the play asked for answers in description to Shakespeare's *Richard II.*, must we not incline to believe that the play was indeed Shakespeare's? Is it likely that there were two plays answering to the same description "in the field" of the Globe—two plays dealing with the closing years of Richard II.?

XVII.

WILY BEGUILED AND THE MERCHANT OF VENICE.

(From the *Athenæum* for July 17, 1875.)

AN interesting Shakespearian chapter has yet to be written, treating of the influence of the great master over his contemporaries. A full description of the way in which his image is impressed upon the contemporary drama would more truly show what his power was during his life, than a long list of direct recognitions and formal eulogies. We wish Dr. Ingleby's very valuable volume might be supplemented by a record of this most significant "prayse." A remarkable instance of it is to be found in *Wily Beguiled*. Whalley noticed how it imitated the *Merchant of Venice* in one passage; but it is, in fact, full of Shakespearian imitations.

As to the date of the play, it seems to have been first published in 1606; but it was certainly written some years before. According to Malone, it "was written before 1596, being mentioned by Nash in one of his pamphlets published in that year" (*i.e.*, *Have with you to Saffron Walden*). Malone's logic is here a little strange. All that he ought to infer is that the play was not written later than 1596. Neither is his statement as to Nash's mention of it accurate, as will be shown in another paper. It was certainly not written before, because it contains a reference to the famous expedition to Cadiz. "Zounds," says Churms, an over-reaching lawyer who is eventually himself over-reached, "I am as proper a man as Peter Plod-all; and though his father be as good a man as mine, yet far-fetched and dear-bought is good for ladies; and I am sure I have been as far as *Cales* to fetch that I have. I have been at Cambridge, a scholar; *at Cales a soldier;* and now in the country a lawyer, and the next degree shall be a coney-catcher; for I'll go near to cozen old father Sharepenny of his daughter; I'll cast about, I'll warrant him." And, unless we believe that the *Venesyon Comedy* mentioned in Henslowe's *Diary*, August 25th, 1594, is the *Merchant*, a belief not easily to be adopted, there is now no external evidence for giving the *Merchant* an earlier date than 1596. Nor do I think that the internal evidence of style and tone points to any earlier date, but this is to some extent a matter of opinion.

The passage which Whalley quotes as manifestly imitating the *Merchant*, is from the scene where Sophos and Lelia are away in the woods together in the starlight, and they converse in this wise:—

> "See how the twinkling stars do hide their borrowed shine,
> As half ashamed their lustre is so stained
> By Lelia's beauteous eyes, that shine more bright
> Than twinkling stars do in a winter's night.
> In such a night did Paris win his love.
> *Lelia.* In such a night Æneas proved unkind.
> *Sophos.* In such a night did Troilus court his dear.
> *Lelia.* In such a night fair Phillis was betrayed.
> *Sophos.* I'll prove as true as ever Troilus was.
> *Lelia.* And I as constant as Penelope."

But, as we have said, the play is full of Shakespearian imitations. Gripe, the usurer, is done out of his daughter and his money, even as Shylock is, and cries out:—

> "I am undone. I am robbed! My daughter! My money! Which way are they gone?"

Again, says Sophos, in an interview with his mistress :—

> "To what fair Lelia wills doth Sophos yield content,
> Yet that's the troublous gulf, my silly ship must pass.
> But, were that venture harder to atchieve
> Than that of Jason for the golden fleece,
> I would effect it for sweet Lelia's sake,
> Or leave myself as witness of my thoughts."

Compare *Merchant of Venice*, i. 1, 172, and iii. 2, 244. Elsewhere—

> *Enter* PEG *sola.*
>
> "I'faith, i'faith, I cannot tell what to do ;
> I love and I love, and I cannot tell who ;
> Out upon this love! for wot you what ?
> I hae suitors come huddle, twos upon twos,
> And threes upon threes ; and what think you
> Troubles me ? I must chat and kiss with all comers,
> Or else no bargain."

Compare *Merchant of Venice*, i. 1, 167-9 ; i. 2, 37 ; ii. 7, 38-47.

In the following passage who can doubt that the writer has in some sort felt the spell of Romeo and Juliet.

> *Enter* LELIA *and* Nurse *gathering flowers.*
>
> "*Lelia.* See how the earth this fragrant spring is clad,
> And mantled round in sweet nymph Flora's robes,
> Here grows the alluring rose, sweet marigolds,
> And the lovely hyacinth. Come, nurse, gather ;
> A crown of roses shall adorn my head,
> I'll prank myself with flowers of the prime ;
> And thus I'll spend away my primrose time.
>
> *Nurse.* Rufty, tufty, are you so frolic ? O that you knew as much as I do; t'would cool you.
>
> *Lelia.* Why, what knowest thou, nurse ? Prythee tell me.
>
> *Nurse.* Heavy news, i'faith, mistress ; you must be matched, and married to a husband. Ha, ha, ha, ha, a husband, i'faith.
>
> *Lelia.* A husband, nurse ? Why, that's good news, if he be a good one.

Nurse. A good one, quotha? Ha, ha, ha, ha! Why, woman, I heard your father say that he would marry you to Peter Plod-all, that puckfist, that snudge-snout, that coal-carrierly clown. Lord! 'twould be as good as meat and drink to me to see how the fool would woo you. .

Lelia. No, no, my father did but jest; think'st thou
That I can stoop so low to take a brown-bread crust,
And wed a clown, that's brought up at the cart?

Nurse. Cart, quotha? Ay, he'll cart you, for he cannot tell how to court you.

Lelia. Ah, nurse! Sweet Sophos is the man,
Whose love is locked in Lelia's tender breast;
This heart hath vowed, if heavens do not deny,
My love with his entombed in earth doth lie.

Nurse. Peace, mistress, stand aside; here comes somebody."

I might add more; but enough is given to show how deeply the author of *Wily Beguiled* was Shakespearianized.

(From the *Athenæum* for Sept. 4, 1875.)

WHAT there was of interest in my communication of July 17th did not at all depend upon the date of *Wily Beguiled.* The object of it was to show how completely the author of it, whoever he was, and whenever he wrote, was permeated with Shakespeare, of which more instances might easily have been given. But, in passing, reference was made to the date of the play, and on this point there have reached me one or two letters from well-known Shakespearian scholars.

Does Nash allude to *Wily Beguiled,* in *Have with you to Saffron Walden?* I was careful to say that the statement he did so was made by Malone. Here is the passage from Nash's pamphlet: "His voiage under *Don Antonio* was nothing so great credit to him, as a French Varlet of the chamber is ; nor did he follow Anthonio neither but was a Captaines Boye that scornde writing and reading, and helps him to set down his accounts, and score up dead payes. But this was our *Gabriel Hagiels* tricke of *Wily Beguily* herein, that whereas he could get no man of worth to cry *Placet* to his workes, or meeter it in his commendation, those worthless Whippets and Jack Strawes hee could get he would seeme to enable and compare with the highest. Hereby hee thought to coneycatch the simple world, and make them beleeue that these and these great men euerie waye sutable to Syr *Thomas Baskeruille*, Master *Bodley*, Doctor *Androwes*, Doctor *Doue*, *Clarencius*, and Master *Spencer*, had separately contended to outstrip *Pindarus* in his *Olympicis*, and sty aloft to the highest pitch, to stellifie him aboue the cloudes and make him shine next to *Mercury*."

Now, so far as the sense goes, there might be here a reference to the play. The title of the play, no doubt a proverbial phrase—see amongst Ray's *Joculatory Proverbs*. *He hath played wily beguiled with himself*—signifies The Cheat Cheated, The Biter bit, The Tables Turned, the lawyer Churms being the wily one who is himself beguiled. Nash might, it is true, use the proverb without any reference to the play. He might mean to say that Gabriel Harvey, while intending to impose on others, had, in fact, made his position worse than it was—the exposure of his trick had led to his own confusion. But also he might directly refer to the play, and mean that Harvey has practised the trick that is practised in it; for in it one Robin Goodfellow in the interest of Churms, his friend and patron, sets up for "a devil," and fails miserably in that line.

But the allusion would not be very happy ; and moreover, we have not only the general sense to consider, but the exact phraseology. And it is not easy to identify the phrase *wily beguily* with *wily beguiled*. Another form of the proverb is found, viz., *wilie beguile himself;* see a passage lighted on by Mr. Furnivall in Dr. John Harvey's *Discoursiue Problem Concerning Prophesies,* 1588 :—

"God, they say, sendeth commonly a curst cow short horns: and doth not the diuel, I say, in the winde-vpall, and in fine, oftner play *wilie beguile himselfe,* and crucifie his own wretched lims, then atchieue his mischieuous and malicious purposes howsoever craftilie conueid, or feately packed, either in one fraudulent sort or other?" But it is not easy to believe that this form any more than the other could be corrupted into *wily beguily.* More probably Nash's phrase is one of those reduplications that are so common in English (see Mr. Wheatley's paper in the *Transactions of the Philological Society*), and of which Nash was particularly fond; see, as Mr. Furnivall notes, his "huddle duddle," "scrimpum scrampum, prinkum prankum," and in the passage quoted above, Gabriel Hagiel.

Nash, then, does not refer to the play, and so Malone's argument as to the date of it must be abandoned. What is the real date there is no space now to discuss. I will only say that Dr. Brinsley Nicholson has kindly placed at my free disposal certain notes of his on the subject, in which he concludes, on the whole, that the play was written "in or after 1601."

XVIII.

A CERTAIN EDITION OF THE MERCHANT OF VENICE.

(From the *Athenæum* for Dec. 15, 1877.)

THE fourth quarto edition of the *Merchant of Venice* appeared, as is well known, in 1652. Such an apparition is not indeed unique in the Commonwealth period: the fourth quarto of *King Lear* came out in 1655, and also in 1655 the third of *Othello;* but there are political circumstances attending the year 1652 which, if they do not explain the re-issue of the *Merchant* just then, yet certainly deserve notice in connection with it. It may have been a mere coincidence—it is undoubtedly a fact worth remarking—that just at the time when the *Merchant* was re-issued, the Jews were beginning to ask for re-admission into England, and the consideration of their request to be seriously entertained. It was not till October, 1655, that Manasseh Ben Israel came over in person; not till the following December that the celebrated discussion at Whitehall took place; but for some years previously that earnest and able patriot had been urging the claims of his people upon English consideration. He had petitioned "Barebone's Parliament," and still earlier had petitioned the Long Parliament—from both these assemblies receiving a passport to come over and represent his case, a permission of which he was prevented from availing himself. And the cause he advocated was not without friends moved by motives far different from his. During the Dutch war, which began in May, 1652, both Blake and Monk recommended the re-admission of the Jews " as a means of damaging the commerce of Holland, and Cromwell appeared favourable to it " (*Annals of England*). Thus, just about the time of the republication of the famous portrait of Shylock, the question of the return of his race was "in the air," was a kindling question, if not yet a burning one. The great Cromwell himself was willing, not only for the reason suggested above, to put an end to the foolish and unjust enactment that exiled from the country a people capable of proving one of its most valuable elements; and some few other of the more enlightened spirits of the day may have agreed with him; but for the most part the feeling was against the Jews. Prejudices are not easily uprooted, and English prejudices are of special tenacity, and this particular prejudice was of unusual strength. So the idea of a Jewish immigration was bitterly resented. The clergy, the lawyers, the populace, were all at one on the subject. William Prynne "headed the cry of Christianity in danger by publishing a manifesto against the Jews, in which 'their ill deportment, misdemeanours, condition, sufferings, oppressions, slaughters, plunders by popular insurrections, royal exactions, and final banishment,' were brought forward in connection with laws and Scriptures, 'to plead and conclude against their re-admission into England.' The old clamour against the Jewerie was revived, especially in the City, where the merchants were jealous of the wealth of the Hebrews; and the Protector, seeing it was in vain to expect any agreement upon this question, sought for no legal sanction to their settling here, but raised no objection to a Portuguese synagogue being opened in 1656." The dispensation Cromwell gave was stoutly protested against when he himself was no more. At Christmas, 1659, one Thomas Violet, a goldsmith, appealed to one of the judges respecting it; and in the following year the same intelligent and broad-spirited person, along with others of a like mind, petitioned against it. Amongst the State Papers of the Restoration is "a remonstrance addressed to the King concerning the English Jews, showing the mischiefs accomplished by them since their coming in at the time of William the Conqueror; the privileges which they purchased by money, their prosperity notwithstanding their oppressions and taxations, their ill dealings and banishment by Edward the First, at the desire of the whole kingdom; yet they have since returned, renewed their usurious and fraudulent practices, and flourish so much, that they endeavoured to buy St. Paul's for a synagogue in the late usurper's time; suggesting the issue of a commission to inquire into their state, and the imposition of heavy taxes, seizure of their personal property, and banishment for residence without licence," &c. (see Mrs. Everett Green's *State Papers*, Domestic Series, 1660).

It must be allowed that the re-exhibition of Shylock in 1652 could scarcely have tended to soften this general disposition. Whether William Leake, in "his shop at the sign of the Crown between the two Temple Gates," had any sinister intentions when he had that quarto reprinted, there would seem no means of knowing. Other volumes published by him, advertised in the *Merchant* quarto, are of various kinds, both religious and general. Amongst them are both *Christ's Passion, a Tragedie by George Sands*, and *A Maid's Tragedie*. There may or may not have been animus in the man, but he certainly did the Jews no good turn when at such a time he re-issued the *Merchant of Venice*.

For by "the general" little heed is paid to the profound skill and the Catholic humanity with which the Jew is interpreted in that play. "The general" sees only a monster, and hisses and hates. A more careful eye observes that this monster is accounted for—that the great poet is considering the problem how such ossifications come to be. He is "anatomizing" Shylock, seeing "what breeds about" his "heart." "Is there any cause in nature that makes these hard hearts?" The Christian who looks frankly and faithfully at this work will not find matter for exultation or for ridicule, but only for shame and sadness. Shylock had been made the hard, savage, relentless creature we see him, by long and cruel oppression. He inherited a nature embittered by centuries of insult and outrage, and his own wretched experience had only aggravated its bitterness. "Sufferance" had been and was the badge of all his tribe; it was his badge. As fetters corrode the flesh, so persecution corrodes the heart. Shakespeare, truly detesting this dreadful being, yet bethinks him, we say, how he became so. He was once a man—at least, his breed was once human; and Shakespeare, no less than the supreme creative genius of our own age, recognized in the Jew splendid capacities and powers, however, so far as he knew the race, misapplied and debased—was no less fascinated by a character of such singular force and ineradicable nationality. But "the general" would see only an atrocious monster, infamous for its greed, execrable for its spite. And such a figure, seen at such a time, could scarcely have promoted the cause of the outcasts of Israel.

XIX.

"WITH GOOD CAPON LINED."

(From the *Antiquary* for March, 1881.)

OFTEN as Jaques' caustic description of the "seven ages" of the drama of life has been quoted, there is a point in one passage in it that has not yet, I believe, been taken. The Justice, as everybody rememembers, is portrayed as

> "In fair round belly with good capon lined,
> With eyes severe and beard of formal cut,
> Full of wise saws and modern instances."

The uninstructed reader probably always misunderstands the word "modern;" and the meaning of "instances" is not so easy to be sure of. But it is not this line to which I now call attention; it is the first of the three quoted. There is an allusion that has been missed in the mention of the "capon," an allusion which adds to the bitterness of a sufficiently bitter life-sketch. It was the custom to present magistrates with presents, especially, it would seem, with capons, by way of securing their goodwill and favour. This fact heightens the satire of Jaques' portrait of an Elizabethan J.P. It gives force and meaning to what seems vague and general. Let us now prove and illustrate it.

Wither, describing the Christmas season, with its burning "blocks," its "pies," its bagpipes and tabors, and other revelries, goes on to sing how

> "Now poor men to the justices
> With capons make their errants;

> And if they hap to fail of these,
> They plague them with their warrants."

That is, the capon was a tribute fully expected and as good as exacted; it was "understood" it should be duly paid in.

> "But now they feed them with good cheer,
> And what they want they take in beer,
> For Christmas comes but once a year,
> And then they shall be merry."

That is, the justices acknowledge the tribute by treating "the poor men" to a good dinner and as much beer as they like. But the more important acknowledgment was yet to come.

Singer, in one of his excellent Shakespearian notes, cites a member of the House of Commons as saying, in 1601: "A Justice of Peace is a living creature that for half a dozen chickens will dispense with a dozen of penal statutes."

Other illustrations will be found in my friend the Rev. T. Lewis O. Davies' *Supplementary English Glossary*, published by Messrs. Bell and Sons, a work of great value to English students. "Samuel Ward," writes Mr. Davies in a letter I have his kind permission to use, "a Puritan Divine, in a sermon undated, but probably preached very early in the seventeenth century, speaks of judges that judge for reward, and say with shame 'Bring you,' such as the country calls 'capon justices.' He does not explain the term further, but I suppose corrupt magistrates were so called because they expected presents of capons and other farm produce from the rustics who came before them."

A further illustration of this morally dubious custom is to be found in Massinger's *A New Way to Pay Old Debts:* but in this case the offering exceeds the dimensions of a capon. Says Mr. Justice Greedy to Tapwell, the ale-house keeper :—

> "I remember thy wife brought me
> Last New Year's tide a couple of fat turkies."

and Tapwell answers:—

> "And shall do every Christmas, let your worship
> But stand my friend now.
>   *Greedy.* How? With Master Wellborn?
> I can do anything with him on such terms."

Then, turning to Wellborn, quoth the disinterested magistrate, aglow with pity for virtue in distress:—

> "See you this honest couple? They are good souls
> As ever drew fossit; have they not
> A pair of honest faces?
>   *Wellborn.* I o'erheard you,
> And the bribe he promised. You are
> . . . . cozen'd in them;
> For of all the scum that grew rich by my riots,
> This for a most unthankful knave, and this
> For a base bawd and whore, have worst deceiv'd me,
> And therefore speak not for them; by your place
> You are rather to do me justice; lend me your ear;
> Forget his turkies, and call in his license;
> And at the next fair I'll give you a yoke of oxen
> Worth all his poultry.
>   *Greedy* (*rapidly converted and forgetting his sympathy with
>   distressed virtue*). I am changed on a sudden
> In my opinion. Come near; nearer, rascal.
> And, now I view him better, did you e'er see
> One look so like an arch-knave? His very countenance
> Should an understanding judge but look on him
> Would hang him though he were innocent.
>   *Tapwell* and *Froth*, his wife (*astounded on this sudden reverse
>   inflicted by the consumer of their turkies*). Worshipful sir!
>   *Greedy* (*full of the righteous indignation inspired by the supe-
>   riority of two oxen to two turkies*). No, though the great
>   Turk came instead of turkies
> To beg my favour, I am inexorable."

In Overbury's *Book of Characters*, the Timist (*i.e.*, Timeserver), has his New-Year's gifts ready at Hallowmass.

How the ministers of justice—too often of injustice—were amenable to influence, whether personal or in the shape of fowls and such matters, is shown by Shakespeare himself in his famous picture of "Robert Shallow, Esquire, in the county of Gloster, justice of peace and *coram* . . . . and *custalorum*, and *ratolorum* too; and a gentleman born, who writes himself *armigero*—in any bill, warrant, quittance or obligation, *armigero*."—See 2 *Henry IV.*, v. 1.

"*Davy.* I beseech you, sir, to countenance William Visor of Wincot against Clement Perkes of the hill.

Shallow. There are many complaints, Davy, against that Visor: that Visor is an arrant knave, on my knowledge.

Davy. I grant your worship, that he is a knave, sir; but yet, God forbid, sir, but a knave should have some countenance at his friend's request. An honest man, sir, is able to speak for himself, when a knave is not. I have served your worship truly, sir, this eight years; and if I cannot once or twice in a quarter bear out a knave against an honest man, I have but a very little credit with your worship. The knave is mine honest friend, sir; therefore, I beseech your worship, let him be countenanced.

Shallow. Go to; I say, he shall have no wrong. Look about, Davy."

"This," notes Singer, "is no exaggerated picture of the course of justice in Shakespeare's time. Sir Nicholas Bacon [alas! that the name of his great son should be in any way mixed up with any of these or kindred abuses!] in a speech to Parliament, 1559, says: 'Is it not a monstrous disguising to have a justice a maintainer, acquitting some for gain, enditing others for malice, bearing with him as his servant, overthrowing the other as his enemy.'"

Latimer denounces this perilous practice of present-taking with characteristic courage and frankness. Referring to the words of Isaiah (i. 23)—"Thy princes are rebellious and companions of thieves; every one loveth gifts, and followeth after rewards; they judge not the fatherless, neither doth the cause of the widow come unto them"—he says: "*Omnes diligunt munera.* They all love bribes. [Observe how easily *munus*, a gift, passes on to mean a bribe.] Bribery is a princely kind of thieving. They will be waged by the rich either to give sentence against the poor or to put off the poor man's causes. This is the noble theft of princes and of magistrates. They are bribe-takers. Now-a-days they call them gentle rewards; let them leave their colouring and call them by their Christian name—bribes: *Omnes diligunt munera.* All the princes, all the judges, all the priests, all the rulers, are bribers. . . . . Woe worth these gifts; they subvert justice everywhere. *Sequuntur retributiones.* They follow bribes. Somewhat was given to them before, and they must needs give somewhat again; for Giff-gaffe was a good fellow; this Giff-gaffe led them clean from justice."

XX.

"CÆSAR DOTH BEAR ME HARD."

(From the Academy for June 30, 1877.)

"IT is remarkable," says Craik in his *English of Shakespeare*, p. 116, "that the expression *bear me hard*, meeting us so often in this one play (*Julius Cæsar*), should be found nowhere else in Shakespeare. Nor have the commentators been able to refer to an instance of its occurrence in any other writer." The instances in *Julius Cæsar* are these:—

"Cæsar *doth bear me hard*, but he loves Brutus."
(I. ii. 317.)

"Caius Ligarius *doth bear Cæsar hard*."
(II. i. 215.)

and

"I do beseech ye, if you *bear me hard*,
Now whilst your purpled hands do reek and smoke,
Fulfil your pleasure."
(III. i. 157.)

So all the Folios, except in the second instance, where the Second, Third, and Fourth read *hatred*. I have to thank a friend for informing me—and I suppose from Craik's remark the fact will be new to most people—that the phrase occurs also in Ben Jonson's *Catiline*, iv. 5, where Sempronia says in answer to Lentulus' praise of Cethegus:—

"Ay, though he *bear me hard*,
I yet must do him right; he is a spirit
Of the right Martian breed."

P.S. Another instance occurs in *The Life and Death of Thomas, Lord Cromwell*. Says Cromwell (Act iv. Sc. 2):—

"Good morrow to my lord of Winchester; I know
You bear me hard about the Abbey lands."

That the phrase was felt to be difficult seems to be shown by the substitution of "*hatred*" as mentioned above. And the phrase *to bear hatred* does occur in *Romeo and Juliet*, II. iii. 53; *to bear hate* several times in Shakespeare, as *Midsummer Night's Dream*, III. ii. 190; *Merchant of Venice*, IV. i. 61; *Titus Andronicus*, V. i. 3; so to *bear a grudge, Merchant of Venice*, I. iii. 48, and *to bear malice, Henry VIII.*, II. i. 62; compare *to bear good will, Two Gentlemen of Verona*, IV. iii. 15. But yet the interpretation is obvious enough. *To bear one hard* = hardly to bear, with difficulty to put up with, to find it no easy thing to tolerate, &c. And in this sense it is used once elsewhere by Shakespeare, with a thing, not a person, for the object. Thus in 1 *Henry IV.*, I. iii. 70, the Archbishop of York is spoken of as—

"Who *bears hard*
His brother's death at Bristol, the Lord Scroop."

Compare *Richard III.*, II. i. 56—

"If I unwittingly or in my rage
Have aught committed that *is hardly borne*
By any in this presence, I desire
To reconcile me to his friendly peace."

where the form *hardly* is specially to be noticed. Thus *to bear hard* is exactly the Greek χαλεπῶς φέρειν, a phrase seemingly used rather of things than persons; as in Plat. *Rep.* 330. A:—καὶ τοῖς δὴ μὴ πλουσίοις χαλεπῶς δὲ τὸ γῆρας φέρουσιν εὖ ἔχει ὁ αὐτὸς λόγος κ.τ.λ.; compare the Latin *graviter ferre*, which also, in classical Latin at least, does not seem to be used of persons. We still say, colloquially at least, "I can't bear him," in the sense of "I detest him;" "I can't 'stand' him." What the phrase we are considering meant was " I can scarcely bear him ; " " It is all I can do to tolerate him ; " or, to use an old verb, " I can scarcely abide him." Thus " Cæsar doth bear me hard," = Cæsar barely endures me, bitterly dislikes me.

Hard then = hardly, as the quotation from *Richard III.* shows. So "to run hard," &c. With this form of the adverb compare such phrases as " speak me *fair* in death," &c.

Dr. Johnson explains *bear* in the phrase before us as = " press," and alongside of it quotes from Addison : " These men *bear hard upon* the suspected party." But *bear upon* and *bear* cannot be bracketed in this way. *Bear upon* is quite a different phrase like χαλεπῶς φέρειν with ἐπὶ and a dative, and is still of extremely common occurrence. Nearer the Shakespearian phrase in sense is " bear with," where perhaps *bear* is used absolutely, be bearing or tolerant, *i.e.*, *patient* in dealing with.

The phrase in *Julius Cæsar*, I. ii. 35 :—

> " You *bear* too stubborn and too strange *a hand*
> Over your friend who loves you."

may perhaps be illustrated by *Lear*, III. i. 27 :—

> " The hard rein which both of them have borne
> Against the kind old king."

In the *Academy* for Dec. 29, 1883, Mr. A. H. Bullen quotes from Beaumont and Fletcher's *Scornful Lady*, iv. 2 :—

> " If he start well,
> Fear not, but cry ' St. George,' and *bear him hard*.
> When you perceive his wind grows hot and wanting,
> Let him a little down ; he's fleet, ne'er doubt him."

Here clearly *bear him hard* is an equestrian phrase, to be

illustrated, perhaps, by the last quotations made above, or to be explained by taking *bear* in the sense of "to hold up." In the *Academy* for Jan. 26, 1884, Mr. W. T. Lendrum aptly quotes an old rime :—

> " Up the hill spare me ;
> Down the hill *bear me ;*
> On the level spare me not."

(Another version of the last line is, I think :—

> " On the level never fear me.")

Of course it is possible the phrase that is the subject of this paper may be identical with this equestrian phrase. But this is far from certain. Undoubtedly there are two phrases *to bear hard :* (i.) the Latinistic phrase which appears beyond question in the quotation given above from 1 *Henry IV.*, I. iii. 70, and (ii.) the equestrian phrase which appears beyond question in the quotation just repeated from *The Scornful Lady*.

XXI.

A NEW VARIORUM EDITION OF SHAKESPEARE.[1]

(From the *Athenæum* for Oct. 20, 1877.)

TO his editions of *Romeo and Juliet* and *Macbeth*, Mr. Furness has now added one of *Hamlet*, in every way sustaining the high character which the preceding volumes of his series have won. The amount of work which these volumes represent almost defies calculation. Whole wildernesses have been traversed, dense forests penetrated, wide bogs and swamps struggled across. For Hamletian literature is now of quite portentous dimensions. *Scribimus indocti doctique.* Everybody believes he has something to say on the subject, and he must needs print it. He cannot be content to explain his views to his family, or disclose them to a few privileged friends. Criticism, like murder, will out; and so library shelves grow crowded with "essays," and "studies," and "lectures"; and chaos seems come again. What do we not owe to one who adventures to grapple with all this infinite host of commentators, who indefatigably encounters each of them, and takes something of him, if anything is found worth taking, and, finally, arranges his spoils for our use in two excellently printed and manageable octavos? It is not easy to overstate our debt, if such a service is executed vigorously and intelligently; and cer-

[1] *A New Variorum Edition of Shakespeare.* Edited by Horace Howard Furness. Vol. III.—*Hamlet.* 2 vols. (Lippincott and Co.)

tainly Mr. Furness's labours may be so described. His researches have extended far and wide, from elaborate volumes to *Notes and Queries*. Germany and France, no less than America and England, are well represented in his pages. In a word, he has produced a work that may fairly be termed encyclopædic.

The first volume contains the text, with various readings, and an abundant selection of notes. The second, which is called "Appendix," consists of some thirty-six pages discussing "the date and the text"; of copies of the 1603 4to., *The Hystorie of Hamblet, Fratricide Punished* (a translation of the old German play), and 250 pages of selected criticisms.

· That there are no faults both of omission and commission we will not undertake to say, or rather we will say it is impossible there should not be such faults. Such a compilation cannot be exhaustive; and, on the other hand, one may now and then wonder whether certain notes quite deserve the room they occupy. Such a suggestion, for example, as Keightley's with regard to "upspring," in a well-known line that has given rise to much controversy—"it is used," he says, "collectively for the risers from the table, a mode of expression not yet obsolete" (as if one should say "the rise" for *the risers*, or "the jump" for *the jumpers*)—is of so little value that we rather grudge it its place. But, on the whole, Mr. Furness has done his part with singular discretion as well as with comprehensive knowledge.

We congratulate Mr. Furness on having proceeded so far with his great undertaking, and wish him all success in his further progress. Our generation sorely needs its *Variorum*. The value of the old one is still considerable. Though it has in it much rubbish, it has, at the same time, much that is extremely useful and suggestive. But it is out of date. Though we would carefully eschew the vulgar error of underrating the services of the old annotators, yet we may fairly assert that many valuable lights have been thrown on the pages of Shakespeare since their time; and the fresh decipherings need a judicious collection. In another century Mr. Furness's work, too, may be superseded—superseded as the standard *Variorum* of the time; as an excellent compendium of Shakespearian knowledge and interpretation as they are in the Victorian age, it is never likely to be superseded.

But that it may soon require additions no one can know better than its editor; for, in the course of his work, he has been forced specially to observe how rapid nowadays is the growth of Shakespearian literature. Every week brings its contributions of more or less value; and it is certain that a more thorough familiarity with other Elizabethan literature will yield yet new aids to the understanding of passages that at present have a wrong interpretation given them, or, when editors speak frankly, no interpretation at all.

The fact is, the subject is simply inexhaustible. The study of Shakespeare is as the study of Nature herself, whose favourite son he was. And the best of Shakespeare-students, if we ask him, as Charmian asked the soothsayer, "Is't you, sir, that know things?" will reply, the more humbly and sincerely the better he is,—

> "In Nature's infinite book of secrecy
> A little I can read."

"A little I can read"—that is all that the truly competent scholar will dare to say.

Even with regard to such a trite subject as Hamlet's madness,—forty pages are devoted to it by Mr. Furness,—there is yet much more to be suggested and considered. It has often been asked what purpose that simulation serves. Certainly one good turn that it did Hamlet, which, we think, has not been sufficiently noticed, was this: it enabled him to break off all relations of civility with the uncle whose nature he detested—towards whom he was filled with a deep-rooted antipathy. To begin with, Hamlet can scarcely bring himself to show common politeness to King Claudius. He instinctively loathes him. What a welcome protection, then, he found in that "antic disposition" he "put on"—put on with so little effort, so overwrought was the sensibility of a keenly sensitive organism. As a madman, he secured for himself a freedom in what he said and did that was not otherwise to be obtained. He could close all communication with what he hated. He could deliver himself from a contact he abhorred. He could give vent to the bitter feelings that oppressed and choked him. And so with regard to Polonius. If the King vexed and irritated his fine-strung nature by his superlative hypocrisy, every word from his lying lips piercing Hamlet like a sting, so Polonius inflamed him with contemptuous anger by his impertinent self-sufficiency. Hamlet could find out nothing; here was a miserable sciolist who could find out everything:—

> "If circumstances lead me, I will find
> Where truth is hid, though it were hid indeed
> Within the centre."

Of this "tedious old fool" Hamlet is little less impatient than of that crowned and sceptred liar, his uncle. And in respect of him, too, his madness provides a safety-valve. He can speak his mind with impunity. He can let the fire that burns within blaze out in the faces of those who kindle it, and such liberty is an unspeakable relief to him. Without it he would be consumed by his wrath and scorn, his *sæva indignatio*—would perish "a cannibal of his own heart," in the midst of the folly and shame and sin that benetted him round.

(From the *Academy* for Dec. 1, 1877.)

THE old *Variorum* with all its faults is still an edition which no really well-appointed Shakespearian library can dispense with. If the homely old saw is quoted that "too many cooks spoil the broth," we may reply—for one proverb may generally have another pitted against it—"where no counsel is, the people fall; but in the multitude of counsellors there is safety." We need scarcely say, then, that a new *Variorum*, edited by one so competent as Mr. Furness, deserves a hearty welcome. Such is the mass of Shakespearian literature that has appeared since the days of Malone, and is annually appearing in growing abundance, that a sifter has become absolutely necessary. Perhaps in the economy of the future a paternal Government may see its way to nominate a public official for this service. Assuredly the labours of such a functionary would not be light. We picture him with his assistant clerks, each provided with a huge sieve, finding all he and they can do too little for the occasion, so rapidly does the heap of Shakespearian matter rise and spread. It is impossible to overestimate the amount of the rubbish that is contributed—and perhaps no age has contributed in this kind more largely than our own; but it must all be looked through on the chance of there being some minute fragment worth preserving—a chance often proved worthless. Of many a critic it must be said that he "speaks an infinite deal of nothing. . . . His reasons are as two grains of wheat hid in two bushels of chaff; you shall seek all day ere you find them; and when you have them they are not worth the search." The best thing would be if this outpouring of rubbish could be stopped: if a would-be Shakespearian author were compelled to come forward in the same guise as a would-be legislator in a certain Greek State—*i.e.*, with a halter round his neck so that he might be hanged incontinently if what he had to say was found of no value; but, as in the present state of modern feeling there is no hope of such vigorous measures—such masterly activity—and these gentlemen are in fact irrepressible, all that can be done is to get somebody to sift or weed for us. Even such a benefactor is the editor of the *New Variorum*.

The *Romeo and Juliet* volume appeared in 1873; the *Macbeth* shortly afterwards; and now we have *Hamlet* in two volumes, one containing the texts and various readings and notes, the other "an accurate reprint of the Quarto of 1603; a reprint of the *Hystorie of Hamblet*; a translation of *Der Bestrafte Brudermord*, together with æsthetic criticism from more than a hundred and twenty-five English, German and French authors."

As before, Mr. Furness has done his part excellently. "The public" may cordially accept the assurance of the publishers "that these volumes contain the essence of a whole library of Hamlet literature."

One omission we must lament—the omission of an index to the second volume. There is one to vol. i.; and vol. ii. has what is called "a table of contents." But this table is not full enough. Convenience of reference is of the utmost importance in such a compilation. We have no wish to "carp"; we are infinitely obliged and indebted to Mr. Furness for what he has done for us; but how welcome a good index to the second volume would have been!

Of course it is impossible that such a work should be exhaustive. Mr. Furness can only undertake to gather for us what seems most suggestive and useful; and, as we have said, he has discharged his part admirably. It is not, therefore, with any intention to accuse him of shortcomings that we mention one or two illustrations not to be found, we believe, in his volumes, which some at least of our readers may care to have pointed out to them.

Apropos of

> "Thrift, thrift, Horatio! the funeral baked meats
> Did coldly furnish forth the marriage tables."

might be noticed a speech of Quicksilver's in *Eastward Hoe* —a play to be specially studied by all who wish to observe and explore Shakespeare's influence on the contemporary drama. When Gertrude asks why her sister does not wait on her to her coach, "Marry, madam," replies Quicksilver, "she's married by this time to Prentice Goulding. Your father, and some one more, stole to church with them in all the haste, that the cold meat left at your wedding might serve to furnish their nuptial table." In his note to "His beard was white as snow," Mr. Furness, we see, quotes Steevens' remark that "this and several circumstances in the character of Ophelia seem to have been ridiculed in *Eastward Hoe*, by Jonson, Chapman, and Marston, 1605;" but Steevens's remark is scarcely extensive enough.

Act. ii. sc. 2. Here is a passage worth quoting from the *Insatiate Countess*:—"Sancta Maria!" cries the Count of Arsena when Roberts announces to him his immediate marriage,—

> "what thinkst thou of this change?
> A player's passion I'll believe hereafter,
> And in a tragic scene weep for Old Priam,
> When fell revenging Pirrhus with supposed

>   And artificial wounds mangles his breast,
>   And think it a more worthy act to me
>   Than trust a female mourning o'er her love."

I. ii. 114. See Chapman's *May-Day* (vol. ii. 373, ed. 1873) :—

> "Come, be not retrograde to our desire."

I. iv. 73. With this use of "deprive," compare *A Hundred Merry Tales*, ed. Oesterley, p. 102 :—"The seventh [commandment] to steal nor *deprive no man's goods* by theft, robbery, extortion, usury, nor deceit."

II. ii. 579. "The play's the thing," &c. See Heywood's *Apology for Actors*, page 57, of the Shakespeare Society's reprint, "Of a Strange Accident happening at a Play," how was awakened the conscience of a murderess at Lynn, "the then Earl of Sussex players acting the Old History of Fryer Francis, and presenting a woman who insatiately doting on a young gentleman, the more securely to enjoy his affection, mischievously and secretly murdered her husband, whose ghost haunted her." See also Massinger's *Roman Actor*, ii. 1 :—

>   "Sir, with your pardon,
>   I'll offer my advice : I once observed
>   In a tragedy of ours, in which a murder
>   Was acted to the life, a guilty hearer
>   Forced by the terror of a wounded conscience
>   To make discovery of that which torture
>   Could not wring from him. Nor can it appear
>   Like an impossibility but that
>   Your father," &c.

III. i. 65-8. Compare Massinger's *Maid of Honour*, ii. 4 :—

>   "How willingly, like Cato,
>   Could I tear out my bowels rather than
>   Look on the conqueror's insulting face;

> But that religion and the horrid dream
> To be suffer'd in the other world denies it."

There is good illustration of Hamlet's remarks on the hard drinking of the Danes and the bad name they have for it—how their "addition" is soiled with "swinish phrase"—in *Pierce Pennilesse*. Nash concludes a violent diatribe against them by declaring that they are "bursten-bellied sots that are to be confuted with nothing but tankards or quart pots. . . . . God so love me as I love the quick-witted Italians, and therefore love them more because they mortally detest this surly swinish generation." See also Lambarde's *Perambulation of Kent*, pp. 318-21, ed. 1826.

That image of the mole—to show how a single defect spoils everything—which Hamlet uses in the same speech, is found also in *Pandosto*—a fact that is worth noticing as perhaps one of the many signs of Shakespeare's familiarity with Greene's writings. "One mole," says Bellaria, "staineth the whole face; and what is once spotted with infamy can hardly be worn out with time."

We do not see that Mr. Furness has pointed out in Armin's *Nest of Ninnies*—on the same page of the "Shakespeare Society's reprint" with the phrase in "the top of question" (which we observe Staunton has noted)—the words, "There are, as Hamlet says, things called whips in store." Though Hamlet does not say so, yet perhaps the ascription of the saying to him may be taken as a mark of his popularity." The nearest approach to the words is in *2 Henry VI.*, II. i. 139, Gloucester *loq.*: "My masters of Saint Alban's, have you not beadles in your town, and things called whips?" Possibly the quotation may come from some earlier form of the play. See Mr. Halliwell-Phillipps's *Memoranda on Hamlet*.

XXII.

HAMLET'S AGE.

(From the *Academy* for March 11, 1876.)

THE following quotation from a well-known book is certainly noteworthy with regard to the question of Hamlet's age:—

"For fashion sake some (Danes) will put their children to schoole, but they set them not to it till they are fourteene years old; so that you shall see a great boy with a beard learne his A. B. C., and sit weeping under the rod when he is thirty years old."—NASH'S *Pierce Penniless's Supplication to the Devil*, ed. Collier, for the Shakespeare Society, p. 27.

So, after all, there is perhaps less inconsistency in the play than has been supposed. I do not mean that there is none.

"AN AERY OF CHILDREN, LITTLE EYASES."

(From the *Athenæum* for Sept. 14, 1878.)

I AM not aware that the following extract has ever been quoted to illustrate a well-known passage in *Hamlet*. It may have been so, for the industry and keenness of

Shakespearian commentators in search of quotations have been no less remarkable than the eager interest of Spartacus in the contents of Roman cellars, whose raids, as we gather from Horace, scarcely anywhere had a bottle been able to elude. However, if ever quoted, it is certainly not generally known. It occurs in neither Malone's nor Mr. Furness's *Variorum*; so I give it here—give it as quoted by Cunningham in his *Handbook of London*:—"He embraced one young gentleman and gave him many riotous instructions how to carry himself . . . . told him he must acquaint himself with many gallants of the Inns of Court, and keep rank with those that spend most. . . . His lodging must be about the Strand in any case, being remote from the handicraft scent of the City; his eating must be in some famous tavern, as the Horn, the Mitre, or the Mermaid; and then after dinner, he must venture beyond sea, that is in a choice pair of nobleman's oars to the Bankside, where he must sit out the breaking up (= the carving) of a comedy; or the first cut of a tragedy; or rather if his humours so serve him, to call in at the Blackfriars, where he should see a nest of boys able to ravish a man."—*Father Hubburd's Tales*, 4to. 1604.

1604 is the date of the first complete quarto of *Hamlet*; 1603 of the imperfect quarto; 1602 of the entry in the Registers of the Stationers' Company of "a book the *Revenge of Hamlet Prince of Denmark* as it lately was acted by the Lord Chamberlain his servants."

The "rather" and the last words exactly illustrate what Rosencrantz says of the extraordinary popularity of certain children-actors—how these are now the fashion. The phrase "a nest of boys" cannot but remind everybody of Shakespeare's " aery of children, little eyases." *Aire* is translated by Cotgrave, "An Airie or nest of hawkes."

The fact that the passage from "How comes it? Do

they grow rusty?" down to "Ay, that they do, my lord; Hercules and his load too" is not found in any of the quartos, does not of course in the least interfere with the value of this illustration.

"THAT CRY OUT ON TOP OF QUESTION."

(From the *Athenæum* for Jan. 8, 1881.)

IT is interesting to note that the great writer who has just gone from us was a native of the same part of the country as Shakespeare, and that her works no less than his illustrate the Midlands, and are to be illustrated from them; and further, that their works illustrate each other. They were both Warwickshire born—Shakespeare of a Warwickshire race, "George Eliot's" father a Staffordshire man. In the veins of both ran some Keltic blood, if, not relying on their literary styles, we may depend upon the names Arden and Evans. Much might be said of the relation of these two great authors to Middle-March, or Mercia, or the Midlands, and to each other. But I only propose now to mention a curious illustration of a certain phrase in *Hamlet* to be found—though never yet noticed, I think—in *Adam Bede.*

It is the phrase used by Rosencrantz of the boy-actors; they are described as "an aery of children, little eyases, that cry out on the top of question." About this "crying out on the top of question" there has been "much throwing about of brains." Some commentators have not understood "on the top of" and others have not understood "question." Not that no one has hit upon the right interpretation—that is the interpretation which I think it will be allowed is justified by the below quotation from Mr. Bartle Massey. Messrs. Clarke and Wright, in their excellent edition of *Hamlet*, say that the phrase "means probably to speak in a high key dominating conversation." Now let us hear the Hayslope schoolmaster, speaking of Martin Poyser's establishment. "There's too many women in the house for me," says the misogynist; "I hate the sound of women's voices; they are always either a-buzz or a-squeak—are always either a-buzz or a-squeak. Mrs. Poyser keeps at *the top o' the talk like a fife*," &c.

That "question" in Shakespeare's language means dialogue, conversation, talk, has been pointed out by Steevens, Elze, and others.

"ASSUME A VIRTUE IF YOU HAVE IT NOT."

(From the *Academy* for May 15, 1880.)

THE idea that Shakespeare teaches false morality in the well-known line—

"Assume a virtue if you have it not"—

arises entirely, not from any misunderstanding of the word *assume* (Mr. Aldis Wright has surely made its meaning plain enough if there could be any doubt about it), but *through cutting off the line from its context*. If it is not so dissociated, "assume" needs no new gloss, but has, and it must have, its ordinary sense. Shakespeare certainly does say, "Wear the guise of a virtue, even if you do not possess that virtue;" but the context explains the seemingly immoral mandate. The guise or habit is to be worn in the hope that it may assist the growth—the acquisition—of the virtue. Now such quoters of the line as so justly offend Mr. Spalding forget the context altogether—forget the worthy purpose for which the virtuous guise is to be worn; and, in fact, suggest that it is to be worn to deceive others—to make others believe that the wearer of it really possesses the virtue.

Once sever a line from its context, and strange things may be made of it. It was Archbishop Whateley, I think, who pointed out that, if we allowed ourselves the liberty of ignoring the surroundings of a phrase, we could discover in the New Testament such a sentiment as "Hang all the law and the prophets"!

XXIII.

KING LEAR.

(From the *Fortnightly Review* for January, 1875.)

THE plays of *King Lear, Cymbeline, Macbeth,* and *Hamlet* are all founded on what passed for historical fact in the sixteenth century, or was then only just beginning to be discredited; and yet it is quite right to rank them, not with the History Plays, but with the Tragedies. They are so ranked in the folio of 1623, which was, as is well known, edited by two of Shakespeare's fellow-actors; and the error made by certain commentators of the last century in putting *Macbeth* among the Histories has been generally corrected in recent editions. And the reason for this classification is, that in these plays the so-called historical facts do not govern the drama, but rather the drama the facts. It is not Shakespeare's purpose in them to attempt an accurate delineation of events, to portray in vivid colours and as faithfully as might be the details of a bygone age, to enable his audience to realize the past of their own or some other country. In these plays he gives himself a license in which he does not indulge in the Histories properly so called. In the Histories, indeed, he frequently departs from chronological order, and he amplifies or contracts the process of events as the case seems to demand; but he never flagrantly disobeys and neglects the authorities he followed—the current authorities of his day—as to the leading issues and results that are related by them. He does not take upon him to amend the decisions of time as so reported, but makes it his work to set them forth graphically and to interpret them with all the intelligence he can command. But in the four plays above mentioned, Shakespeare does not restrict himself in this way ; he readjusts, and alters, and adds as his art requires. The old stories are merely clay in his hands, which he reshapes and moulds with just the same freedom that he allowed himself in dealing with confessed fiction.

But yet it must not be forgotten that there is in these plays a historical element. We shall seriously misunderstand them, or at least fail to take up the right position for understanding them, if we do not recognize this. It is a fact that there were such persons as Cymbeline, Macbeth, and Hamlet; and it is a fact, whether *we* believe in King Lear's existence or not—and there is not the slightest evidence of it—that the Elizabethan age believed in it. What our latest historical inquiries have determined about him is not the question. The question is what Shakespeare's era thought about him. In every age there are hosts of beliefs in circulation which are of no intrinsic trustworthiness, and which a better instructed time will scatter to the winds; and yet a student would make a fatal mistake if he ignored them. Now King Lear was a reality to the ordinary Elizabethan. The narrative of his reign had a place in the ancient British history then commonly received, as it still has in the less critical of histories of Britain by Welshmen. It was first brought into general currency by that very dubious work, Geoffrey of Monmouth's *History of the Britons*, where in a veracious list of monarchs stretching from Brutus, the great-grandson of Æneas, down to Cadwallader, who died at Rome in 689 A.D., appears, tenth in order, King Lear, who, we are told, reigned sixty years somewhat before the times when the prophets Isaiah and Hosea flourished, and Rome was built upon the eleventh before the kalends of May by the two brothers

Romulus and Remus. So Lear was definitely located in the first half of the eighth century before Christ. Through the Middle Ages this dynasty of which he was a member was universally regarded as something substantial. Thus Sir John Fortescue, the eminent lawyer of the fifteenth century, remarks gravely in his work on the laws of England: "Concerning the different powers which kings claim over their subjects, I am firmly of opinion that it arises solely from the different nature of the original institutions. So the kingdom of Britain had its original from Brutus and the Trojans who attended him from Italy and Greece, and was a mixed government, compounded of the regal and democratic." And even so late as the reign of James I., Lord Chief Justice Coke declared that the original laws of this land were composed of such elements as Brutus first selected from the ancient Greek and Roman institutions. Holinshed, whom Shakespeare uses so extensively, is never troubled with a doubt as to these primeval potentates. Perhaps the first Englishman who dared to suspect them—an Englishman possessed of learning and a sagacity rarely surpassed—was Camden. In his *Reliquiæ Britannicæ*, published in 1604, he, to quote a contemporary, "blew away sixty British kings with one blast." Their majesties would not bear criticism; and when it dared to touch their royal persons, they grew paler and paler, thinner and thinner, mistier and mistier, till at last there was nothing of them tangible or visible. The day of historical science was dawning, and these imperial phantoms that had walked the earth in the night-time with so positive a tread and so commanding a presence faded and vanished, their sceptres melting into thin air, their crowns dissolving like glittering bubbles.

But I say that to appreciate duly this play of *King Lear* we must remember that the central figure of it was in Shakespeare's time commonly believed in as a veritable personage. For, though Shakespeare shows no minute observance of the traditional tale, yet he by no means totally ignores it. And so the plays of *Cymbeline*, *Macbeth*, and *Hamlet* have marks upon them of the various centuries to which their stories belong. Like their author, they are not of an age, but of all time; but yet they are not absolutely and recklessly severed from their age. *Cymbeline* is placed by Shakespeare in the century in which the old chronicles place him, and in both *Hamlet* and *Macbeth* there are features that associate these plays with the eleventh century, in which the historical Hamlet and the historical Macbeth did in fact live. Now let us notice what signs there are in *King Lear* of a far-away pre-Christian century, such as that eighth in which I have already said the Lear of the legends was supposed to have reigned.

The fact I wish particularly to point out is that Shakespeare has in this play purposely and deliberately conducted us into heathen times, and by this heathenizing acknowledged the chronology of the old traditions. Anachronisms no doubt there are, as when Regan speaks of Edgar as "my father's godson." Shakespeare is never over-careful about such matters. . Does not Hector, in *Troilus and Cressida*, quote Aristotle? Indeed, he sometimes trespasses in this way "of malice prepense"—as when he makes the Fool, in act iii. scene 2, utter a prophecy after the manner of Merlin :—

> "When priests are more in word than matter,
> When brewers mar their malt with water,
> When nobles are their tailors' tutors,
> No heretics burned but wenches' suitors,
> When every case in law is right,
> No squire in debt, nor no poor knight,
> When slanders do not live in tongues,

> Nor cutpurses come not to throngs;
> Then shall the realm of Albion
> Come to great confusion;
> Then comes the time, who lives to see't,
> That going shall be us'd with feet."

and then calmly add: "This prophecy Merlin shall make; for I live before his time." It is none the less true for these and similar slips, intentional or unintentional, that the atmosphere of *King Lear* is the atmosphere of heathendom. In this play the poet has, for a certain purpose, travelled back into the ages of darkness and barbarity. He has consciously quitted the light that surrounded with more or less splendour his own times, and passed into a land where the rays of civilization were only just beginning to glimmer, where the passions of men yet raged in all their violence, untamed and unshackled, and nature still reigned, wild, unredeemed, ferocious.

Amongst all Shakespeare's plays there is not one that resembles *King Lear* in this respect. The king himself, with his swiftly-kindled furies and his terrible fierce curses, seems at times scarcely human as Shakespeare for the most part drew humanity. Goneril, and Regan, and Edmund—what strange, savage figures are these, whose eyes burn with mere hate, and feet are swift to shed blood! "Then let them anatomize Regan—see what breeds about her heart. Is there any cause in nature that makes these hard hearts?" This Cornwall plucking out Gloster's eyes—

> "Out, vile jelly,
> Where is thy lustre now?"—

there is nothing nearly so frightful in all the Shakespearian theatre, or so little capable of defence so far as the perpetration of this crime on the stage is concerned. What crowding horrors, atrocities, ghastlinesses! One seems to be among "the dragons of the prime." It is true that there are beings in the play of a far different order. There is Kent, the true and faithful, whom the outrageous wrath of Lear cannot alienate; but even Kent is characterized by a certain impetuosity and vehemence; he returns wrath for wrath:—

> "Be Kent unmannerly
> When Lear is mad. What wilt thou do, old man?
> Think'st thou that duty shall have dread to speak
> When power to flattery bows? To plainness honour's bound,
> When majesty falls to folly. Reverse thy doom,
> And in thy best consideration check
> This hideous rashness.
>
>   *   *   *   *   *
>
> *Lear.* Now, by Apollo,—
> *Kent.*   Now, by Apollo, king,
> Thou swear'st thy gods in vain.
> *Lear.*   O, vassal! miscreant!
> *Alb. & Corn.* Dear sir, forbear.
> *Kent.* Do; kill thy physician, and the fee bestow
> Upon the foul disease. Revoke thy doom;
> Or, whilst I can vent clamour from my throat,
> I'll tell thee, thou dost evil."

And, when he encounters the steward, who is indeed his opposite, as base as he is noble, as faithless as he is trusty, as self-loving as he self-sacrificing, he cannot contain his passion, but breaks out into a very torrent of abuse. There is Cordelia, too, all truthfulness and piety, so that one may well marvel how she can be sister to Goneril and Regan. And may clearly understand Kent's perplexity when he cries out:—

> "It is the stars,
> The stars above us, govern our conditions;
> Else one self mate and mate could not beget
> Such different issues."

And there are Edgar and Albany, also, to counterweigh the deformities that constitute those other characters. But still it is true that such deformities abound in such a degree in no other Shakespearian play.

And for this reason much adverse criticism has been levelled at *King Lear* and its author. Inferences have been drawn from it highly unfavourable to the culture of the Elizabethan age. It has been forgotten how in other pieces Shakespeare has shown himself capable of depicting the highest possible refinement and the truest conceivable humanity, and remembered only that here he has painted monsters. Such criticism, like the greater part of the unfriendly criticism that prevailed mainly under French leadership during the last century, and yet lingers on in less informed quarters in our own day, is based on an imperfect conception of Shakespeare's purpose. It has not been seen that, as I have already said, it was his design in this play to depict an age unruly and turbulent, only now emerging from barbarism, in whose ears the still voice of conscience was scarcely yet audible, when Passion was yet lord of all, and the influences that broaden the division between men and brutes were as yet but faintly exercising their divine dominion.

If then we would appreciate this masterpiece of Shakespeare's art, we must turn our eyes back into that cruder and wilder world of which it is an image, and see in those remorseless, callous forms, in whose lineaments we cannot readily discern the emotions of humanity, the proper inhabitants of such a sphere.

Christianity is indeed conspicuous by its absence in the play. "It is the stars," cries out Kent, as we have already heard:—

"The stars above us govern our conditions."

Observe, too, Lear's heathen oaths :—

> "by the sacred radiance of the sun;
> The mysteries of Hecate, and the night;
> By all the operation of the orbs,
> From whom we do exist, and cease to be."

It is "the gods" he cites in another passage as "themselves throwing incense upon such sacrifices" as Cordelia and himself, when they have fallen in the hands of their enemies.

And not only are there such certain and designed indications of a far remote paganism in *King Lear*, but also—and this is a point I believe not hitherto perceived—Shakespeare is not unmindful of the race to which his story belonged. Shakespeare had a keen sense of national character. This appears in several of his plays: eminently in the *Merchant of Venice*, where he paints his immortal portrait of the Jew: in *Romeo and Juliet*, where he depicts the swiftly susceptible temperament of Italy: in *Othello*, where the hot blood of North Africa glows in the veins of his hero. To this list I propose to add *King Lear* as a strikingly faithful picture of the Celtic race.

If it is asked, where he had studied this race, the answer is, not so much through books as through direct observation. It was not Shakspere's way to look at nature through spectacles, or any such instruments, if he could help it. He looked at her face to face; dared, not irreverently, but yet steadily, to gaze into her very eyes, and listen for himself to the beatings of her heart. And this is why his works are so inestimable; they are not mere copies of copies, but taken directly from the original. Nature herself visited the studio of this artist, and sat serene and patient while his pencil traced her imperishable features. So, wishing to portray Celts, Shakspere gave his attention, not to printed descriptions, but the living and breathing specimens of the race as they were to be seen and known in Great Britain. In the older play the king of Cambria is specially addressed as "Welshman." It was as well known in the sixteenth century as now that the Welshmen were the direct descendants of the Ancient Britons. Therefore, if anywhere, the posterity of King Lear was to be found (in the original story his family is not extinguished as in Shakespeare's version, but perpetuated through the children of Goneril and Regan), it was to be found amongst the Welsh. Some years before he wrote *King Lear* Shakespeare had studied and portrayed the Welshman. In his *Henry V.*, written in 1599, he has brought together representatives of the various components of our nation. There is Macmorris the Irishman, Jamy the Scotchman, besides of course Englishmen of different grades and various characters; and there is Fluellen, the brave, high-spirited, quick-blooded, fantastic Welshman, full of natural pride, and a determined avenger of all insults offered to " the leek."

"I do know Fluellen valiant,
And touched with choler, hot as gunpowder,
And quickly will return an injury."

King Lear takes us into the midst of such a race—a race highly inflammable, headstrong, flushed with sudden angers, and breaking out into wild violences, but also, in its better children at least, of a deep tenderness and sincerity; in short, a highly emotional race, quickly stirred to good and to evil; swift to love, swift to hate; blessing and cursing with the same breath; with eyes, now full of a gentle solicitude and regard, now flashing into an intolerant frenzy of detestation; a blind hysterical race, if not wisely counselled and judiciously led; but under good auspices springing forward, with a splendid vivacity, to the highest prizes of glory and honour. This is a perilous temperament, and there is no prophet who shall say what its career shall be—whether it will reconcile itself to the bonds and the bars of existence, or dash itself to pieces in a fierce revolt. It is perhaps true that there is no middle path for it; it must either triumph or perish. Look now at the characters in our play. Is not the king himself the very type of his race? The Teutonic mind can scarcely follow the rapid revolutions of his fiery spirit. Here we see an intensely sensitive nature, that yearns for love, and even for the mere profession of it, suddenly flaming out into an outrageous wrath, and banning and banishing the dearest and truest treasures of his life. Look at Kent, as we have already seen him, no less swiftly convulsed and frenzied than the master, whom, for all his wildness, he serves to the very death. Look at Cornwall:—

> "You know the fiery quality of the duke,
> How unremovable and fix'd he is
> In his own course."

and note Lear's frantic reply:—

> "Vengeance! plague! death! confusion!
> Fiery? what quality?"

And Cordelia—is she too not a true daughter of her father of her race? Is not the Celtic impulsiveness her characteristic? Why will "our joy, although the last, not *it*," not respond when the old man asks her for some expression of her love? Was it well that she should harden self against that yearning cry? Ah! she was a child of race, and the indignation that was kindled in her fine l by the falsehoods of her sisters overcame every other ling; and not to draw

> "A third more opulent than her sisters,"

t, not to pleasure that father for whom she was ready, as

she proved, to give up everything that she might cherish him, would she then make a single overture of affection!

Thus in *King Lear* we pass into a remote pre-Christian age, and into the midst of another race than our own; and so the play has a certain historical and a certain ethnological interest. But it has another interest far transcending these —a great human interest; and it is on this only we will now fix our thoughts. Seen in a certain light, the distinctions of ages and of races are merely trivial. "A touch of nature makes the whole world kin;" or, as the Latin poet expresses it, "I am a man, and nothing that is human do I deem alien." And the reason why, to the end of time, men will stand and gaze, all rapt and absorbed, on this picture, is because it represents human life, not any special time or people. The picture is individual, but it is also typical; it is of men, but it is also of mankind; it is of an age, but it is also of all time.

King Lear deals especially with the natural man as opposed to the artificial man. When the King saw Edgar, then a Tom o' Bedlam, in the great storm scene, he exclaims—

"Is man no more than this? Consider him well. Thou owest the worm no silk, the beast no hide, the sheep no wool, the cat no perfumers. Ha! here's three on 's [himself, the Fool, Kent] are sophisticated: Thou art the thing itself: unaccommodated man is no more but s in a poor, bare, forked animal as thou art. Off, off, you lendings! Co and unbutton here."

in

And he tears his clothes off him. And this bare-stripping figure, in that awful scene, may serve as an image of of society the play represents. It is a society with all its dec guises torn off. The passions walk abroad, bold and confideing Greed lifts up its head unabashed; Lust scorns all holy ti of Wrath rages like a tempest. A fearful earth, indeed, if givn over to such accursed powers! But it is not so. There is also the passion of Love, and throughout the play love is performing its secret ministry. Good and evil close in a fierce struggle, as always where there is life, and not mere death; and in the end good prevails, as in the end it must prevail: for evil has not only good to encounter, but it has to fight with itself: it is essentially self-consuming. So that in this play we have presented to us humanity in its purest and simplest elements—humanity unsophisticated, denuded of all its "lendings," with its natural impulses all unchecked and potent.

Now, in the space at our disposal, it is impossible to attempt to examine in detail a work of such multiform interest as this play. It might be well worth our while to observe Goneril and Regan, and see how like and how different they are; how in both there reigns a certain shameless effrontery of selfishness, while in the elder sister there is an originality of crime with which the other is not endowed; so that while in the matter of morality there is little to choose between them, in intellectual activity Goneril has the advantage, or disadvantage.

Or we might attend to the striking contrast developed between the Steward and Kent—a contrast already mentioned; how the one is the very image of the time-server, the other of the truth-server; how the one lends himself to all vile uses, the other maintains his integrity at any cost, and finds it banishment, and not freedom, to be where loud lies prevail over modest sincerity; how the one lives and moves only for himself, the other only for others.

Or the Fool might attract us with his strange, keen sense of his master's folly in his abdication—a sense quickened by the tender love he bears him and the daughter that resembles him,—the Fool who, "since my young lady's going into France, hath much pined away," and whose heart breaks amidst the fell distresses that presently fall upon the house,—tenderest of jesters!

Or we might follow the course of the Earl of Gloucester, from the ominous carelessness of his first appearance, to the time when the clouds, which indeed his own act has formed, gather and burst upon his miserable head; how his whole being is astonished and amazed, and he thinks himself the mere victim of a malignant or a reckless Heaven—

> "As flies to wanton boys, are we to gods;
> They kill us for their sport."

and he is eager to reach that cliff,

> "whose high and bending head
> Looks fearfully in the confined deep:"

but at last learns submission,—

> "Henceforth I'll bear
> Affliction, till it do cry out itself,
> 'Enough, enough,' and die."

for indeed, however imperfectly he recognizes the lesson,

> "*The gods are just, and of our pleasant vices
> Make instruments to plague us.*"

Or we might watch the true and sound nature of Albany; how it severs itself from that of Goneril, with a divine discordance—not quick to suspect evil or to condemn, but inflexible towards it when once unveiled and patent—

> "O Goneril!
> You are not worth the dust which the rude wind
> Blows in your face. I fear your disposition:
> That nature, which contemns its origin,
> Cannot be border'd certain in itself;
> She, that herself will sliver and disbranch

From her material sap, perforce must wither
And come to deadly use.
  Gon. No more : the text is foolish.
  Alb. Wisdom and goodness to the vile seem vile :
Filths savour but themselves. What have you done?
Tigers, not daughters, what have you perform'd?
A father, and a gracious aged man,
Whose reverence even the head-lugg'd bear would lick,
Most barbarous, most degenerate ! have you madded.
Could my good brother suffer you to do it ?
A man, a prince, by him so benefited ?
If that the heavens do not their visible spirits
Send quickly down to tame these vile offences,
It will come ;
Humanity must perforce prey on itself,
Like monsters of the deep."

Or the two brothers, Edmund and Edgar, the false and the true, might well occupy us : Edmund, whose very spirit is stained by the stain of his birth, and mutinies against " the plague of custom " that so brands him, and, recklessly mutinying, discerns nothing binding or holy in the ties of brotherhood or sonship or marriage.

  " Thou, Nature, art my goddess; to thy law
  My services are bound."

Edgar, the good angel of his house, with his bright, keen, ready intellect, but yet brighter soul; whose own sufferings but yield him opportunities to minister to others, and, himself in desperate fortunes, to lead them on to hope and peace,
  " Ever bearing free and patient thoughts."

Perhaps, if we so stand and muse, we should presently notice that this play deals specially with domestic and social relations, and shows how all order, indeed all civilization, rests and reposes upon them ; how the rending of the bonds that bind child to parent, and child to child, involve the rupture and ruin of the whole human fabric. "It is not good to live alone;" nay, it is not possible. We cannot isolate ourselves, if we would. We cannot repeal the ordinances of our birth. We cannot re-adjust the ties of blood and of kindred. *King Lear* is a magnificent exhibition of what the Latins call "piety"—of the affection to which we are bound by duty, as distinguished from the affection which springs from taste and selection. Virgil's "pious Æneas" is a less effective figure than Shakespeare's pious Edgar or the pious Cordelia. And, for impiety, what portraits have ever been drawn to compare with Edmund, Goneril, and Regan?

From such a multitude of interests I propose now to select only two. Let us look only at the King himself, and at Cordelia. What means this strange, hoary-headed figure, wildly rushing into the storm, appealing madly to the cloud-coped heavens—

> "Contending with the fretful element:
> Bids the wind blow the earth into the sea,
> Or swell the curled waters 'bove the main,
> That things might change or cease: tears his white hair;
> Which the impetuous blasts, with eyeless rage,
> Catch in their fury, and make nothing of;
> Strives in his little world of man to outscorn
> The to-and-fro-conflicting wind and rain.
> This night, wherein the cub-drawn bear would couch,
> The lion and the belly-pinched wolf
> Keep their fur dry, unbonneted he runs,
> And bids what will take all.
>   *Kent.* But who is with him?
>   *Gent.* None but the fool; who labours to outjest
> His heart-struck injuries."

And Cordelia, why must she die? Is it not anguishing that it is so? Does not one feel as if one would give years of one's own life, if one might, to retain her, when "Enter

Lear, with Cordelia dead in his arms"? "Cordelia, Cordelia, stay a little". Whence is sped the arrow that strikes down that lovely presence? Is it from the quiver of a just and law-abiding heaven? or are we indeed the mere game of wanton gods, and the earth but a hunting-ground for their high majesties, when they care to leave their nectar for a season, and exercise their celestial limbs in the chase?

To understand the terrific sufferings of King Lear, we must closely examine him as he is when we first see him. He is a man of keen affectionateness, and a nature that wins affection, but of a nature altogether uncurbed and headstrong. He is an absolute king, a very sultan, whose will, whose whim, has been and is his law. The amiable Goneril and Regan describe him as he has been only too accurately :—

> "*Gon.* You see how full of changes his age is; the observation we have made of it hath not been little : he always loved our sister most; and with what poor judgement he hath now cast her off, appears too grossly.
> *Reg.* 'Tis the infirmity of his age: *yet he hath ever but slenderly known himself.*
> *Gon. The best and soundest of his time hath been but rash ;* then must we look to receive from his age not alone the imperfections of long-engraff'd condition; but, therewithal, the unruly waywardness that infirm and choleric years bring with them."

An indulgent, kindly, impetuous, obstinate man, with whom life has flowed smoothly, simply because no firm, irremovable obstruction ever made it whirl and foam. Lear has had his own way, and his way has not been all selfish and evil. "When he did stare, see how the subject quaked." Thwartings and crossings have not formed part of his experience. And now we see him,

> "Fourscore and upward, not an hour more or less,"

laying Thin almightily a programme for his closing years.

S

> "Meantime we shall express our darker purpose.
> Give me the map there.—Know, that we have divided
> In three our kingdom : and 'tis our fast intent
> To shake all cares and business from our age ;
> Conferring them on younger strengths, while we
> Unburden'd crawl toward death."

What an irony is here! Read these words in the light of what was to come! The test he proceeds to make of the affections of his daughters must be pronounced foolish enough. Goethe, indeed, called this opening scene "absurd ;" but it is scarcely so, if we remember what Lear's experience had been. His unhappy position as autocrat had prevented his ever learning the worthlessness of mere words, or realizing the abysses that may separate words from deeds. He listens with a foolish satisfaction and a fatal credulity to the "large speeches" of his elder daughters. And now at last, in the very hour of his calm, when there are to be no more troubles, and he has said to his soul, "Soul! take thine ease," even now begins for him a new and terrible time.

The instant that he encounters a check, and this queer caprice of his is challenged and denied, all the wildness of his nature shows itself; for, indeed, for all his long life, he is yet wild and untutored and untamed—the exact reverse of what Edgar, in one of his various shifts, describes himself to be—

> "A most poor man, made tame to fortune's blows,
> Who by the art of known and feeling sorrows
> Am pregnant to good pity."

That instant, when his whim is traversed, he flames out into a demoniac fury, and hurls his curse at his "joy."

It is not, nor it cannot come to, good. What*e* y'deous rashness," to use Kent's words. He tells us him¹ "F*r*

> "I lov'd her most, and thought to set my rest
> On her kind nursery."

"He has always loved our sister most," says Goneril. Yet he shrieks out :

> "Hence, and avoid my sight!
> So be my grave my peace, as here I give
> Her father's heart from her."

What of the long years of affection and love that they had lived together? Can these be uprooted like weeds, and flung away to the winds? Is man omnipotent over his past, and can he tear all its traditions in pieces? When Lear fulminates against Cordelia, it is no less on himself that the thunderbolts fall. From this time he is a maimed and broken man. The best influence of his life is turned out of his doors. Who can say how much his excitable nature had already owed to the better-controlled temperament of Cordelia? When Kent interferes, he rages only the more vehemently,—

> "Come not between the dragon and his wrath ;"

and at last, in his fury, banishes him :—

> "Hear me, recreant!
> On thine allegiance, hear me!
> Since thou hast sought to make us break our vow,
> (Which we durst never yet,) and with strained pride
> To come between our sentence and our power
> (Which nor our nature nor our place can bear,)
> Our potency made good, take thy reward :
> Five days we do allot thee, for provision
> To shield thee from diseases of the world ;
> And on the sixth to turn thy hated back
> Upon our kingdom : if, on the tenth day following,
> Thy banish'd trunk be found in our dominions,
> The moment is thy death. Away! by Jupiter,
> This shall not be revoked."

From this ferocity nothing can be hoped. We are prepared for all that follows. After this paroxysm against the darling of his heart, the next wild outburst against Goneril surprises us not at all. Here we know there has been some serious provocation; yet here, too, what frightful intemperance and excess. If the voice of a better nature had not ceased appealing to Goneril, would not this loud curse have hushed and scared it away for ever? Well may Albany exclaim,

"Now gods that we adore, whereof comes this?"

This wild father finds himself all of a sudden in the midst of a world of hate and scorn. Already had Cordelia's "fault," he says,
"like an engine, wrench'd my frame of nature
From the fixed place."

Regan supports Goneril, and there seems no longer firm ground under his feet. His brain reels under the pressure of such huge reverses, and the storm that now breaks out in the physical world is less terrible than that which rages in his soul.

Perhaps there is nothing in all literature to equal the scene upon the heath that presently follows, as the old King stands exposed to all the whirling fury of the winds and the rains, and, what is more dreadful far, with all his faith in humanity convulsed and uprooted. He seems the victim of a dreadful league between the powers of nature and yet more remorseless man.

"I tax not you, you elements, with unkindness;
I never gave you kingdom, call'd you children;
You owe me no subscription : then let fall
Your horrible pleasure ; here I stand, your slave,
A poor, infirm, weak, and despised old man :—
But yet I call you servile ministers,
That will with two pernicious daughters join'd

> Your high engender'd battles, 'gainst a head
> So old and white as this. O! O! 'tis foul!"

The very earth quakes under his feet, and truth and honour seem buried in the gulfs that suddenly yawn around. When and where shall he find comfort? Virtue is no longer a reality, but a merely simulated thing. A darkness worse than that of the unstarred night falls upon his spirit, so that the mere material inclemencies that assail him are hardly perceived.

> "Thou think'st 'tis much that this contentious storm
> Invades us to the skin: so 'tis to thee:
> But where the greater malady is fix'd,
> The lesser is scarce felt. Thou 'ldst shun a bear;
> But if thy flight lay toward the raging sea,
> Thou 'ldst meet the bear i' the mouth. When the mind's free,
> The body's delicate: the tempest in my mind
> Doth from my senses take all feeling else,
> Save what beats there."

Slight indeed his bodily ailments by the side of the anguish of his mind—the sharper than serpent's teeth that gnaw and tear his inmost heart.

> "Oh! that torment should not be confined
> To the body's wounds and sores,
> With maladies innumerable
> In heart, head, breast, and reins;
> But must secret passage find
> To the inmost mind;
> Then exercise all his fierce accidents,
> And on her purest spirits prey,
> As on entrails, joints, and limbs,
> With answerable pains, but more intense,
> Though void of corporal sense." (*Samson Agon.*)

His self-command gradually deserts him. Patience has never been one of his virtues, and patience is not a virtue that can be extemporized. And it is in vain that he cries out, "No, I will be the pattern of all patience; I will say nothing:" it cannot be. The long years will bear their proper fruit.

It is a very relief, exquisitely piteous though the sight is, when he becomes unconscious of his infinite wrongs, and, amid the phantasies of delirium, wears once more his crown and administers justice upon a world of hypocrites. You may see, if you listen to his speeches—speeches that are not all wild and wandering,—

> "Or matter and impertinency mix'd!
> Reason in madness!"—

how there are reflected upon the broken fragments of his mind his own bitter experiences.

But do not for a moment fancy that these awful sufferings, to which this old man is subjected, are mere idle visitations, or that Shakespeare represents them to us merely to display his mastery of his art; for, indeed, madness has never been represented in art with at all comparable skill. Shakespeare was too human-hearted so to trifle with us. Can we think he would not have altered this "side-piercing sight," if the facts of life would have let him? Can we think his own most gentle heart did not yearn towards this so piteous old king—

> "that noble and most sovereign reason,
> Like sweet bells jangled, out of tune, and harsh"?

 But he would have us remember that the sufferings of King Lear were partly at least the result of his own wild and cruel impulsiveness. Lear had lived long, but he had not learned wisdom. The great school of the world never breaks up. Lear, in his old age, was yet low in the great world-school, and had yet to master a quite elementary lesson. He was slow at it, as might be expected; but it had to be learned. Amidst storm and tempest and agonies, he learned it.

He learned to know himself, how frail and feeble he was, how narrow all his prerogatives; and that the glozings, that in old days had charmed and enervated his soul, were born of falsehood, and not of truth.

"They flattered me like a dog; and told me, I had the white hairs in my beard, ere the black ones were there. To say 'ay,' and 'no,' to everything I said!—'*Ay' and 'no' too was no good divinity.* When the rain came to wet me once, and the wind to make me chatter; when the thunder would not peace at my bidding; there I found 'em, there I smelt 'em out. Go to, they are not men o' their words: they told me I was everything: 'tis a lie; I am not ague-proof."

And so he learned to mistrust all mere appearances.

"A man may see how this world goes with no eyes. Look with thine ears: see how yond justice rails upon yond simple thief. Hark, in thine ear: Change places; and, handy-dandy, which is the justice, which is the thief?"

He learned, too, sympathy with his poorer fellows.

"Poor naked wretches, wheresoe'er you are,
That bide the pelting of this pitiless storm,
How shall your houseless heads and unfed sides,
Your loop'd and window'd raggedness, defend you
From seasons such as these? O, I have ta'en
Too little care of this! Take physic, pomp;
Expose thyself to feel what wretches feel;
That thou may'st shake the superflux to them,
And show the heavens more just."

Lear is a changed man when he awakes out of that healing sleep in Cordelia's tent.

"In him the savage virtue of his race,
Revenge, and all ferocious thoughts were dead,"

as he sees that sweet ministering spirit standing by. Ah!

think when he had last seen her! He cannot believe but that she is of another world, or that such tenderness is not for him.

> "Pray, do not mock me:
> I am a very foolish, fond old man,
> Fourscore and upward, not an hour more nor less;
> And, to deal plainly,
> I fear, I am not in my perfect mind.
>
> * * * * *
>
> "You must bear with me:
> Pray you now, forget and forgive: I am old and foolish."

The old rage had passed away, and now only the love of a loving and lovable nature—only his better part—survives. Blessed with his restored darling, he wants nothing more.

> "Come, let's away to prison:
> We two alone will sing like birds i' the cage:
> When thou dost ask me blessing, I'll kneel down,
> And ask of thee forgiveness. So we 'll live.
> And pray, and sing, and tell old tales, and laugh
> At gilded butterflies, and hear poor rogues
> Talk of court news; and we 'll talk with them too,—
> Who loses, and who wins; who's in, who's out," &c.

He is now ripe for death; and when that new blow falls, and his Cordelia is taken from him, he dies quietly and at once. In fact, her death is not so much a fresh misfortune for him, as the signal for his release. The gate of the unseen is not yet closed upon her, when it re-opens for him; and so his weary and heavy-laden spirit finds rest at last.

> "Vex not his ghost: oh, let him pass! he hates him
> That would upon the rack of this tough world
> Stretch him out longer."

It remains that I try to say something of Cordelia, though I do not forget Schlegel's words, "Of Cordelia's heavenly beauty of soul I do not dare to speak."

She tells us of herself, and you may accept every word her true lips utter, that

> "what I well intend,
> I 'll do 't before I speak."

Her whole nature shrinks from loud avowals and protestations. She loves to be, not to seem. When Goneril's tongue overflows with fine phrases of filial affection, her very soul recoils.

> "*What shall Cordelia do? Love, and be silent.*"

When Regan rivals her elder sister in professions, she whispers to herself:

> "Then poor Cordelia!
> And yet not so; since, I am sure, my love 's
> More richer than my tongue."

When at last her turn comes in this strange *vivâ voce* examination, all her truthful instincts are aroused, and it seems to her it would be treason to add her voice to the lying chorus. Also the question is put to her in a way dreadfully offensive to her disinterested spirit:

> "What can you say, to draw
> A third more opulent than your sisters? Speak."

Is love to be traded in so? Are the treasures of the soul to be bought and sold? She will not say a word! Perhaps, one might say she *cannot* say a word. It is true that she "cannot heave her heart into her mouth." Still less does she care to "mend her speech a little, lest it should mar her fortunes." Blame her, if you please, and tell us what a perfect person would have done. What you say may be all very true, but the world is not populated by perfect persons, and Shakespeare does not make it his business to draw perfect persons. And you must take her as she is. She will have to suffer for this waywardness, perhaps. Let us only think for the present of the impulses of truth that govern her being. The poor king, when he curses her, does indeed bless her—

"*Thy truth, then, be thy dower.*"

It is so: this is the divine "settlement" nature has made for her! Truth is indeed her jointure. And so the King of France is right when he declares "she is herself a dowry." Who does not applaud and envy his high choice?—

> "Fairest Cordelia, that art most rich, being poor;
> Most choice, forsaken; and most loved, despised!
> Thee and thy virtues here I seize upon:
> Be it lawful, I take up what's cast away.
> Gods, gods! 'tis strange, that from their cold'st neglect
> My love should kindle to inflamed respect.
> Thy dowerless daughter, king, thrown to my chance,
> Is queen of us, of ours, and our fair France:
> Not all the dukes of waterish Burgundy
> Can buy this unprized precious maid of me.—
> Bid them farewell, Cordelia, though unkind:
> Thou losest here, a better where to find."

We see nothing more of this fair, true woman till towards the end of the piece, when she lands with forces to avenge her father's wrongs. But Shakespeare has contrived to keep her perpetually before our mind's eye. She is present, though absent, like

> "That silver sphere,
> Whose intense lamp narrows
> In the white dawn clear,
> Until we hardly see—we *feel* that it is there."

The Fool, as we have heard already, pines much for "my young lady," and we find that, though dismissed with such outrageous resentment by her father, her first thought has been for him. She has kept herself in communication with the court, that if ever she is wanted to *do*, not to *say*, anything for him, she may be at once informed. She stands watching the poor old man's fortunes, like some sweet, wistful-eyed angel with wings ready to be spread on a mission of mercy. Kent, in the stocks before Gloucester's castle, draws forth a letter to read from her.

> "I know, 'tis from Cordelia;
> Who hath most fortunately been inform'd
> Of my obscured course; and shall find time
> From this enormous state,—seeking to give
> Losses their remedies."

Presently he sends to her for the news of how things are going, and in a later scene we hear how she received it.

> "*Kent.* Did your letters pierce the queen to any demonstration
>   of grief?
> *Gent.* Ay, sir; she took them, read them in my presence;
> And now and then an ample tear trill'd down
> Her delicate cheek : it seem'd, she was a queen
> Over her passion; who, most rebel-like,
> Sought to be king o'er her.
>   *Kent.*   O, then it moved her?
>   *Gent.* Not to a rage : patience and sorrow strove
> Who should express her goodliest. You have seen
> Sunshine and rain at once : her smiles and tears
> Were like a better way: those happy smilets,
> That play'd on her ripe lip, seem'd not to know
> What guests were in her eyes; which parted thence,
> As pearls from diamonds dropp'd.—In brief,
> Sorrow would be a rarity most beloved,
> If all could so become it.
>   *Kent.*   Made she no verbal question?
>   *Gent.* 'Faith, once, or twice, she heaved the name of 'father'
> Pantingly forth, as if it press'd her heart;
> Cried, 'Sisters! sisters! Shame of ladies! sisters!
> Kent! father! sisters! What? i' the storm? i' the night?
> Let pity not be believed!'—There she shook
> The holy water from her heavenly eyes,
> And clamour moisten'd :—then away she started,
> To deal with grief alone."

At last we are permitted to see her again, all eager to find the poor King, "as mad as the vex'd sea," and nurse him with her own sweet tendance. She is pure devotion, earnest in thanking others for their services, but never dreaming of any thanks for her own or conscious of any merit in them.

> "O thou good Kent, how shall I live, and work,
> To match thy goodness? My life will be too short,
> And every measure fail me."

While her father sleeps, she stands by praying:

> "O you kind gods,
> Cure this great breach in his abused nature!
> The untuned and jarring senses, oh, wind up,
> Of this child-changed father!"

And presently, to the playing of music, the old man awakes himself and sobered, as we have seen, and father and daughter are once more happy in each other's arms.

And now why must she die? I have said Shakespeare was no arbitrary homicide. Was it not possible, then, that Cordelia should live? In the first place, it must be noted that Cordelia lands in England at the head of a French army, and the national sentiment, strong always—boisterously strong in the Elizabethan age—demanded that the enterprise should therefore fail. Albany, for instance, was on Lear's side, and would not have opposed any means of avenging him, compatible with his patriotism. But he could not let foreign troops overrun the dear free soil of this island.

> "Where I could not be honest,
> I never yet was valiant; for this business,
> It touches us as France invades the land
> Not bolds the king, with others, whom, I fear,
> Most just and heavy causes make oppose."

But quite apart from this national reason, there are two others of deep ethical moment that may explain the awful catastrophe. One is this: her own nature betrays her. Is she not, as we have seen, the child of impulse? Was it not so in her first appearance, and is it not so in her last? And can such natures thrive in our air? Does not the sword ever overhang them? And in times of violence, like that pictured by Shakespeare in *King Lear*, will it not fall? She cannot take care of herself in this world. She is all for truth, as we first see her. Home and wealth, and even her father's smile, are nothing to her by the side of that sumless treasure. Later on in her pure life, she is all for love; she thinks of nothing else but relieving her father; she gives not a thought to her own safety and protection in an enemy's country. Now, here on this earth it goes hard with such natures. They belong to a different sphere; they cannot conform to our habits of self-consideration and prudence. These are the martyrs of this world, and in their hands are palms.

"Upon such sacrifices
The gods themselves throw incense."

Lastly, when evil powers are let loose, mischief and ruin will ensue not only on those who have unchained them, but on the innocent who fall within their baleful reach. They are like the winds in that bag Æolos gave Odysseus in the old story. Once let them fly out and rave, and who shall count the shipwrecks that shall strew the shores? The foolish sailors, who did the deed, may cry and moan with a real repentance; but the waves will soon smother their wretched shrieks, and the blasts but howl a dirge for them. Can we think that Goneril and Regan could have power placed in their hands, and no harm come of it except to the unwise donor? Does not the rain fall on the just and the unjust? Yes; and so does the rain of ruin, in the hour and power of evil. The whirlwind, when once it rages, does not pick and choose its victims. Goneril's spite will not spare

Cordelia, when once it has a chance of venting itself upon her; the chance comes, and it does not spare her. Let Lear bemoan his folly as he may, yet, alas! alas! he cannot cancel it. By all means let the wicked man repent, let him turn away from his wickedness, and let him save his soul alive, as best he may; but do not let him flatter himself that he can certainly undo his crime.

"Nescit vox missa reverti."

When blood is shed, can it be gathered up again?

And so Cordelia dies: not only Goneril and Regan consumed by their own guilt as by a living fire; and Cornwall stabbed by outraged humanity in the shape of a peasant; and Edmund pierced by the righteous sword of Edgar; and Gloucester crushed by the weight of his own troubles; and the King broken-hearted.

In that last scene, when the house of Lear is on the verge of extinction, as the dying King stoops over the corpse of Saint Cordelia, well may Kent, who has himself a journey shortly to go, ask, "Is this the promised end?" He means, "Is this the day of judgment?" "Or image of that horror?" says Edgar. Yes; it is an image of that horror, if we can understand. So

"draw the curtain close,
And let us all to meditation."

XXIV.

CORDELL ANSLYE.

(From the *Athenæum* for Sept. 2, 1876.)

MY friend, Mr. S. J. Low, sends me a copy of the following epitaph from a slab let in the wall of what was formerly the tower of the church at Lee, Kent :—

"Here lyeth buried the bodyes of Bryan Anslye Esquier, late of Lee in the county of Kent, and Audry his wife, the only davghter of Robert Turell, of Bvrbrocke in ye county of Essex Esquier. He had issue by her one sonne and three daughters, Bryan who died wthout issve; Grace married to Sr John Wilgoose, Knight; Christian married to the Lord Sands; and Cordell married to Sir William Hervey, Knight. Ye said Bryan the father died on the Xth of Jvly 1604; he served Qveene Elizabeth as one of ye band of Gentlemen Pencioners to her Matie the space of XXX^{tye} yeares. The said Awdry died on ye XXVth of Novebeber (*sic*) 1591. Cordell, the youngest daughter, at her owne proper cost and chardges, in further testimonie of her dvtifvll love vnto her father and mother, caused this monvment to be erected for the p'petvall memorie of their names against the ingratefvll natvre of oblivious time.

"Nec primus, nec ultimus; multi ante, Cesserunt, et omnes sequetitur" (*sic*).

The mention of "ye band of Gentlemen Pencioners" is interesting. How gay and grand they were we know from the *Midsummer Night's Dream*, II. i. 10 :—

"The cowslips tall her *pensioners* be ;
In their gold coats spots you see."

and *Merry Wives of Windsor*, II. ii. 78, where Mistress Quickly is boasting of Mrs. Ford's suitors :—

"The best courtier of them all, when the Court lay at Windsor, could never have brought her to such a canary . . . And yet there has been earls, nay which is more *pensioners;* but I warrant you all is one with her." "As brave as any *pensioners*" is a phrase of Nash's (*Piers Penniless*).

But more interesting is the last sentence, where Cordell is not unmindful of her greater namesake, for there is certainly in it an echo of the old story. And it is not impossible that she may have been influenced by Shakespeare's version of it; for that in all probability was just come out at the time she was erecting her filial monument. But it is not necessary to suppose so, for the popularity of the old tale, which her very name illustrates, is shown by many various sixteenth century versions, to say nothing of the old play, of which we first hear in 1593 as acted at the Rose Theatre, and have a printed edition in 1605.

The form of the name is worth noting. Other forms that occur are Cordilla, Cordeilla, Cordoille, or Gordoylle. In the pre-Shakespearian play it is Cordella. Spenser has Cordeill, and also Cordelia.

We may fondly trust that Grace and Christian, the elder sisters, by no means corresponded to Goneril and Regan.

XXV.

THE PORTER IN *MACBETH.*

(Read at the Fifth Meeting of the New Shakspere Society, May 22, 1874.)

"I pray you remember the Porter."—ii. 3.

AS is well known, the earliest extant copy of the play of *Macbeth*, is that of the Folio of 1623. Perhaps the earliest allusion to the play occurs, as Mr. Halliwell points out, in the year 1607, in the *Puritan*[1] (iv. 3); where the words "We'll ha' the ghost i' th' white sheet sit at upper end o' th' table," seem distinctly to refer to the apparition of Banquo. So that *Macbeth* had been exhibited at least sixteen years before its publication in the first Folio. . And it has been suspected that in more than one part the play is not preserved in the Folio in the exact shape in which it left the hand of its creator. Thus the passage in the 3rd scene of the 4th act, where the touching for the "King's evil" is described, has been supposed to be an interpolation, and it certainly has the air of being so. In the preface of the Clarendon press edition of the play, many other passages are mentioned which the editors, rightly or wrongly, incline to believe were written by Middleton. Amongst the passages that have been doubted are the soliloquy of the Porter, and the short dialogue that follows between the Porter and Macduff. And the doubts concerning it deserve

[1] See Hazlitt's *Shakespeare's Plays and Poems*, vol. v. p. 293, ed. 1852. Hazlitt's note is :—"Dr. Farmer thinks this was intended as a sneer at Macbeth."

all consideration, because they were supported, if not originated, by the best Shakespearian critic this country has yet produced. "The low soliloquy of the Porter," says Coleridge, "and his few speeches afterwards, I believe to have been written for the mob by some other hand, perhaps with Shakespeare's consent; and finding it take, he, with the remaining ink of a pen otherwise employed, just interpolated the words, 'I'll devil-porter it no further: I had thought to let in some of all professions, that go the primrose way to the everlasting bonfire.' Of the rest not one syllable has the ever-present being of Shakespeare."—(*Literary Remains*, ii. 246-7.) Coleridge is not be followed implicitly, because he has in other Shakespearian matters erred strangely;[1] but yet this doom of his must not be lightly disregarded. It cannot be said, however, to have convinced the world. Many editors do not even acknowledge that a doubt should exist. Gervinus does go just so far. "Coleridge and Collier," he says, "are in favour of this omission, as they consider his [the Porter's] soliloquy to be the unauthorized interpolation of an actor. It may be so." And then he proceeds, in fact, to show how it may not be so.

I propose in this paper to consider whether the Porter is not after all a genuine offspring of Shakespeare's art. It is possible to show beyond controversy, that he is an integral part of the original play; and therefore we must conclude, if he is not the creation of Shakespeare, that the play was originally the fruit of a joint authorship, and not merely amended by some reviser. But if, in addition to this, it can

---

[1] Thus, in 1802, he places *The London Prodigal* amongst Shakespeare's plays, *The Merchant of Venice* after *Henry V.*, &c.; in 1810, *The Tempest* in the 2nd Period, *Othello* amongst the latest plays; in 1819, *The Tempest* in the same epoch with *The Merchant of Venice*, &c. See *Literary Remains*, ii. 86-91.

be shown that his appearance is in accordance with the artistic system by which Shakespeare worked, that it relieves the awful intensity of the action, and permits the spectator to draw breath,—further, that he satisfies that law of contrast which rules, not unfrequently in a manner that perplexes and astonishes, the undoubted compositions of Shakespeare—that his speech has a certain dramatic pertinence, and is by no means an idle outflow of irrelevant buffoonery;—if such theses can be maintained, then certainly the Porter is the result of Shakespeare's direct dictation, if not his own manufacture. Lastly, if his particular style and language prove to be Shakespearian, it must surely be a confirmed hypersceptic that persists in believing that he is not of the family of Shakespeare, but begotten by some skilful mimic. Certainly these are the five points which should be thoroughly considered before any final verdict is pronounced. On each one of them I shall try to offer a few suggestions. For the sake of clearness I recapitulate them:—

(i.) That a Porter's speech is an integral part of the play.
(ii.) That it is necessary as a relief to the surrounding horror.
(iii.) That it is necessary according to the law of contrast elsewhere obeyed.
(iv.) That the speech we have is dramatically relevant.
(v.) That its style and language are Shakespearian.

(i.) *That a Porter's speech is an integral part of the play.* This is a very simple matter. No one will deny that the knocking scene is an integral part of the play. In the whole Shakespearian theatre there is perhaps no other instance where such an awful effect is produced by so slight a means, as when, the deed of blood accomplished, in the frightful silence that the presence of death under any circumstances ever imposes on all around it, when the nerves of Macbeth are strained to the uttermost, and without any external provocation he hears an unearthly voice crying "Sleep no more"—

> "Still it cried, 'Sleep no more' to all the house :
> Glamis hath murder'd sleep, and therefore Cawdor
> Shall sleep no more ; Macbeth shall sleep no more—"

at this ghastly moment there is a knocking heard. The spiritual and the material seem merged; and one half fancies that it is Conscience herself that has taken a bodily form, and is beating on the gate, or that Vengeance has already arisen and is clamorous for its victim.

> "'Whence is that knocking?' cries Macbeth.
> 'How is't with me, when every noise appals me?'"

It comes again, and his wife now hears it, and recognizes it as made at the south entry. To her with her marvellous self-command it is intelligible enough; but even for her how terrible, and, as in due time appears, how burnt in on the memory this first arrival of the outer world, now that the old conditions of her life are all deranged and convulsed.

> "I hear a knocking
> At the South entry ; retire we to our chamber ;
> A little water clears us of this deed ;
> How easy is it then ! your constancy
> Hath left you unattended.   [*Knocking within*]
>   Hark ! more knocking.
> Get on your night-gown, lest occasion call us,
> And show us to be watchers. Be not lost
> So poorly in your thoughts.
>   *Macbeth.* To know my deed, 'twere best not know myself.
>   [*Knocking within*]
> Wake Duncan with thy knocking ! I would thou couldst !"

And then, as he leaves the stage, "Enter a Porter," the

knocking continuing with slight intermissions; and at last, when the door is opened, Macduff interrogates the opener as to his lying so late. And when Macbeth appears, after whom he is at the moment inquiring, he says,

"*Our knocking* has awaked him; here he comes."

Later on in the play, when Lady Macbeth's overtasked physique gives way under the pressure of vast and truceless anxieties, and reason dethroned, we see something of the impressions which, in spite of herself, have been stamped and branded upon her mind; we learn how that knocking thrilled and pierced her too. "To bed, to bed!" she exclaims, in the awful scene of the delirium; "there's *knocking at the gate;* come, come, come, give me your hand."

The knocking scene, then, is of no trivial importance.[1] But with the knocking the Porter is inseparably associated. If we retain it, we must retain him. And if we retain him, he must surely make a speech of some sort; or are we to picture to ourselves a profoundly dumb functionary? Are we to conceive him as crossing the stage, thinking a great deal but saying nothing?—nodding perhaps with all the amazing volubility of Sheridan's Lord Burleigh, or brandishing his keys with a mysterious cunning, or perhaps rushing headlong to his post as if his life was at stake, but with his tongue fast tied and bound? There is probably no student of Shakespeare who is prepared to accept such a phenomenon. Clearly, then, the Porter speaks, to whatever effect.

(ii.) *That some speech of a lighter kind is necessary to relieve the surrounding horror.* In the scene that includes the enactment of Duncan's murder, the latter part of which

---

[1] See *On the knocking at the gate in Macbeth*, De Quincey's Works, xiii. 192-8, ed. 1863.

has already been discussed and quoted, the intensity of the Tragedy reaches the highest possible point of endurance. Such is the mighty power of the dramatist, that we find ourselves transported into the midst of the scenes he portrays. They are not images for us, but realities. We verily see Macbeth pass into the King's chamber, and share his frightful excitement. "The owls scream, and the crickets cry." And we hear one "laugh in 's sleep," and one cry "Murder." And the wild weird fancies that overcome him are vivid with us too, and the air is filled with ominous visions and ghastly voices, and the shadows of horror encompass us round as with a cloak. We reach the *ne plus ultra* of dramatic terror. Nature can bear no more. We cannot breathe in so direful an atmosphere. The darkness is crushing us like a weight. "Fearfulness and trembling are come upon us; and a horrible dread" threatens to "overwhelm us."

As between the sublime and the ridiculous, so between pleasure and pain there is but one step. But the great artist never takes this step. The pleasure he imparts is often strange and inexplicable, and not to be defined; but it is pleasure. When we speak of his moving terror in us, we use the word in a modified sense. It is an inferior and a coarser art that thrills with positive fear and affright. If the old story is true that the Furies of Æschylus were so dreadful [1]

---

[1] They might well be so if they answered to the Priestess's description of them :—

πρόσθεν δὲ τἀνδρὸς τοῦδε θαυμαστὸς λόχος
εὕδει γυναικῶν ἐν θρόνοισιν ἥμενος.
οὔτοι γυναῖκας ἀλλὰ Γοργόνας λέγω,
οὐδ' αὖτε Γοργείοισιν εἰκάσω τύποις.
εἶδον ποτ' ἤδη Φινέως γεγραμμένας
δεῖπνον φερούσας· ἄπτεροί γε μὴν ἰδεῖν
αὗται, μέλαιναι δ' ἐς τὸ πᾶν βδελύκτροποι·

to see that women in his audience were thrown into fits and convulsions, then the representation was not truly artistic, but rude. Certainly Shakespeare does not ever so miscomprehend his craft. He has the strength of a giant, but he does not use it as a giant. He understands and he observes the proper limits within which his power may be exercised. There was a certain profound humanity in him which forbade all idle torturing of those whom his irresistible fascination placed at his mercy. And so in his excitement of the feelings he knew when to stay his hand, and he acted faithfully according to his knowledge. He does not turn pleasure into pain by an excessive prolongation of any state of extreme emotion.

Now if ever in the plays of Shakespeare some relaxation is needed for the nerves tense and strained to the utmost, if ever some respite and repose are due to prevent the high mysterious delight which it is the province of the artist to kindle within us, corrupting into a morbid panic, if ever, as we read or listen, one's heart threatens to suspend its beating, and a very palsy seems imminent, should the awful suspense be protracted, it is so in the terrible scene now before us. In Davenant's version of the play, in which all the vigour of the context is miserably weakened and diluted, no such imperious necessity exists. But I submit that any

> ῥέγκουσι δ' οὐ πλάτοισι φυσιάμασιν·
> ἐκ δ' ὀμμάτων λείβουσι δυσφιλῆ λίβα·
> καὶ κόσμος οὔτε πρὸς θεῶν ἀγάλματα
> φέρειν δίκαιος οὔτ' ἐς ἀνθρώπων στέγας. κ.τ.λ.
> *Eum.* 46-56.

'The appearance they have in Æschylus was more or less retained by the poets of later times. . . . On the stage, however, and in works of art, their fearful appearance was greatly softened down,' &c. See art. "Eumenides" in Smith's *Dict. of Greek and Roman Biog. and Myth.*, vol. ii.

one of imagination, who studies this scene as we have it with all his power, who realizes it in all its finished terribleness, and is keenly sensible of the darkness of it, as of a darkness that may be felt, will be truly thankful for a temporary release and diversion.

"Neque semper arcum
Tendit Apollo."

A monotony of horror cannot be sustained. In that appalling night scene the very air seems poisoned; and any disturbance of it is infinitely welcome. The sound of a fresh voice, after we have listened so long to that guilty conference, is a very cordial. If it would be going too far to say, with an important alteration of the poet's words, that

"We must laugh or we must die,"

one may fairly maintain that the terror must be drawn out no further, or our sensibilities will be either numbed and stupified, or roused into a wild fever of excitation.

That this view—that some relief is indispensable—is not an idle conjecture, founded on an exaggerated estimate of the fearfulness of the murder scene, is curiously illustrated by the experience of one who attempted to thoroughly study that scene apart from its surroundings. Mrs. Siddons, so studying it, found the horrors of it completely overcome her. The following is the account she herself gives of the result of such an isolation:—

"It was my custom to study my characters at night, when all the domestic cares and business of the day were over. On the night preceding that on which I was to appear in this part for the first time, I shut myself up, as usual, when all the family were retired, and commenced my study of Lady Macbeth. As the character is very short, I thought I should soon accomplish it. Being then only twenty years of age, I believed, as many others do believe, that little more was necessary than to get the words into my head ; for the necessity of discrimination, and the development of character, at that time of my life had scarcely entered my imagination. But to proceed. I went on with tolerable composure in the silence of the night (a night I can never forget) till I came to the assassination scene, when the horrors of the scene rose to a degree that made it impossible for me to get farther. I snatched up my candle, and hurried out of the room in a paroxysm of terror. My dress was of silk, and the rustling of it, as I ascended the stairs to go to bed, seemed to my panic-struck fancy like the movement of a spectre pursuing me. At last I reached my chamber, where I found my husband fast asleep. I clapt my candlestick down upon the table without the power of putting the candle out ; and I threw myself on my bed, without daring to stay even to take off my clothes."[1]

(iii.) *Some lighter speech is necessary according to the law of contrast elsewhere observed by Shakespeare.* Perhaps there is no characteristic of the Romantic drama more striking than the frequent or rather the habitual, juxta-position of opposites. It delights in the meeting of extremes. The Tragi-Comedy, or Comi-Tragedy, was a form of its own peculiar invention. The Masque had its Antimasque. This law of contrast may seem at first sight identical with the law of relief just discussed. But it is not so. It springs not from the practical restraints of the drama in its demands upon human endurance, as does that law of relief, but from far wider considerations. It springs from the grand ambition of Teutonic art to embrace in its representation life in all its length and

[1] See Campbell's *Life of Mrs. Siddons*, ed. 1839, p. 184. The passage may also be found in Knight's Cabinet Edition of Shakespeare, ix. 4.

breadth. This art is not content with a mere excerpt from life, a mere fragment, a single side of life, as the phrase is. It yearns to comprehend life in its totality. It would put its arms round the whole world—a girdle around the entire earth. The artist, if you think of him as a reaper going forth with his scythe, will not be confined to this single acre or that. He must have free scope, and he will gather his harvest everywhere. Of an audaciously aspiring soul, he will not acknowledge the artificial barriers that are reared around him. And as he gazes at life as a whole, he sees it full of amazing contrasts, and the most fantastic paradoxes, and it is life he aims at portraying, this oxymoron life, as the grammarians might call it, so bitter-sweet, so teeming with strange reverses, so dull and so bright, so low and so lofty, so mean, so noble. To the true humorist these various shades and colours are inextricably interwoven. He cares nothing for the superficial distinctions that pass current around him. For him there is a transcendent unity that binds all things together. He does not trouble himself about the labels that are placed by conventional persons on the various departments of existence. He laughs everywhere, and he cries everywhere. It is all infinitely sad, and infinitely comic. Heraclitus and Democritus meet in him. As you look at him you cannot say whether his eyes are filled with tears or with smiles. The beauty of summer and the bleakness of winter, the gaiety of youth and the torpor of age, the gladness of life and the dulness of death;—these are omnipresent with him. And so to him there is nothing shocking or abhorrent in the inter-proximities of things apparently alien to each other. For him the very jaws of death are capable of laughter.

And so in the Shakespearian drama we find strange neighbourhoods. Jesters and jestings in the midst of that stupendous storm in *King Lear*.[1] In *Hamlet* the gravedigger is one with the clown! In *Othello*, amidst all its bitter earnest, there are foolings and railleries. In fact, *Macbeth* would be unique amongst the tragedies of Shakespeare if the comic element were utterly absent from it.

This law of contrast might be supported also from a purely æsthetic point of view, no less than that of truthfulness to nature; and we might see in this mattter as in others how

"Beauty is truth, truth beauty—that is all
Ye know on earth, and all ye need to know;"

and be reminded of that fine mandate delivered to poets by one, herself, of no mean poetic rank:

"Hold, in high poetic duty,
Truest Truth, the fairest Beauty."

(iv.) *The Speech of the Porter is dramatically relevant.* In order to justify this speech as it stands, it is not enough to point out, as I have tried to do, the general laws of relief and contrast by which Shakespeare works. For in his modes of providing relief and contrast he does not proceed recklessly. He does not ignore harmony when he aims at securing variety. There is a real concord in the seeming discord. All things work together to one general effect. Amidst apparent confusion and chaos there is absolute subordination and symmetry.

"Many things, having full reference
To one consent, may work contrariously:
As many arrows loosed several ways

---

[1] "He complained of the Fool in *Lear*. I observed that he seemed to give a terrible wildness to the distress; but still he complained." See Wordsworth's Notes of his conversations with Klopstock. *Wordsworth's Memoirs*, i. 130, or Coleridge's *Biographia Literaria*, Satyrane's Letters, iii. p. 172 of the one-volumed edition.

> Come to one mark; as many ways meet in one town;
> As many fresh streams meet in one salt sea;
> As many lines close in the dial's centre."

Now, is the Porter's speech incurably discrepant and incongruous with the play of which it is a part?

"After all," says Bodenstedt, "his uncouth comicality has a tragic background; he never dreams, while imagining himself a porter of hell-gate, of how near he comes to the truth. What are all these petty sinners, who go to the everlasting bon-fire, compared with those great criminals whose gates he guards!"

"Yet, at all events," says Gervinus of this soliloquy, after mentioning, as we have seen above, the theory of those who would excise it, "it is not inappropriate; there is an uncomfortable joviality which by way of contrast is very suitable to the circumstances, when the drunken warder, whom Duncan's gifts or festivities of the evening have left in a state of excitement, calls his post 'hell-gate,' in a speech in which every allusion bears point."

Surely what these two comments put forward must have occurred to every thoughtful reader. The whole speech of the Porter is in fact a piece of powerful irony, "If a man were porter of hell-gate." But is this man not so? What then is hell? and where are its gates? and what is there within them? What of the "scorpions," of which Macbeth's mind is presently full? Knowing what we know of the hideous doings that night has witnessed in his castle, may we not well say: "How dreadful is this place! This is none other but the house of the devil, and this is the gate of hell?"

It may be well to notice here that the Porter of Hell was a not unfamiliar figure in the old Mysteries. We find in Virgil, indeed, what might have suggested some such official to the medieval mind, if any suggestion were necessary. Virgil speaks of Cerberus as "janitor" (*Æn.* vi. 400) and as "janitor Orci." (*Ib.* viii. 296.) So Silius after him speaks of "Stygius Janitor" (*Punic.* iii. 35); and so Fletcher in his *Honest Man's Fortune* (III. ii.) of "hell's three-headed porter." But no classical suggestion was necessary for such a creation. It was natural enough, when so much was talked of St. Peter with his keys keeping the gate of Heaven, that there should be conceived an infernal counterpart of that celestial functionary. In the *Coventry Mysteries*, Belial seems serving in this capacity; at least it is he who, when the "Sowle," "Anima Christi," "goth to helle gatys, and seyth, 'Attollite portas, principes, vestras, et elevamini, portæ eternales, et introibit Rex Gloriæ.'"—

> "Ondothe youre gatys of sorwatorie!
> On mannys sowle I haue memorie
> Here comyth now the kynge of glorye,
>   These gates for to breke!
> Ye develys that arn here withinne,
> Helle gatys ye xal unpynne,
> I xal delyvere mannys kynne;
>   From wo I wole hem wreke.—"

it is "Belyalle" who on this summons exclaims:

> "Alas! alas! out & harrow!
> Onto thi byddynge must we bow,
> That thou art God now do we know;
>   Of the had we grett dowte.
> Agens the may no thynge stonde,
> Alle thynge obeyth to thyn honde;
> Bothe hevyn & helle, watyr & londe,
>   Alle thynge most to the lowte."

Belial, perhaps, is "the other devil" in the Porter's speech. In a print engraved for Hearne from an old drawing we have a portrait of this gate-keeper. It represents that Harrowing of Hell which is dramatized in the *Coventry Mysteries*. Christ is in the act of releasing various souls from the mouth of "the pit," to the severe annoyance of the appointed Custodian, who appears to be blowing a horn as a signal of alarm. Above his head is the legend, "Out out aroynt."[1] In Heywood's *Four P's* the Pardoner tells how he was anxious to find out in what estate stood the soul of a female friend who had died suddenly. His knowledge of her, as it would seem, not leading him to look for her in Paradise, he proceeded to Purgatory, and not finding her there he went to Hell.

> "And first to the devil that kept the gate
> I came, and spake after this rate:
> 'All hail, Sir Devil,' and made low courtesy;
> 'Welcome,' quoth he thus smilingly.
> He knew me well, and I at last
> Remembered him since long time past:
> For as good hap would have it chance,
> This devil and I were of old acquaintance;
> For oft in the play of Corpus Christi
> He hath played the devil at Coventry.
> By his acquaintance and my behaviour
> He showed to me a right friendly favour;
> And to make my return the shorter,
> I said to the devil, '*Good Master Porter*
> For all old love, if it be in your power
> Help me to speak with my lord and your.'
> 'Be sure,' quoth he, 'no tongue can tell
> What time thou couldst have come so well;
> For as on this day Lucifer fell,
> Which is our festival in hell.
> Nothing unreasonable craved this day
> That shall in hell have any nay.

[1] A reprint of this grotesque picture may be seen in Hone's *Ancient Mysteries described*.

"But yet beware thou come not in
Till time thou may thy passport win," [1] &c.

(v.) *Are the style and language of the Porter's speech Shakespearian?*

Surely the fancy, which is the main part of the Porter's speech, must be allowed to be eminently after the manner of Shakespeare. He was well acquainted with the older stage, as his direct references to it show, as those to the Vice in *Twelfth Night*, IV. ii.; 1 *Henry IV.*, II. iv.; 2 *Henry IV.*, III. ii.; *Richard III.*, III. i.; *Hamlet*, III. iv.; and this conception of an infernal janitor is just such a piece of antique realism as he would delight in. He has it elsewhere; see *Othello*, IV. ii. 90, where Othello cries out to Emilia:

"You, mistress,
That have the office opposite to St. Peter,
And keep the gate of hell."

The manner in which Macduff "draws out" the Porter is exactly like that of Shakespeare in similar circumstances elsewhere. "What three things does drink especially provoke?" says Macduff; and then the Porter delivers himself of his foolery, which is coarse enough, and to our taste highly offensive, it must be allowed. Compare the way in which Orlando is made to elicit the wit of Rosalind in *As You Like It*, III. ii. 323, et seq., &c. If this likeness of manner has no positive, yet it has some negative value. We see that the manner is not un-Shakespearian, if it cannot

---

[1] See Hazlitt's *Dodsley's Old Plays*, i. 373-4; see also, ib. ii. 171, *The Nice Wanton*:—

"I would not pass
So that I might bear a rule in hell by the mass,
To toss firebrands at these pennyfathers' pates
I would be porter, and receive them at the gates;
In boiling lead and brimstone I would seeth them each one."

be pronounced definitely Shakespearian; and we need not go to Middleton's plays for an illustration of it.

The passage is written in the rhythmic, or "numerous," prose, that is so favourite a form with Shakespeare. Compare it in this respect, for instance, with Mrs. Quickly's account of Falstaff's end. See *Hen. V.*, II. iii. 9-28.

And so for the language, there is certainly nothing in it un-Shakespearian. The use of "old" in "old turning of the key" occurs in 2 *Henry IV.*, II. iv. 21, "*old* Vtis;" *The Merry Wives of Windsor*, I. iv. 5, "an *old* abusing of God's patience and the king's English;" *Much Ado about Nothing*, V. ii. 98, "yonder's *old* coil at home;" *equivocation* in *Hamlet*, V. i. 149; *French Hose* in *Henry V.*, III. vii. 56; comp. *Merchant of Venice*, I. ii. 80. *Devil-porter it* is according to a very frequent Shakespearian construction, as "prince it," in *Cymbeline*, III. iii. 85; "dukes it," in *Measure for Measure*, III. ii. 100. Compare, especially, "I cannot daub it farther," in *King Lear*, IV. i. 54; and "I'll queen it no inch farther," in *Winter's Tale*, IV. iv. 460.

The most striking phrase in the passage is certainly "the primrose way to the everlasting bonfire;" and in *Hamlet* (I. iii. 50) Ophelia speaks of "the primrose path of daliance." See also *All's Well that End's Well*, IV. v.: "I am for the house with the narrow gate, which I take to be too little for pomp to enter: some that humble themselves may; but the many will be too chill and tender, and they'll be for the flowery way that leads to the broad gate and the great fire."

I have not been careful to allude in this Paper to what is commonly said as to the disputed passage by those who allow it to be by Shakespeare, that it was inserted for the sake of the groundlings, or the gods, as we should say, because I am not inclined to think that Shakespeare would have made any undue sacrifice to that part of his audience. They were certainly to be considered by a theatrical writer, and certainly Shakespeare did not forget them. But to suppose that he would have glaringly disfigured—if the passage is to be regarded a disfigurement—one of the greatest passages of his art from any such consideration, is surely audacious and extravagant. Moreover, is it so certain that such an interruption of the terror would have gratified the "groundling?" Would not the genuine animal—and individuals of his species were and are to be found in other parts of the theatre besides that from which he derives his name—have rather had

"On horror's head horror accumulate?"—

the darkness deepened, his blood yet more severely chilled his every hair made to stand on end? The thorough-bred sensationalist would surely vote the Porter to be an obnoxious intrusion. He would long for a draught of raw terror, and it is from such a potation that the Porter debars him.

The argument on which the rejectors of the passage take their stand is the intrinsic inferiority of it. An unsatisfactory argument. It involves two questions: First, is the inferiority of it so signal and admitted? and, secondly, if it is so, yet is the passage therefore not by Shakespeare? As to the former question, without contending that the soliloquy is a masterpiece of comedy, and the following dialogue a supreme flight of wit, yet surely the Porter holds his own well enough as compared with corresponding persons in other plays. Is the wit of the grave-digger in *Hamlet*, for example, so very superior? Again, have those who thus condemn him taken well into account that coherence of his speech with the main action of the drama, which has been dwelt upon above? With regard to the second question, suppose the inferiority of the Porter be conceded, are we to believe that Shakespeare is always equal to himself—that he is always at his best, and never slumbers nor sleeps? "Interdum dormitat Homerus." Homer is sometimes caught napping. But Shakespeare never? No one would deliberately say so; and yet perpetually critics argue on this presumption. If anything distinctly un-Shakespearian, or thought to be un-Shakespearian, can be pointed out either in the language or the style or the thought or the connection, then of the authenticity of the passage containing it our suspicions may be justly encouraged. But we cannot be too cautious in condemning a passage simply because it seems to us comparatively weak and forceless. Our eyes may not be good. And, if they are ever so good, yet it must be remembered that in Shakespeare's life, no less than in the lives of lesser men, there must have been times when all the wheels of his being were slow, when the "nimble spirits" seemed prisoned[1] up in the arteries, and the divine energy of his genius fainted and languished.

The general conclusion justified by what has been advanced in the course of this paper seems to me to be this: that the Porter is undoubtedly a part of the original play, and that the general conception of his speech is certainly Shakespeare's: with regard to the expression, that part of it is most certainly Shakespeare's, and, for the rest, no sufficient reason has yet been urged to countenance any doubt that it too is by Shakespeare.

[1] "Poysons up," in the 1623 Fol.

XXVI.

MACBETH A GOOD CHURCHMAN.

(From the *Academy* for March 2, 1878.)

IT may be a satisfaction to some minds to be assured that, after all, Macbeth was a good Churchman. Shakespeare has overlooked this side of his character, though Holinshed has recorded it, and the fact is verily so, as was long since remarked by Mr. J. H. Burton. What I wish now to point out is the mention of Macbeth in this aspect in a famous Elizabethan work, even in *Laws of the Ecclesiastical Polity*, "Will any man deny that the Church doth need the rod of corporal punishment to keep her children in obedience withal? Such a law as Macabeus made among the Scots, that he which continued an Excommunicate two years together, and reconciled not himself to the Church, should forfeit all his goods and possessions." Keble's note quotes from Boece the Latin of this, as Hooker thinks, commendable enactment:—"Qui pontificis authoritatem annum totium execratus contempserit neque se interim reconciliavit, nostis reipublicæ habetor; qui vero duos annos in ea contumacia perseveravit fortunis omnibus multator."

XXVII.

"THE COAL OF FIRE UPON THE ICE."

(From the *Academy* for July 20, 1878.)

THERE being other reasons for supposing that Shakespeare wrote *Coriolanus* in 1608, I may perhaps point out that there is in it what may be a reference to the famous frost of 1607-8, when fires were lighted on the Thames. Says Marcius, in his favourite vein of contempt for the commons:—

> "You are no surer, no,
> Than is *the coal of fire upon the ice*
> Or hailstones in the sun."

It must be allowed that this is a somewhat out-of-the-way image. Coals on ice are not usually a common spectacle; but it would seem they were so in the winter of 1607-8, and at that time the image would be by no means far-fetched or unfamiliar; it would, in fact, be obviously suggested. Of course one would lay no great stress on it if there was nothing else to connect the play with that time; but there being other things that so connect it, the allusion may perhaps be taken as confirmatory.

"Above Westminster," writes Chamberlain to Carleton, January 8th, 1607-8, "the Thames is quite frozen over, and the Archbishop came from Lambeth on Twelfth Day over the ice to Court. Many fantastical experiments are daily put in practice, as certain youths burnt a gallon of wine upon the ice, and made all the passengers partakers."

An account of this frost, written during its prevalence, is given in a tract called "The Great Frost: Cold Doings in London, a Dialogue," reprinted by Mr. Arber in his most useful collection, *An English Garner*, Vol. I.—a volume soon, we hope, to be followed by others not less valuable. The citizen in this dialogue tells—to quote a side-note—of beer, ale, wine, victuals, and fires on the Thames. "Are you cold with going over?" runs the text, "You shall, ere you come to the middle of the river spy some ready with pans of coals to warm your fingers." I will just mention that the passage in this tract: "Amongst many other things upon the frozen Thames . . . . It was a marvellous deliverance," pp. 97-9 of Mr. Arber's reprint, is evidently out of its place.

XXVIII.

"THE WASHING OF TEN TIDES."

(From the *Academy* for Sept. 1, 1877.)

TURNING over, the other day, Murray's *Handbook* of *Kent*, I read:—"*Execution Dock*, Wapping, was th usual place at which pirates and persons committing capit: crimes at sea were hung at low-water mark, there to remai till three tides had overflowed them," and at once Antonio kindly wish for the Boatswain in the *Tempest* came into m mind as interpreted or illustrated by the custom describe(It seems unlikely that this suggestion should not have bee made before, but I do not myself remember having seen it.

Nor, I find, does Dr. Elze, whom I have to thank for copy of certain *Noten und Conjecturen zu neu-englischen Dic. tern*. The same idea has occurred to him, prompted by passage in Harrison's *Description of England*:—

"Pirates and robbers by sea are condemned in the Cou of the Admiraltie, and hanged on the shore at low-wat mark, where they are left till three tides have overwashe them."

Evidently Antonio's phrase is a mere exaggeration of suc a sentence. For such a "wide-chapped rascal" as tl Boatswain, three tide washings are not enough—let him ha· ten.

Here is another allusion to this form of punishment, fro a well-known play, Green's *Tu quoque; or, The City Gallar* Staines is dismissing his faithful servant Bubble:—

Bub. But, master, wherefore should we be parted?
Staines. Because my fortunes are desperate, thine are hopeful.
Bub. Why, whither do you mean to go, master?
Staines. Why, to sea.
Bub. To sea! Lord bless us, methinks I hear of a tempest already. But what will you do at sea?
Staines. Why, as other gallants do that are spent—turn pirate.
Bub. O master, have the grace of Wapping before your eyes, remember a high tide; give not your friends cause to wet their handkerchiefs. Nay, master, I'll tell you a better course than so; you and I will go and rob my uncle; if we 'scape, we'll domineer together; if we be taken, we'll hang together at Tyburn; that's the warmer gallows of the two."

Stow—this reference is given in Hazlitt's *Dodsley's Old English Plays*, xi., 188—points out " the usual place of execution for hanging of Pirates and Sea-rovers at the low-water mark," there to remain till three tides had overflowed them.

CHISWICK PRESS: C. WHITTINGHAM AND CO., TOOKS COURT, CHANCERY LANE.

INDEX.

Abbott's *Grammar*, 171.
Adam Bede, 239.
Addison, 68, 74.
Aery of children, 237.
Æschylus' *Furies*, 278.
Aetion, 196.
Alderminster, 14.
Allusions (possible) to conspiracy in Shakespeare, 50, 51, 52.
Anslye, Cordell, 271.
Ariel, 196.
Aristophanes' *Frogs*, quoted, 81 *n*.
Armin's *Nest of Ninnies*, 236.
Assembly of Foules, 92.
Aston Rowant, 22.
Austen, Jane, 72.
Avon, the river, 13.

Bacon, Sir Nicholas, 222.
Barckley's *Discourse of the Felicity of Man*, 115.
Bates, Thomas, 29.
Beaumont and Fletcher, 62, 66, 68, 86, 88, 226.
Belleforest, 109.
Benfield, Robert, actor, 156, 158.
Blackfriars Theatre, 154, 155, 156, 160, 163.
Boccaccio, 101.
Bodenstedt, 284.

Boece, 291.
Browning, Robert, his dramatic power, 67, 68.
Brudermord, Der Bestrafte, 233.
Burbages, the, 155, 156, 159, 160, 161, 162, 163, 192.
Burney, Frances, 72.

Camden, 244.
Capons as presents to magistrates, 219.
Catesby, Robert, 4, 27, 32.
Caxton, 101.
Chapman's *Odyssey*, 110; *May-Day*, 235.
Chaucer's characters, 65; Prologue and Inter-prologues, 62.
Children of the Chappel, 162, 163.
Chipping Norton, 13.
Clopton Bridge, 14.
Clopton House, 27.
Coke, Lord Chief Justice, 244.
Coleridge on the Porter in *Macbeth*, 274.
Collier, 111, 121, 124, 274.
Colne, the river, 23.
Combe Abbey, 30.
Combe, John, 39; William, 39.
Condell, or Cundall, 155, 161, 162, 163.

298 INDEX.

Cornbury Hall, 19.
Coughton, 27.
Countess, Insatiate, 234.
Coventry Mysteries, 285, 286.
Cromwell, Thomas, Lord, *Life and Death of*, 224.
Cunningham's *Handbook of London*, 238.

Daniel, Samuel, 86, 87.
Dante, 59.
Davenant, 12, 134, 279.
Defoe, 71.
Delius, 178.
Dickens, 73, 75.
Digby, Sir Everard, 31.
Ditchley Park, 18.
Dogberry, where "studied," 2.
Dowden, Professor, 196, 197.
Drayton, Michael, 10, 86, 88.
Dryden, 83, 127.
Dunchurch, 47.
Dyce, 121, 138.

Eastward Hoe, 234.
Ebert, Professor, on Chaucer's *Knight's Tale*, 77 n.
Eden's *History of Travayle*, 113.
Elze, 240, 294.
Enstone, 18.
Equivocation, 51, 52.
Essex, Earl of, 35, 36, 205, 206.
Execution Dock, 294.

Fielding, 71, 74.
Fletcher, see Beaumont.
Fletcher, Laurence, 140.
Florio, 136.
Fortescue, Sir John, 244.
Frost, The Great, of 1607-8, 293.

Garish, 204.

Garnet's complicity in the Gunpowder Plot, 51.
Garter, Host of the, 94.
Gascoigne, 102, 198.
"George Eliot," 74.
Gerard's, or Jarrett's Cross, 23.
Gernutus, 123.
Gervinus, 274, 284.
Gesta Grayorum, 122.
Ghost in *Macbeth*, 194.
Gifford, 81.
Globe Theatre, 154, 156, 157, 162, 208.
Goethe, 81, 258.
Goldsmith, 67, 71.
Goulart's *Admirable and Memorable Histories*, 122.
Gower, 63, 84, 85.
Gray, 70.
Greek drama, its rapid development, 149.
Greene, 108, 126, 133, 236.
Green's *Tu quoque, or the City Gallant*, 294.
Grendon Underwood, 12.

Hall, his *Satires*, 199, 200.
Halpin, Rev. W. J., 132.
Hamlet, Memoranda on, 236.
Harvey, Dr. John, 214.
Heming, actor, 155, 159, 161, 162, 163.
Henryson, Scottish poet, 97.
Henslowe's *Diary*, 109, 210.
Herods of literature, 75.
Heywood, Thomas, 113, 235.
High Wycombe, 21.
Hillingdon Hill, 24.
Holinshed, 244, 291.
Holyoke's *Dictionary*, 193.
Hone's *Ancient Mysteries*, 286.

Hooker, 291.
Hundred Merry Tales, ed. Oesterley, 235.

Jews, re-admission of, into England, 215, 216.
Jonson, Ben, 12, 66, 74, 81, 86, 87, 94, 106, 109, 127, 135, 163, 183, 198, 199, 224.

Kempe, actor, 156.
Kiddington, Over and Nether, 18.
Kimbles, the, 22.
King Richard II., 205.
King's evil, touching for, 273.
King's Players, 163.
Kirke, Edward, Spenser's friend, 86.

L'Allegro, 201-204.
Lambarde's *Perambulation of Kent*, 236.
Lapworth, 27.
Latimer, Bishop, 85, 223.
Lee Church, Kent, 271.
Lodge, 126.
London Prodigal, The, 274.
Long Compton, 16.
Lowen, actor, 155, 156.
Luther, Martin, on the Jews, 139.
Lydgate, 82, 89, 101.

Macdobeth, 195.
Malone, 153, 209, 212, 232.
Manasseh Ben Israel, 215.
Marlowe, 60, 98, 136, 137, 138.
Marston, John, 199, 200.
Massinger, Philip, 67, 68, 217, 220, 235.
Masters of the Revels, 153.

Merlin, 245.
Merrick, Sir Gilly, 205, 206, 207.
Middleton, 273, 288.
Midsummer Night's Dream, 136, 201, 204.
Milton and Forest Hill, 22.
Mirrour of Magistrates, 99.
Monmouth's, Geoffrey of, *History*, 243.
Monstrelet, Johnes's, 121.
Montaigne, *Essai XIX.*, 136.
Morecroft, Robert, 160.
Morris, William, 68.

Nash, 108, 209, 212, 213, 214.
Nicholson, Dr. Brinsley, 214.
Norbrook, 27.
North's *Plutarch*, 115, 122, 123, 126.

Occleve, 82, 89.
Othello, 192.
Overbury's *Book of Characters*, 221.
Ovid, 90, 105.
Oxford, 10, 11.

Pandosto, 236.
Pembroke, Earl of, 156.
Pensioners, Gentlemen, 272.
Phillips, Augustine, actor, 161, 163, 206.
Pierce Pennilesse, 236, 237, 272.
Pope, 83, 190.
Prynne, William, 216.
Puritan, The, 194, 273.

Ratcliffe, Anne, 72.
Retzsch, 185.
Richardson, 71, 74.

INDEX

Roads, state of, temp. Eliz., 4.
Robbers, especially in Chiltern Hills, 2, 3, 9,
Rollrich-stones, 16.
Romano, Julio, 141, 142.
Rookwood, 42.
Rose Theatre, 272.
Routes to London from Warwickshire, 10.
Ruskin, 108.

Sackville, 84.
Sandblind, 193.
Schlegel, Aug. Wilh. von, 78.
Scott, Sir Walter, 59, 72.
Shanks, actor, 156, 159.
Shelley, 67.
Shipston-on-Stour, 15.
Shirburne Castle, 22.
Siddons, Mrs., 280.
Sidney, Sir Philip, 192.
Smollett, 71.
Sonnets, Shakespeare's, 2, 3.
Southampton, Earl of, 36, 144, 205.
Spenser, 56, 84, 196.
Steele, see Addison.
Steevens, 153, 183 *n.*, 184, 234, 240.
Sterne, 71.
Stour, the, Warwickshire, 13.
Supp'ementary English Glossary, 220.

Surrey, Earl of, 84, 89.
Sycorax, origin of the name, 197.

Taylor, the actor, 155, 156.
Teniers, 74.
Tennyson on Chaucer, 83.
Thackeray, 73.
Theobald, 190, 191.
Thirlwall on Sophocles' "irony" 78.
Travelling, temp. Eliz., 7.
Tredington, 15.
Two Noble Kinsmen, 88, 96, 169.
Tyrwhitt, 56.

Vasari, two epitaphs quoted from, 142, 143.
Verstegan, 56.

Walsh, Sir Richard, 48.
Warner's translation of *Menæchmi*, 122.
Welcombe Hills, 26, 27, 40.
Whateley, Archbishop, 241.
Wicliffe, 67.
Wilson, Professor, 132.
Wily Beguiled, 209, 212.
Woodstock, 19.
Wordsworth, 82, 129.
Wright, Mr. Aldis, 240.
Wright, Christopher and John, 31.
Wyatt, 84.

CHISWICK PRESS:—C. WHITTINGHAM AND CO., TOOKS COURT,
CHANCERY LANE.

www.ingramcontent.com/pod-product-compliance
Lightning Source LLC
Chambersburg PA
CBHW031905220426
43663CB00006B/776